PUTTING THE
SCIENCE
IN FICTION

EXPERT ADVICE FOR WRITING WITH AUTHENTICITY IN SCIENCE FICTION, FANTASY, & OTHER GENRES

EDITED BY DAN KOBOLDT
FOREWORD BY CHUCK WENDIG

WRITER'S DIGEST BOOKS

D0905756

DEDICATION

To those who work or teach in S.T.E.M. fields.

For more resources for writers, visit www.writersdigest.com.

22 21 20 19 18   5 4 3 2 1

Distributed in the U.K. and Europe by F+W Media International
Pynes Hill Court, Pynes Hill, Rydon Lane
Exeter, EX2 5AZ, United Kingdom
Tel: (+44) 1392-797680, Fax: (+44) 1626-323319
E-mail: postmaster@davidandcharles.co.uk

Library of Congress Cataloging-in-Publication Data

ISBN-13: 978-1-4403-5338-3

Edited by Amy Jones
Designed by Katelyn Summers and Jason Williams
Cover Designed by Alexis Estoye
Production coordinated by Debbie Thomas

TABLE OF CONTENTS

PART ONE: RESEARCH LABS, HOSPITALS, AND REALLY BAD WAYS TO DIE

PART TWO: GENOME ENGINEERING: IT NEVER ENDS WELL

PART THREE: THE BRAIN IS WIDER THAN THE SKY

PART FOUR: FROM ZERO TO SIXTY (LEGS, THAT IS)

PART FIVE: THINGS TO KNOW FOR WHEN SKYNET TAKES OVER

PART SIX: EARTH AND OTHER PLANETS. YES, PLUTO COUNTS!

PART SEVEN: SOMETIMES, IT REALLY IS ROCKET SCIENCE

PART EIGHT: *STAR WARS* AND THE FAR FUTURE

FOREWORD
by Chuck Wendig

The piece of advice we writers often hear is this: *Write What You Know.*

It is good advice. Until it's not.

This is true of all of the so-called "sacred cows" of writing advice—from *Kill Your Darlings* to *Never Open Your Story With Weather* to *Don't Use Adverbs Because Adverbs Eat Babies*. They're a good place to start but not always a great place to finish. They work well as *guidelines*, but far less as *rigorous authorial gospel*.

If we give *Write What You Know* (aka WWYK) too much authority—too much weight as a supposed *rule*—we run the very likely risk of never actually writing anything interesting, because what we "know" as writers is often quite limited. Many of us write in the genre space, from science fiction to fantasy to horror, and we are automatically walled away from those genres if we interpret WWYK too literally. I've never ridden a dragon, henceforth, I should never write about riding a dragon. I'm not a robot from the future sent to kill the mother of the leader of a future human resistance movement, so how the hell could I write about it? Chased by a masked killer holding a bloodthirsty machete through the woods? Thankfully, no. So I guess I can't write about it? The only thing I can write about is …

Being a writer?

Or worse, being a writer who is writing about writing?

Ye gods, what a thrilling novel *that* would be.

PAGE ONE: THE WRITER WRITES. Scribble, scribble.

PAGE 300: THE WRITER IS ABOUT TO FINISH HIS MASTERPIECE ON THE SUBJECT OF A WRITER WRITING. It's writers writing about writing all the way down.

Ugggh.

However, flip the script a little. If we view WWYK as less of a law and more of an opportunity, what does that afford us?

First, it lets us, when we're struggling in the work, to reach to our own lives and find something in there that is as true as we remember it. No, I've never flown on the back of a dragon, but you know what? I've stood up out of the open sunroof of a speeding limousine; I've ridden a Waverunner; I've stood atop lighthouses and skyscrapers and other tall structures, feeling the wind whipping so hard that it brings tears to my eyes. That gives me something. Something to hold onto. An experience, or sensation, to borrow from when it comes to the work.

Second, it gives me the chance to view the world through the lens of *emotional truth*, too. Sure, I don't "know" a lot of very specific things, but I know how a lot of things make me feel. I know what it is to feel exhilarated, or terrified, or what it is to fall in love, or lose someone to disease. I have a lot of emotional truths, and fiction is my chance to speak about those truths no matter what the dragon-robot-monster context I choose to place them in.

Third, and now we're really getting to the meat of it, WWYK is not a condemnation or a limitation, but rather an *invitation*—

In particular, it's an invitation to *know more stuff*.

It is an invitation to learn.

And that's what this book is all about.

* * *

Let's switch gears a little bit.

I'm kind of a dope. A ding-dong. A wee bit of a goofball. I've also more or less ruined myself for what some might consider a "real" career at this point. I've gone so far down the rabbit hole of writing about hackers and genetically-modified killer ants and space wizards that I've sullied myself as a proper recipient of gainful employment. If ever the bottom falls out of this whole writing stories thing, I am in the deepest ordure with no rope to pull myself up and out. (Plus, I think the writing career has made me go savage. I imagine two days in a cubicle and I'd probably be covered in flies, using fast food wrappers as clothing, cooking a granola bar over a trash can fire. The copier would be my only friend. He would be named Aragorn and we would have adventures and wait, what do you mean I'm fired?)

I suppose it's never too late to start over, but at this point, could I ever really be a scientist? A chef? A detective? A dragon-tamer? A time-traveling space doctor?

More to the point, do I really *want* to be those things, when I can, as an author, be *all* of those things? And more? The author's purview is limitless. Our opportunity to explore everything and anything is only framed by the extent of our imagination.

But imagination really isn't enough.

Let's talk about hacking—not chopping at something with a hatchet, but rather, the art of penetrating computer systems. I don't know how to do that. I've never done that. Because, spoiler alert, I'm not a hacker. Now, when you watch most pop media on the subject of hackers, we get the same thing over and over again: someone has a computer screen open and there's like, a HACKING PROGRESS BAR slowly creeping toward 100%, and meanwhile there's a helicopter outside whose front cannon is whirring bullets, chewing apart the wall as the hacker waits for The Hack to be complete. And then, just as the wall is gone and the helicopter descends, the hacking progress bar *dings* 100% and—

KABOOSH, the helicopter explodes.

The helicopter got hacked, boom.

The hacker, an angsty white guy in his black hoodie, *wins again*.

It's nonsense, of course. That's not even remotely how you do it. So, when writing *Zer0es*, I very distinctly wanted to do the opposite of that—to portray a series of hackers from a variety of backgrounds and cultures with a diverse series of motivations who actually do something on the page that looks, at least at a distance, like *actual hacking*. (The caveat there being *actual hacking* is a little boring in terms of writing it in prose, so you have to spice it up a bit.)

I don't know how to hack a computer.

As I said: I'm a total ding-dong. Barely fit for public life!

And yet, sysops and hacker-folk said I got a lot of stuff right.

How did I do that?

Well, here's the trick: I talked to experts. And I read books.

That's it. That's the secret, and it's really no secret at all. And that's the secret non-secret of *this* book. This book will: a.) Put experts in front of you b.) Let you read about a wide variety of smart, science-flavored subjects.

And it doesn't do so with the singular purpose of teaching you the breadth and depth of a single subject—be that subject genetics or climate change or space travel—but rather, to teach you how to get started, and how to ask questions, and how to seek out even more information on the topic at hand. To play off the old cliché, it doesn't do the fishing for you: It teaches you how to fish.

(Er, again, not literally: This book will not teach you how to fish. It's a metaphor for "fishing for information" and—well, you're picking up what I'm laying down, right?)

So, sure, go ahead, write what you know. But if you don't know enough about the subject at hand? *Know more stuff.*

And this book is ground zero for doing exactly that.

—Chuck Wendig, June 2018

INTRODUCTION

by Dan Koboldt

Science, medicine, and technology have starring roles in a wide range of genres, most notably science fiction, but in other genres as well. Unfortunately, many depictions of technical subjects in literature, film, and television are pure fiction. This is perhaps not very surprising, since most writers don't hold advance technical degrees or have years of laboratory training under their belts. Furthermore, popular myths about scientific and technological concepts have pervaded mass media for decades.

Public misconceptions are especially common in the field of genetics, which happens to be my area of expertise. Most often, nonexperts tend to simplify the concepts of genetic inheritance to the point where first-degree relatives are expected to have the same eyes. Or hair. Or nose. Also prevalent is the idea that someone's entire future is written in his genetic code (à la the 1997 SF thriller *Gattaca*). In reality, genetics is usually more complex than most people realize, and there's so much we don't know. I felt it was my duty, as a scientist and SF writer, to try to help others avoid these pitfalls in their own writing.

So I wrote an article for *Apex Magazine* called "Eye-Based Paternity Testing and Other Human Genetics Myths," which debunked some of the worst of them (simple inheritance, mutations being "good," etc.). The response to that article was astonishing. I began asking people who worked in other disciplines to share their expertise. And so the Science in Sci-fi blog series was born. Each week, I discuss the scientific, medical, or technological aspects of science fiction with help from an expert in the field. Over a few years, I gathered a wealth of material, much of which you hold in your hands.

The forty or so contributors in this anthology represent a wide array of scientific, technological, and medical expertise. They've collectively endured more than one hundred years of graduate study in their chosen fields so you don't have to. They won't bore you with dense treatises on the latest scientific theory. Instead, they're going to cover the fundamentals of each topic, addressing common misconceptions and offering tips on how to get the details right. In other words, they'll teach you just enough to be dangerous.

This book aims to be a reference for the genre fiction writer. While your story doesn't have to adhere to every scientific fact—it is *fiction*, after all—a basic understanding of biology, physics, engineering, and medicine empowers you to create more realistic stories that satisfy even the most discerning readers. It will not only help you write realistic, compelling technical elements (and avoid common pitfalls), but might provide the seeds of new story ideas by showcasing the current state of the art. Whether you're writing about mutant monsters, rogue viruses, giant spaceships, or even murders and espionage, *Putting the Science in Fiction* will have something to help you craft better fiction.

PART ONE

RESEARCH LABS, HOSPITALS, AND REALLY BAD WAYS TO DIE

CHAPTER I

HOW TO ASK AN EXPERT

By Eric Primm

Stories require a delicate balance between too much and too little world building. Authors must always know more about their fictional setting than the reader, but the story needs only the information necessary to make the reader believe it is real. Authors research and research and research a subject necessary to their stories to increase the verisimilitude. One possible research method is asking an expert, and the following tips will help you ask more efficient questions.

PREPARATION

When seeking information, make sure to contact the correct expert. As the world gets more and more technologically advanced, professions become increasingly specialized. For example, while engineers have general knowledge of other fields, an aerospace engineer probably won't know the answer to a chemical engineering question. Just as no one would go to a doctor to learn why a car engine is rattling, they also wouldn't go to a mechanic for a flu shot. Specialization matters. Therefore, seek an expert with experience and knowledge in the relevant field. If your "go-to" expert can't help, it's acceptable to politely ask if she knows anyone who can, but the author needs to respect the expert's right to say no. Finding the correct source is as important as finding the information itself. Some questions are general enough that the expert may not need graduate-level knowledge to explain some basics, but the author should follow up with an expert who understands both the basics and the complexities of the subject. For example, a doctor may be able to explain how brake systems work, but it's best to verify that information with a mechanic who knows for sure. Just like precision jobs need the correct tool, a smart author needs the correct expert.

How the question is asked matters as much as the information you are looking for. Requirements analysis is one phase of project planning. This is an attempt to clarify what is really needed. In the example question "Would water, telephone lines, and other utilities function in a postapocalyptic world without a major power grid?" the requirement is information about how utilities operate. Information about utilities or the definition of a power grid is unnecessary to fulfill the minimum requirement. You could likely get to the needed information with a more general question—"How would utilities and power grids function in a postapocalyptic world?"—but it's a less efficient use of time and the expert's expertise. By understanding what is really needed, you can create a succinct question that allows the expert to provide the appropriate answer. Only meeting the minimum requirement leaves more questions and more information to wade through.

FILL IN THE BACKGROUND

To avoid a vague answer, provide the expert with a little background information. Details direct the expert toward a response that best fits the story. The example question defines a requirement: utility function. But many different methods of failure will cause nonfunctional utilities. As the question stands, there are too many unknowns for a useful answer. This isn't to say it's a bad question; it's an example showing how laypeople often communicate with experts. While the requirement is how utilities function, the phrase "postapocalyptic world without a major power grid" is vague and needs clarification to determine whether utilities could function. In other words, the cause changes the answer. For the example question, clarification of the following questions changes the story as well:

1. What does "without a major power grid" mean? Does this mean that the power stations are no longer working? Or are the power stations working but the "grid" itself—the wires and transformers—are somehow destroyed?
2. What caused the power grid to go down? For example, a hacker shutting down power generation plants has different physical consequences than if an electromagnetic pulse (EMP) is the cause of the apocalypse. Whereas a hacker can shut down the generation of power, an EMP will fry nonshielded circuits in all electronics. Massive tornadoes could tear apart the wires while missing the power generation stations.

A plot synopsis is not necessary to answer the question well. A sentence or two should suffice. The expert doesn't need to know about the terrorists' years of being dosed with LSD by the CIA to understand why they distributed the zombie plague upon the world. But the expert does need to know that the power plant doesn't work because instead of doing their jobs, the uninfected workers chose to hide out in their local Costco to wait out their eventual death. (In this scenario, the power plant would eventually shut down, and the electricity used in the utility plants would shut off at some point. But the grid is not affected, and the wires inside Costco are not harmed. Thus, with a few generators, the last humans in Costco can party like Prince did in 1999.) Be careful of providing too much plot detail because red herrings work well for the story, but not for research.

THE RESPONSE

Expect to receive more information than will end up in the story. An expert is an expert for a reason; he has invested time and effort into his chosen profession. The information provided will contain nuggets that are important for the world building but may not be necessary for the story. Remember that you need to know more than the reader. It's your job to figure out what is and isn't pertinent. If necessary, ask the expert whether she believes a certain piece is necessary to support the story. For example, in the power grid question, you could ask if Faraday cages would shield electrical equipment from an EMP blast. In answering that, the expert might note that the cage is made from copper. Is that really important? Maybe—it depends on how you use it. Ultimately, the author determines what ends up in the story, but more information allows for better, more realistic choices.

You should not expect a one-stop solution. Asking an expert isn't as easy as googling an answer, but it's an opportunity for a more holistic knowledge than just reading a Web page. Follow-up questions might be required to get the answer that works. If so, patience on both sides is the key. Ask for clarification where needed; this may lead to more questions. By asking an expert, a deeper knowledge of the subject is possible.

Depending on how much information is needed, the expert may point you to a different resource. Experts don't know everything and use resources to bolster their own knowledge. Part of becoming an expert is learning how and where to find the correct information. Take advantage of this by asking for books, articles, websites, etc. on which experts rely. Then, the expert can clarify specific questions about information found in the sources. Going to the same sources as an expert is more efficient and allows you to ask specific questions.

If the expert's reply doesn't answer the question, it probably asked a different question than you intended. In this case, it's likely you didn't fully understand your own requirements. Asking the expert why she provided the answer she did lets you see into her process. So, the next time you ask a question, it will be clear enough for the expert to answer.

A BETTER EXAMPLE

Taking into account all of this advice, the example question from earlier should look something like this: "Would utilities function in a postapocalyptic world where major power grids were destroyed by nuclear detonations in the atmosphere? A war between Belgium and Costa Rica escalates to a global conflagration. Nuclear nations set off enough nukes to ensure that the entire surface of the earth is bathed in EMP. Would cell phones still work? Would home faucets have running water?" Another example might be: "Tornados rip through the middle of Kansas, shearing all power lines between Opolis and the Wichita power plant. Would utilities function if all power transmission lines were destroyed?"

To answer the question, utilities require electricity. So, if the power goes down, water will only flow for as long as the pressure in the pipes remains because the pumps will be without power. The electricity required to power switchboards and server farms will eventually run out, leaving phones useless. (For the EMP scenario, all the circuits would be fried by the magnetic blast, thus, nonfunctional.) Either way, if the electricity stops flowing or the paths that the electricity travels are damaged, the ending is the same.

Asking an expert is a powerful, interactive research tool for an author. It can help speed up fictional world building. Talking about ourselves is a universal human trait, and experts are no different. Most enjoy spreading knowledge about where they excel and are willing to help educate others. For fiction, the best use of an expert's knowledge is to make the author think deeply about the story. Because in the end, the more thought-out the author's world, the better the story.

CHAPTER 2

RESEARCHERS GONE WILD

By Gabriel Vidrine

We've read it before: mad scientists, weird science, and horrific experiments. Or maybe it's heroic scientists working in state-of-the-art laboratories who produce miracles in minutes. Both of these portrayals of science are misguided; research just isn't done that way. Here are some common myths about scientists and research.

MYTH #1: EXPERIMENTS TAKE A FEW MINUTES

We're all pretty familiar with *CSI: Crime Scene Investigation* (the books are actually better than the TV show, in my opinion; Max Allan Collins and Jeff Mariotte are fantastic writers). The criminalists collect their samples from the crime scene, get them sent back to the lab, and within pages (or minutes) are getting their results. Of course, to hold a reader's interest, an author can't really say six months go by while Nick, Greg, and Sara work other cases and wait for the lab to work through the backlog to their samples. But that's really what happens.

Science takes time. Even a fairly simple experiment can take days. Gene sequencing? Even with the best, most advanced equipment, it can take hours. And that doesn't include the backlog, which can stretch that time out to months.

MYTH #2: SCIENTISTS ARE GREEDY AND HAVE NO MORALS

I find this one to be personally insulting. How many books have been published that paint scientists as greedy, amoral jerks who run whatever experiment seems likely to gain them the most money? How many books have an apocalypse caused by the release of a deadly virus by a careless or crazy scientist?

Hey, come on people, scientists are just like anyone else. We go to work, do our jobs, and collect our paychecks. Most of us aren't in it for the fame (haha!), riches (HAHA!), or the power to destroy the human race. We do it for the science. News flash: Science doesn't (usually) pay that well.

MYTH #3: SCIENTISTS DO RIDICULOUS, ILLOGICAL EXPERIMENTS FOR FUN

Ever wonder why scientists are putting human genes into plants and animals? No, it's not for fun, or because we're amoral, weird, or evil. The reasons depend on what gene we're talking about, but there's almost always a logical reason, like trying to understand cancer or improving the food supply. "Frankenanimals" or "Frankenfood" are not "part-human" or "part-animal," though some mice are considered "humanized" (due to the expression of human-like genes in some tissues).

This does not mean that the strawberry you are eating is part fish. DNA is DNA, and a "fish" gene is not inherently "fishy" any more than any of your genes are fundamentally "human." There are many gene sequences, called *conserved*, that are extremely similar across multiple species, so the DNA itself is not human or animal.

So while that strawberry is expressing a protein normally found in fish, it is not "part fish." It's not ridiculous to put some gene into an animal or plant it normally wouldn't be found in; that "fish gene" actually protects that strawberry from a killing frost and has nothing to do with "being a fish." Scientists don't do ridiculous experiments. There's not enough funding for that.

When I read Kim Harrison's *Dead Witch Walking* (Harper Voyager, 2008) I nearly threw the book across the room when I realized her apocalypse was caused by an attack of the killer tomato. While it is true that animal and human genes are used in plants or bacteria (and yes, sometimes animals like mice or rabbits), it is not true that a human virus put into a tomato plant can kill the vast majority of humans on the planet.

Proteins from viruses can, and have been, expressed in tomatoes and other plants. But there is no scientifically valid reason to grow a full human virus in a tomato. There are human cell lines designed for that (this is called *in vitro* culture, where cells are grown in flasks, which is much simpler than growing an entire organism, like a tomato).

GETTING RESEARCH RIGHT IN FICTION

1. **YOUR SCIENCE—AND YOUR SCIENTIST!—SHOULDN'T BE RIDICULOUS**

   Think like a scientist! There needs to be a reason why the experiment is being done. If you can think of no reason other than "My bad guy is a scientist, so he needs to do icky things like putting human eyeballs on tomato plants," you may need to rethink your plot. Your villain should have more dimension than that anyway, and scientists aren't typically evil geniuses bent on world domination.

2. **SCIENCE SHOULD BE (A LITTLE BIT) BORING**

Yeah, it might not be fun to read, but it will be much more realistic. Think of that time kind of like when your characters are going to the bathroom or eating lunch. Readers know it happens, but it doesn't need to be in the story in detail (or even there at all). Plan your plot to include the time it takes for major discoveries (years, not hours), and if it just drags the story down, rearrange the timeline so your characters have already put in the work before the book starts.

There are ways to work pacing into science so the exciting stuff happens in the story. But make it clear that it took a lot of time and work to get there.

3. **ASK A SCIENTIST OR DO RESEARCH ON YOUR OWN**

Look up what the scientific method is and why it's important to science. Researchers are happy (usually) to share their knowledge about research methods, so contact one with questions. The Internet is now one of the most powerful research tools on Earth. While Wikipedia or Google itself might be of limited use, Google Scholar can link you to many published research articles. You might need a license to access them (try your local college library), but many are available for free.

All of the articles on PubMed Central are free and available to anyone and everyone to access. If you think someone might have done research similar to what you are writing about, check it out, and make your fiction much more realistic! (And keep scientists from chucking your book across the room.)

CHAPTER 3

PROPER LAB TECHNIQUE

By Rebecca Enzor

Whether it's the first semester of chemistry class in high school, any laboratory course in college, or the first day at a new job, every lab experience starts with a class on proper lab technique and safety. Which means, if you have a character who works in a lab, she's gone through at least three lab safety courses to get there.

At the environmental testing lab where I work, we have an entire week of safety courses before we ever step foot in the lab. My job is to test water, soil, and tissue samples for radioactivity, pesticides, herbicides, and polychlorinated biphenyls (PCBs). There are a lot of steps in this process—a lot of places where it can go dangerously wrong—and we have to have defensible data in court (sometimes needed by our clients), so I have to be very careful when I'm working. Which is why it bugs me so much when scientists in books and movies have a laissez-faire attitude toward how they use their equipment.

What are some of the things you need to keep in mind when writing about lab work? Let's start with proper protective equipment (PPE).

PROPER PROTECTIVE EQUIPMENT (PPE)

Most books and movies get at least the basics of PPE right. After all, what's a scientist without the white lab coat and oversized safety glasses? And gloves, because no self-respecting scientist is going to touch anything in a lab without gloves on.

But did you know that you can't wear tennis shoes in some labs? My lab requires shoes with leather on top, preferably slip-on, so if you spill something on them you can quickly slip them off. You wouldn't want to have to untie your shoes when there's hot acid all over the laces. Not to mention the hot acid will seep through the cloth quicker than you can slip the shoe off, even if you don't have laces. And if you spill hot acid anywhere on your clothing, trust me, the first thing you're going to do is strip it off as fast as you can.

Does your character have long hair? She'll have to put it in a ponytail. Long necklace? Leave it at home. Deep V-neck shirt? She should wear something else. Expose as little skin as possible. Speaking of exposing as little skin as possible: Never wear a thong in the lab. It's *really* embarrassing when you spill something dangerous on your pants and have to rip them off, only to leave your butt cheeks flapping in the breeze for all to see.

Just trust me on that one.

LAB EQUIPMENT

Once you're properly clothed you can get to work, but depending on what you're doing, you might need some special equipment. Working with chemicals? You're going to need a fumigation hood. (Unless you're isolating radium-228, which they'll let you do on a counter with no hood, even though the acetic acid will give you a headache.)

The most important thing to know if you're working with a fume hood is *don't stick your head inside*. The whole point of the fume hood is to capture the dangerous fumes, and if you stick your head in there your nose will capture the fumes instead. There's also usually a glass or plastic moveable "door" on the hood that you want to keep closed as often as possible, not only because fumes will escape but because it's a great barrier to all those dangerous chemicals you're working with. When you add chemicals to other chemicals, they often splash—sometimes they explode. If you don't want them to explode all over *you*, there needs to be a barrier.

Other things you might be working with?

- **ACID DISPENSERS:** These are pumps that fit on top of 1.5-liter acid containers and are used to squirt the same amount of acid with each pump (anywhere from one to ten milliliters at a time). Definitely use these inside the hood with the barrier between you. Most acid containers are glass and can shatter if dropped (the exception being hydrofluoric acid, which eats through glass and is stored in plastic containers).
- **CENTRIFUGES:** These spinning machines are used to separate sediment from liquid by drawing the sediment to the bottom of the centrifuge tube. Make sure they've stopped before you go sticking your fingers in there.
- **SYRINGES:** I'm pretty sure you can figure this one out on your own. Don't stab yourself (or anyone else) with the needle.
- **GLASSWARE:** From beakers to flasks to graduated cylinders, these are easy to break and cut yourself. Bonus points if there's acid, radioactive contamination, or other nasty things on the glassware to infect your cut! They also make an excellent amount of noise when your character gets fed up with everything and throws them on the ground.

- **VACUUM FLASKS:** These cone-shaped glass flasks are used to separate two liquid layers, or a layer of liquid from sediment that's too large to fit in the centrifuge. When these explode they make an awful noise and an even more awful mess! Never mix acids and bases in a vacuum flask and always make sure the flow is good before you start using them. You can usually tell if the flow is good by the sound: if there's a blockage there will be a higher pitch than usual. Unfortunately that's something you have to learn through practice.

And then we get to pipettes, which is the whole reason I wrote this article on proper lab technique.

HOW *NOT* TO USE AN EPPENDORF PIPETTE

I'm sure most of you have seen, or at least heard of, James Cameron's *Avatar* (as opposed to the *Avatar* TV show where the characters can control the elements). That movie came out in 2009—almost ten years ago—and there's a scene in it that to this day bugs me. Sigourney Weaver is using a pipette, which is a tool we use in the lab to transfer a specifically measured amount of liquid from one container to another.

You hold the pipette upright, depress the plunger, stick it in the liquid you want to transfer, and release the plunger. It sucks the exact same amount of liquid up each time (we calibrate the pipettes daily so we know that they are, in fact, sucking the exact same amount of liquid up each time). You then place the pipette tip over the container you want to put the liquid into and depress the plunger again so all the liquid exits. It's a super easy and mostly fail-proof way to get the exact same amount of liquid into each sample. You could do the same with a syringe, but there's a lot more human error involved in a syringe and it takes much longer.

So Sigourney Weaver is using a pipette, gets the appropriate amount of liquid into it, and then *turns it upside down*. Friends, I have done this exact same thing by accident, and do you know what happens when you turn a pipette full of liquid upside down? The liquid goes into the pipette's mechanism and you can't use it anymore because it's contaminated. Part of the liquid can squirt out, too, which is very dangerous if you're using it to transfer radioactive sources or acids. I've done this—by accident—more times than I'd like to admit. And pipettes are expensive. My boss probably hates me.

I can tell you I'm not the only one who's noticed this, either. If you Google "Sigourney Weaver, pipette, Avatar" the first hit is a YouTube video entitled "How Not to Use an Eppendorf Pipette" and then pages and pages of scientists like myself gasping in utter horror over her misuse of said pipette. It would be funny if I wasn't still horrified all these years after watching a science fiction/fantasy film. Obviously this one stuck with me.

RESPECT FOR SCIENCE

The last thing you need to know about writing a scientist in a lab? We care about what we're doing. We check constantly to make sure we're safe and the people around us are safe. We make sure we're doing every step correctly, because a misstep could lead to bad data ... or an explosion. So never, ever, ever write this sentence: "Scientists have their heads in the clouds and don't bother with maintenance."

Because I will throw your book across the room.

CHAPTER 4

ORGANOGENESIS IN 3D

By Megan Cartwright Chaudhuri

Vat-grown flesh—whether to eat as meat or transplant as organs—has always been one of my favorite science fiction tropes. What's not to love about eating a delicious steak without the slaughterhouse and replacing your cholesterol-clogged heart after you've eaten too many steaks?

But when I became a scientist and started growing cells in petri dishes, I became skeptical about how easily so many characters picked up new hearts, hands, and nervous systems. It wasn't just the ease that bothered me, but the missed chances to tell an even better story full of the awesome, gross, and fun things possible with vat-grown organs!

I'll dig into the misconceptions behind some common science fiction tropes about organogenesis—the complex process by which cells grow into organs. Then, I'll offer some tips on how to make your story's vat-grown flesh more believable.

TROPE #1: ORGANS GROW IN VATS

I know: I keep saying "vat-grown flesh." That makes it sound like you just need a bucket of chicken broth and some stem cells (Worst. Soup. Ever.) To grow something as big and complex as an organ out of billions of different specialized cells, your characters will need at least six things: cells, a cell scaffold, nutrient broth, stimuli, the right location, and money.

1. **CELLS.** Your story's organs will probably start as a small number of unique cells, like stem or pluripotent cells, that can divide and specialize into various types. Whether embryonic (from a fetus) or induced pluripotent (from an adult), stem cells might need some genetic tweaks to make them compatible with the recipient. Another cell source could be the recipient's progenitor cells from their own bone marrow.

2. **CELL SCAFFOLD.** Now that you have your cells, you'll need to grow them on something! For something large and complicated like an organ, you'll need either a temporary scaffold to brace the cells until they can support themselves, or a permanent "skeleton." This skeleton could be a frame made from some-

thing natural, like cartilage, or a synthetic polymer. For temporary scaffolds, cells could also grow on soft, gelatinous substances such as hydrogels.

3. **NUTRIENT BROTH (MEDIUM).** Your growing organ will need to be immersed in a liquid that transmits oxygen and nutrients, carries away carbon dioxide and waste products, and keeps the cells' environment at the right acidity. But unless there are blood vessels (or something similar) to circulate medium throughout the growing organ, it won't be able to grow much bigger than a few millimeters.

4. **STIMULI.** A growing organ is constantly sending and receiving signals—both biochemical and mechanical—that direct and shape its growth. Your organ will need the right mix of signals (particularly a group called *growth factors*) and mechanical cues to avoid becoming a blob of confused, disorganized tissue. For internal organs, these cues might involve pressure that simulates crowding against neighboring organs; for others, like muscle, these cues could involve being stretched and relaxed. Currently, scientists simulate these cues by growing cells in light-sensitive hydrogels—scaffolds that stiffen and stretch cells when exposed to light, then relax when the light is gone.

5. **THE RIGHT LOCATION.** Bacteria, fungi, and viruses would all love to grow in the medium or in the cells! To stop these buggers from contaminating cultures, scientists work in sterile conditions, such as in a dedicated room with positive air pressure, which blows away bacteria that try to get inside. And they only open the cultures when the dishes are inside a tissue culture hood.

6. **MONEY.** The equipment, personnel, and chemicals for growing and implanting these organs will cost some serious cash. To give you an idea, mass-produced skin grafts for diabetic foot ulcers are estimated to cost from $1,400 per small ulcer to $11,800 for a big one. And that's for a simple, mass-produced tissue like skin!

TROPE #2: REPLACEMENT ORGANS WORK GREAT!

As if growing organs wasn't hard enough, here are a few problems your characters could face after their shiny new organs are implanted:

- **IMMUNE REJECTION.** If that organ grew out of cells from a donor, it could get rejected and attacked by the recipient's immune system—just like transplants nowadays. Alternatively, the immune system could attack and break down the organ's synthetic scaffold.
- **CANCER.** Unfortunately for your character, that new organ could be a source of cancer. If the organ's cells had some genetic tweaks, they might carry some

unintended mutations caused by the techniques used to edit the genome. Those mutations could lead to cancer. And if your character received an organ that still harbored some immature embryonic stem cells, those stem cells might grow into a tumor called a *teratoma*.

- **POOR FUNCTION**. I'll say it again: Organs are complex, with billions of different cells specialized into various forms and structures. That shiny new organ might lack some important structures; for example, the "mini-guts" currently grown in laboratories to study colon cancer lack the tentacle-like villous structures critical for absorbing food nutrients and drugs. Compared to the natural organ, a lab-grown organ may only be able to do a few simple tasks. This means your character might still need the occasional dialysis treatment to complement her new kidneys, or take highly concentrated supplements that can diffuse across her villous-free replacement gut.

HOW TO DO IT RIGHT

When it's time to start growing and grafting some organs onto your characters, here are a few questions to think about to make your "vat-grown flesh" more believable:

- How big and complex is the organ—is it just a few outer layers of skin or a massive, complicated beast like the liver?
- Where are its cells coming from?
- What are the cells being grown on—a temporary scaffold made from some soft hydrogel, or a permanent skeleton made out of something like cartilage?
- How well does the organ function?
- Does the character need to do or take anything (immune suppressants, extra nutrients, dialysis, etc.) to keep the organ going, and to keep himself alive?

—————●—————

CHAPTER 5

MEDICAL MISCONCEPTIONS, PART I

by Karyne Norton

I haven't been able to watch shows with hospital scenes for the last decade, and I cringe when I run into medical misconceptions in books. I wish I could ignore the errors, but they stand out to me like bad grammar stands out to an English teacher. My hope is to help writers who don't have medical training get through some of the common pitfalls of writing about medical situations.

MISCONCEPTION #1: CPR IS FOR LIVING PATIENTS

I can't tell you how many times I've seen writers mess up cardiopulmonary resuscitation (CPR). One of the first things they teach us in Basic Life Support classes is that you can't screw up CPR because the person is already dead. Your goal is to bring them back to life. But if the patient is talking, moving, or breathing, you should *not* be doing CPR.

Real CPR Training

If your character comes across an unconscious person and they have any medical training, here's what they'll do.

1. They'll gently shake the unconscious person and call their name (or shout something) to see if they wake up.
2. They'll ask nearby people to call for help/911. They also might ask for an automated external defibrillator (AED).
3. Sometimes (especially on children) they'll check for breathing. It used to be taught as ABC (airway, breathing, circulation), but for strangers it's no longer recommended to do mouth-to-mouth resuscitation, and recent studies have shown that circulation should be prioritized because our blood has plenty of oxygen to circulate without rescue breaths. Children tend to have healthy hearts, so if they're unconscious it's usually because they choked or drowned.
4. Most often they'll immediately check for a pulse on the neck or wrist. If there's no pulse, they start chest compressions. Real chest compressions look awful. If they don't look awful, you're not pushing hard enough. Bones break.

5. When an AED is available, they use it to shock the heart back into a viable rhythm. AEDs come with written instructions, but the machine also talks you through the steps to use it. Feeling confident with this machine could save a life, so don't be afraid to read more about how they work: www.nhlbi.nih.gov/health/health-topics/topics/aed/howtouse.

6. They continue administering CPR until an ambulance arrives.

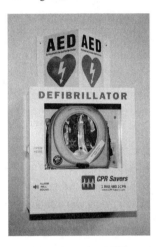

Figure 5.1: An AED

Keep in mind these are not the same steps used to revive a baby at birth. To accurately depict this, you'll want to refer to the Neonatal Resuscitation Program (NRP) guidelines.[1]

CPR in the Hospital

When a patient needs CPR in a hospital setting, the same general steps are followed, except when someone calls for help, they push a code button on the wall that alerts an entire team of medical professionals to come to the room with a code cart. This is often depicted as a chaotic moment, but in larger hospitals it's more like a highly intricate dance.

The first person to find the patient is generally the one to do chest compressions. The next person to come will start giving oxygen through a bag and mask. If there isn't already an IV, someone starts one. Another person sets up the code cart and hooks the patient up to the EKG monitor. Another simply records every-

---

1 American Academy of Pediatrics. "Neonatal Resuscitation Program." AAP.org. www.aap.org /en-us/continuing-medical-education/life-support/NRP/Pages/NRP.aspx (accessed May 4, 2018).

thing that's being done at what time so they can chart it all later. Usually there are five to ten people that walk in within a minute (if not sooner).

When the anesthesiologist arrives, the person in charge of airway assists her while she gets the patient intubated (compressions are paused during this process). The patient's primary doctor usually watches everything that's being done and gives out orders. Others in the room are encouraged to voice any ideas or steps that might have been missed.

There's a lot happening at one time, but don't think for one second that it's disorganized. The code teams in hospitals are trained to respond to every code in the hospital, and depending on the size of the hospital, there can be a handful each day.

MISCONCEPTION #2: BABIES FLY OUT IN ONE PUSH

This is the absolute hardest one to please me on because it's *my* area. If I love a book and a delivery scene shows up, I tend to skim it out of fear that I will forever close the book. Your personal labor experience is yours and probably shouldn't be your character's. If you barely made it to the hospital and your babies practically slid out, please realize it's not common. According to the Centers for Disease Control and Prevention's National Vital Statistics Reports, 23.8 percent of women were induced for their labor in 2015.[2] Many of those inductions last *days*. So your character will very likely have time to make it to the hospital. She will even have time to get to the labor and delivery unit so she doesn't have to have a hectic and dramatic delivery in the emergency department, where they do everything possible to avoid taking care of a pregnant patient. The emergency department sends pregnant patients to labor and delivery even if the patient checks in for a broken toe.

Another 32 percent (there's definitely crossover with the inductions) end up with C-sections.[3] Yes, your character can have a C-section. It could even be planned. Your character can also have an epidural, and if she lives in present-day America, she probably should because about 90 percent of laboring Americans do. I'm sure your character is a very strong woman with a high pain tolerance, but that doesn't have anything to do with whether or not she would get an epidural. And the women who don't get epidurals? They don't all scream bloody murder. Some don't make a sound.

2 Martin M.P.H., Joyce A., Brady E. Hamilton, Ph.D., Michelle J.K. Osterman, M.H.S., Anne K. Driscoll, Ph.D., and T.J. Mathews, M.S., Division of Vital Statistics. "Births: Final data for 2015." *National Vital Statistics Report* 66, no. 1 (2017): 53.
3 Ibid., 53.

MISCONCEPTION #3: IVs ARE NEEDLES

This is a pretty quick fix, but I see it often enough that it's worth mentioning. When an IV catheter is inserted a needle is used, but the needle is immediately removed and a plastic catheter is all that remains. This is a common misconception among patients, too (especially ones who like to complain). Don't have your characters notice the needle in their arm or complain about it being sharp. Or if they do, have your nurse character set them straight so you get a smile out of this reader.

MISCONCEPTION #4: MEDS ARE USED TO SHUT PEOPLE UP

This is incredibly illegal, and for some reason writers like to have their characters being given meds that knock them out left and right. "You have a scrape on your elbow? Here, let me start an IV for no reason other than to give you an incredibly potent narcotic that I happen to have in my pocket and I can't possibly already have an order for. That way you'll fall asleep super confused and the reader will want to turn the page."

That's seriously how I read those scenes. In the hospital setting, we need a physician's order to give any kind of medication. Even oxygen requires an order. In emergency situations, there's almost always a doctor present to give us that order, but we can't just pull it out of our hat. Narcotics (and most other medications) are kept locked up in medication dispensers that require passwords and fingerprints to access.

We also have to get permission from the patient to give any medication. If a patient is in hysterics and needs to be restrained in some way, most hospitals have policies requiring two physicians agreeing that the physical restraints or medication (never both) be used. And these are very rare occurrences.

Now, I'm not going to lie. Medications get used to shut people up, but it's usually done by the nurse strongly encouraging the patient to ask for the medication. Nursing licenses are too hard to earn just to lose over a stupid narcotic and an annoying patient.

MISCONCEPTION #5: TEENS GET TREATMENT WITHOUT PARENTAL SIGN-OFF

Be careful what you have your young adult characters getting done without parental figures present. In emergency situations, minors are treated in order to save their lives. But pain medications won't be given out to every crying kid. You may not always need parental permission to get an abortion, but if that same girl decides to show up at the hospital six to nine months later wanting an epidural, mommy or daddy might need to sign for her. Some of these issues are state-specific, so do your research. For example, in Arizona pregnant teens are considered emancipated and can sign for their care in labor and delivery. Once the baby is born they can sign for the baby, but they then revert back to needing parental consent for their own care.

HOW TO GET THE MEDICAL STUFF RIGHT

I'm only scraping the surface of medical misconceptions. Someone who works in an oncology unit or cardiac unit might have very different things to point out. Some medical standards vary regionally, while others are affected by specific hospital policies. So what's a writer to do? Make a nursing friend. Or two. Or twelve. Honestly, we're very friendly people and we love talking about our jobs. Just be aware that you might hear more than you want, and you might not want to eat while we talk.

CHAPTER 6

MEDICAL MISCONCEPTIONS, PART II

By Stephanie Sauvinet

Popular medical shows are full of dramatic, emotionally draining situations such as a beloved primary character "flatlining," or a poor child impaled by some foreign object. Often, these scenarios are overdramatized for maximum emotional engagement with the audience. Unfortunately for those of us working in the medical profession, it's often difficult to look past the gross scientific and medical errors repeatedly shown that could be downright dangerous and life-threatening if performed on a living patient.

I find myself wondering if production and/or writing staff enlist the aid of medical consultants, or if the goal is simply to maximize the drama (at a cost of reducing the scientific accuracy). Anyone who has faced one of these scenarios "in real life" will undoubtedly tell you that these fleeting seconds are already packed with enough drama to last a lifetime. There is no reason to insert additional drama into the equation when a real person's life is on the line; you already have Thor's hammer pounding your chest. If you don't want to end up with a dead/incompetent character, follow along.

MISCONCEPTION #1: THE DEFIBRILLATOR MYTHS

Shocking a Flatline

Electrical signals are the enablers of a beating heart: They run through it creating the familiar "lub-dub" sound. The electrical pulses are unique to the heart and are created by three main bundles of specialized cells. Similar to the pistons in a car engine, the parts of the heart need to beat in a specific rhythm to pump blood effectively throughout the body and provide oxygen to your organs and cells through a process called *oxygenation*. A heart monitor is used to display the rhythm a person's heart is following. The "rhythm" is another way of describing the behavior of the current running from bundle to bundle.

The purpose of a defibrillator is to "reset" the heart's rhythm by disrupting ("shocking") it—think CTRL+ALT+DELETE for a PC or COMMAND+OPTION+ESCAPE for you folks who like machines named after red fruits. If the rhythm isn't appropriate to circulate the blood to the rest of your body, shocking it will hopefully "reboot" the rhythm to its normal (effective) rhythm by forcing the bundles to communicate once again in an organized pattern.

When a flatline occurs (also called asystole), no electrical current is running through the heart. If pulseless electrical activity (PEA), a condition that looks very similar to a flatline occurs, there may be a tiny bit of quivering occurring in the heart. This quivering is usually not enough to make the heart contract and the patient has no pulse. In these cases, shocking the heart won't do anything. Remember that shocking only resets the electrical current's rhythm and does not add or produce current within the heart.

So how do we add current to the heart? Think batteries! What creates current in a battery? A chemical reaction! Each electrolyte has a specific electrical charge, and their movements across various cells within the body create an electrical charge. That is why medications like epinephrine are administered. These medications will affect electrolytes within the body, forcing them in or out of a cell in an attempt to create current and "jump-start" the heart.

Only after the flatline or PEA event stops and we begin to see current within the heart can we begin to worry about whether it is beating in the correct rhythm. If the rhythm is not correct (based on the output of the cardiac monitor), defibrillation can be applied.

Rubbing the Defibrillator Paddles

A defibrillator uses either paddles or pads that are applied to the patient's body. When defibrillator paddles are used, a conductive gel is usually applied to assist with conduction and prevent severe burns to the patient's chest. While rubbing the paddles together may add to the drama, it is completely unnecessary because the gel will spread once the paddles are placed on a patient's chest.

The most up-to-date cardiopulmonary resuscitation (CPR) guidelines prefer self-adhesive pads over paddles. The self-adhesive pads are placed on the patient's chest and remain there for the entire duration of a cardiopulmonary arrest (or "code"). They help minimize any delay between pausing CPR, "clearing" everyone touching the patient (or "CLEAR!"), shocking the patient, and resuming CPR.

The self-adhesive pads also allow for heart pacing. After the shock is administered to the patient, the heart's rhythm may be too slow to perfuse blood adequately to all of his organs. In these cases, the defibrillator can then be set as a pacer to provide additional shocks with just enough electricity through to pace the heart rate to a faster range.

A Patient Is Shocked, and Her Entire Body Lifts Off the Table

Muscular contraction and movement occur based on input from the "processing center" of the body: the brain. This is the reason why a patient's body may jerk around during certain seizure episodes: The brain misfires, resulting in random muscle movement and sharp jerking.

In order for a patient's body to completely lift off of a surface, many different muscle groups would need to simultaneously contract. The heart sits in the center of the chest, with its apex slightly to the left. As a result, one defibrillator pad/paddle is placed on top of the right chest and the other under the left breast, laterally. The purpose of this placement is for the shock to travel from right to left and up to down, following the same direction that current normally flows through the heart.

Current immediately ceases to be applied once it reaches the left pad/paddle. With the electrical current localized to this region of the body (and therefore only applied to a limited set of muscle groups), it is physically impossible for the person's body to violently lift off the table.

MISCONCEPTION #2: INJECTING MEDICINE STRAIGHT INTO THE HEART

Very dramatic, but also very deadly!

The heart is a very fragile organ protected by a bone directly on top of it called the *sternum*. This biological construct should provide a not-so-subtle hint that attempting to access the heart in this manner is probably a bad idea. The vascular system is a closed system for a reason. Piercing the body's main pumping station would result in an imminent death sentence by bleeding!

The only time a needle is used to pierce the heart, other than during major cardiac surgeries, is for a procedure called *pericardiocentesis*. The heart is enclosed in a double-walled sac called the *pericardium*. The sac contains a small amount of fluid that lubricates the moving part of the heart as it beats. Under the affliction of certain diseases, the pericardium sometimes fills up with too much fluid, creating a pericardial effusion. If significant enough, it can develop into cardiac tamponade. This extra fluid is life-threatening as it squishes the heart to the point where it is unable to beat efficiently. During pericardiocentesis, a physician uses a needle to drain some of the fluid to relieve the pressure around the heart using an ultrasound machine as a guide.

At the present time, the best way to administer lifesaving medication is through an IV placed by a medical professional. Outside of a hospital, you may not have an

IV already in place. In these cases, a needle is used to inject the medication into a peripheral vein. Much like a blood draw, some type of tourniquet can be applied to help find a vein and the needle can be threaded in the vein to administer the injection directly into the bloodstream.

If an IV is not available during an emergency situation, medications can also be administered through intraosseous access (IO). This type of needle is inserted into the bone marrow of specific, highly vascular bones that cause the medication to be absorbed in a fashion similar to that of an IV access. It is extremely dangerous to access the sternum because the heart sits right behind it. Other bones are used for IO access such as the head of the humerus (shoulder area) or the proximal and distal tibia (right below the knee and above the ankle).

Remember: If medications are administered to a person who has no pulse, CPR should also be performed. In addition to being life-sustaining, chest compressions also help circulate the medication throughout the body.

MISCONCEPTION #3: PULLING OUT FOREIGN OBJECTS

Many fictional characters have pulled foreign objects out of the human body in a fit of rage/courage. This is another thing that looks great on the big screen (or in small print), but it might have the unintended consequence of ending our hero's world-saving career! The arrow/pole/knife/other foreign object may be the only thing compressing a severed artery and slowing the bleeding down. As soon as it is removed, the hero may quickly bleed to death.

In these situations, the best course of action is to stabilize the object as best as possible and remember that movement may do more harm than good. After doing this, immediately seek professional medical attention to have the object safely removed (this usually involves surgery).

GET MEDICAL FACTS RIGHT

Social media is your friend: There are so many venues to start a conversation with someone "in the know." Most people in the medical field, myself included, love to talk about what we do. Trust me, we'd rather stab ourselves in the eye than read a novel or watch a movie where false medical practices are propagated and facts, if they ever were facts, degrade into dramatic fiction. Strike up a conversation with us. Ask around; do your research before your pen hits the (digital) page!

CHAPTER 7

THE SCIENCE OF TOXINS AND POISONING

By Megan Cartwright Chaudhuri

One of the most dramatic scenes in George R.R. Martin's *A Storm of Swords* (Bantam, 2000) [*SPOILER ALERT*: Skip this paragraph if you haven't read it] is the agonizing death of psychopathic King Joffrey. While being an ass at his wedding feast, Joffrey begins to choke on some wine. Gagging, he claws at his swelling throat, his face darkening as he fights to breathe amid the screams of his guests. When Joffrey collapses and dies, the reader in me wants to cheer. But the toxicologist in me wants to groan: *Another instantaneous death from poison sprinkled in food.*

There is so much more that a writer can do with poisons. The next time you reach for something to torment your characters (psychopaths or not), I hope you build a better, more interesting poisoning that avoids these common tropes and misconceptions.

TROPE #1: ALL POISONS DO IS KILL

Whether it's arsenic or table salt or water, *every* chemical can kill you, if you take enough of it in a short span of time. Some chemicals, like cyanide or the "strangler" in *A Storm of Swords*, are so potent they will overwhelm anyone at miniscule doses. However, most chemicals have a gradient of effects that get worse as more chemical gets into your body. The amount of chemical that causes those effects varies from person to person, with people being extra vulnerable when they are very young or if they have, for example, failing kidneys that can't filter chemicals out of their blood.

You can do a lot with this gradient of effects, which toxicologists call a *dose-response*. Why kill a character right away when you can force him to empty his bowels in public, riddle his scrotum with tumors, or make her give birth to one-eyed children? Here are a few examples of the different effects of real poisons and their gradients:

- **NEUROTOXICITY.** Many animal and insect venoms, as well as pesticides, poison the nervous system by interfering with neurotransmitters—the chemical signals relayed between nerve cells. While sometimes lethal, these poisons can also cause embarrassing and painful effects like drooling, uncontrolled diarrhea, convulsions, and paralysis.

- **CANCER.** At high doses, many poisons kill quickly. But at low doses, taken over time (such as in drinking water, or encountered at work), many can cause terrible diseases. Arsenic is a perfect example. Small amounts of this element contaminate drinking water in Bangladesh, where it causes skin cancer and heart disease. Another example is a benzo[a]pyrene, a component of soot, which caused scrotal cancers in chimney sweeps during the Industrial Revolution.
- **REPRODUCTIVE TOXICITY.** Many chemicals have little effect on healthy adults but do awful things to a developing fetus. One infamous example is cyclopamine, a toxin in a pretty flower called *corn lily*. Cyclopamine causes babies to be born with one eye and a missing nose and/or mouth. Another example is methylmercury, which slips across the placenta and concentrates inside the fetus's brain to devastating levels.

TROPE #2: POISONS WORK WHEN YOU EAT AND DRINK THEM

A poison works when it can interact with a vulnerable part of the body. While George R.R. Martin's character's throat is clearly the part that's vulnerable to the strangler, for many other poisons the vulnerable organ is tucked away (like the brain). That means that these poisons have to get into the bloodstream to reach the vulnerable organ.

Eating and drinking—ingestion—are surprisingly inefficient ways to get poison into the blood. If the stomach's full of food, the poison travels more slowly out of the stomach and into the bloodstream, giving the body more time to potentially clear it. A lot of poisons (especially metals like the elemental mercury in thermometers and toys) also don't cross easily from the stomach to blood, meaning they mostly pass out of the body as toxic poop.

Ingestion aside, here are other ways you can get poisons into your characters:

- **INJECTION.** Whether it's through fangs, poisoned arrows, or a needle, a poison injected directly into the bloodstream usually finds its vulnerable organ the quickest.
- **INHALATION.** The lungs are a marvelous way to quickly get a poisonous gas or vapor into the blood (just think about how anesthesia is usually administered). But the lungs offer another, unique way to get poisoned. Very small particles—from asbestos fibers to nanomaterials like quantum dots and single carbon nanotubes—can get lodged in the lung and keep damaging the delicate tissue.

- **ABSORPTION (SKIN, EYES, VAGINA, ANUS).** Some poisons just sit on your skin and do nothing. Others, like certain pesticides and chemicals that dissolve in fatty oils, can slowly slide inside and enter the bloodstream. Skin absorption is usually a slow way to get a poison into the blood, although it gets a little speedier if the skin is delicate, warm, or damaged. By comparison, a splash of poison to the eyes can hurt the eyes and move more quickly into the blood. And a poison applied to the thin tissues inside the vagina or anus is going to get into the blood even faster (but I'll leave it to the writer to figure out how to deliver that poison!).

HOW TO DO IT RIGHT

Whether you're devising your own poison like the strangler or picking one from real life, here are some questions to think about to make your poisoning as unique and believable as possible:

- How much poison is needed—a single speck like cyanide, or a heaping handful like lead?
- What is a poison's gradient of effects at different doses?
- Who is the most sensitive to its effects?
- What is the vulnerable part or system of the body?
- How does it come into contact with the vulnerable part?
- If the poisoned character survives, what are the long-term effects on his body?

RESOURCES

- *A Is for Arsenic: The Poisons of Agatha Christie*, by Kathryn Harkup (Bloomsbury Sigma, 2017)
- Agency for Toxic Substances & Disease Registry: Toxic Substances Portal (www.atsdr.cdc.gov/toxfaqs/index.asp)
- American Association of Poison Control Centers (www.aapcc.org)
- American College of Medical Toxicology FAQs for the Public (Disclosure: I've received money from this group to write continuing medical education materials on toxicology) (www.acmt.net/Public_FAQ_s.html)
- *Casarett & Doull's Toxicology: The Basic Science of Poisons*, by Curtis D. Klaassen (the bible of toxicology) (McGraw-Hill Education, 2013)
- Me! I love answering questions about toxicology. Feel free to contact me at meganchaudhuri@gmail.com, and I'll give it a shot (or forward you to another expert if I can).

PUTTING THE SCIENCE IN FICTION

CHAPTER 8

THE MANY FACES OF DEATH

By Bianca Nogrady

There's a great scene in the 1987 film *Outrageous Fortune,* which starred Bette Midler and Shelley Long, where Long's character is asked to perform a death scene in her acting class.

Her character, desperate to please the acting coach, delivers the most overblown Baroque impression that drags on and on with its flourishes, gasps, and gestures until finally, mercifully, she "dies." She gets utterly roasted by the coach, but gets her revenge later in the film (*SPOILER ALERT!*) when, to save her life, she must convince him that he has succeeded in shooting her.

That death performance is a little different. There are no flourishes, no dramatic gestures. Just *bang*, and she's down.

Thanks to Hollywood, our ideas of what death looks like are pretty skewed from the reality, either to serene closing-of-the-eyes or a Tarantino-style bloodsoaked blaze of glory.

The truth is generally a long way from either of these. Watching a life end is like watching a life begin. Sometimes it's a calm, peaceful, even beautiful experience. Sometimes it's a horrible bloody mess. Mostly, it's a bit of both.

THE EXPECTED

There's no such thing as a "typical" death, but there are events often reported by those who work in hospitals, hospice care, or other environments.

Cheyne-Stokes respiration is a characteristic breathing pattern that often heralds death, although it is also encountered when sleeping at very high altitudes (which can lead to some unintended alarm on the part of the sleeper's companions!). The person's breathing gets deeper—and sometimes faster—but then gets shallower and shallower until it appears to stop altogether … and then it resumes.

The aptly named "death rattle" is an unpleasant sound that does not necessarily imply the dying person is in discomfort. It can be a rasping, rattling, gurgling, moaning sound that is thought to be the result of saliva in the throat. Generally not a lot can be done about it.

Death often comes as one long, last exhalation, but one thing that many people report is a very sudden change in the skin appearance of the person who's died. As the circulation stops, the skin very quickly—in a matter of a minute or two—takes on a waxy appearance as blood stops moving through the skin.

THE UNEXPECTED

There are few things more shocking than having someone who has exhaled their final breath suddenly take a choking gasp, sometimes a minute or two after they have apparently died.

Agonal gasps, as they're called, sound a lot worse than they actually are (at least for the person who has died). They're considerably less pleasant for the people sitting by the bedside who have begun to mourn. It doesn't mean the dead have returned to life—agonal gasps are thought to be a final reflex as the brain seeks one last burst of oxygen, but they are also a clear sign that death has occurred.

An equally surprising but much more welcome event that can occur just before death is called *terminal lucidity*, or "lightening up." Many tell stories of people with dementia, Alzheimer's disease, or brain tumors: In the final minutes of life, whatever fog has clouded their minds seems to lift. For a brief, shining moment, they are themselves again. They might acknowledge a loved one they have not recognized for years or crack a joke that gives a glimpse of the person they once were.

However, this moment is all too brief and usually only happens within minutes of death. We still don't understand why or how it happens, but for those who experience it, it is a huge gift when they need it most.

Something similar is *pre-terminal agitation*, where a person who might have been bedridden and barely conscious suddenly finds the strength to get out of bed, walk, dance, or even run.

Perhaps the strangest explainable phenomenon around death is the Lazarus reflex, which is very occasionally seen in brain-dead individuals in the minutes after they are taken off artificial ventilation. They might lift their arms up in the air and let them drop crossed over their chest. It's thought to be a very basic, primal reflex, but no amount of explanation could reduce the shock of seeing it.

THE UNEXPLAINABLE

"There are more things in Heaven and Earth, Horatio, than are dreamt of in your philosophy." So said Hamlet to Horatio upon encountering the ghost of Hamlet's father.

PUTTING THE SCIENCE IN FICTION

As someone coming from a background of science, there were many things I encountered while researching death that seriously challenged my ability to explain. It is possible that all the following phenomena can be attributed to oxygen-deprived brains, happenstance, coincidence, or just a desperate search for meaning. Whether that is the only explanation becomes a matter of faith, not science.

Deathbed visitations are one such phenomenon. People sitting with the dying person often report that person having animated, excited conversations with an unseen person in the room who has long since died (usually a spouse, parent, or friend).

Whether these can be explained by science or not is a moot point: For the person experiencing them, they are as real as anything else around them. Interestingly, the type of visitor seems influenced by culture. In the West, the visitor tends to be a loved one. In countries such as India, it's more likely to be a deity.

These visitations often have a positive effect on the person who is dying, resulting in a change of attitude and language toward a sense of journeying onward. It's usually a source of comfort to the dying person, and to those around them.

There are many stories of pets and animals behaving strangely around the moment of death: dogs howling at a distance when their owner dies, birds flocking to the windowsill. Cats in particular have been associated with death. Oscar the cat achieved global fame when a report about his ability to pick which nursing home resident was going to die next was published in *The New England Journal of Medicine.*

Other unexplained phenomena reported at the moment of death include strange lights surrounding someone, clocks stopping (recall the song "My Grandfather's Clock" by Henry Clay Work—"But it stopped short—never to go again—when the old man died"), and familiar machinery breaking down at a person's workplace.

Death is an extraordinarily varied moment and from the perspective of a writer, there is much that can be explored through it.

PART TWO

GENOME ENGINEERING: IT NEVER ENDS WELL

CHAPTER 9

A WHIRLWIND TOUR OF THE HUMAN GENOME

By Dan Koboldt

The human genome is present in virtually every cell of our bodies and contains the complete set of instructions to build a human being. The first effort to read that instruction book—the Human Genome Project—wrapped up in 2001. Even then, it was clear that our genome was a large, complex, and puzzling thing. Seventeen years later, we're still working to unravel all of its mysteries. Here's a whirlwind tour of what we know so far.

THE BIG PICTURE

The human genome comprises 3.2 billion base pairs, spread across twenty-two autosomes and two sex chromosomes. The autosomes are generally ordered by size; chromosome 1 is the largest (about 250 million base pairs), while chromosomes 21 and 22 are the smallest (48 and 51 million base pairs, respectively). Amusingly, the two sex chromosomes are dramatically different in size: Chromosome X is 155 million base pairs (about the size of chromosome 7), but chromosome Y is just 59 million.

There's also a tiny chromosome in mitochondria, the energy-producing organelles found in human cells. The mitochondrial genome is miniscule in size (16,500 base pairs), but a single cell might have as many as 2,000 copies of it. Unlike autosomes and sex chromosomes, the mitochondrial genome is only inherited from the mother. Between that and the multiple copies, it can give rise to some odd patterns of genetic inheritance. If one mitochondrion acquires a disease-causing mutation, it usually doesn't cause symptoms because there are hundreds or thousands of other mitochondria in the cell. Over time, however, more mitochondria pick up mutations. The cell continues to function until this reaches a certain threshold, which can take many years. As a result, many of the diseases caused by mitochondrial mutations (such as Leber optic atrophy) are inherited at birth but don't cause symptoms until late into adulthood.

CHROMOSOME STRUCTURE

Most of us picture chromosomes as the X-shaped things we learned about when studying mitosis in high school biology. That's how they look under a light microscope during metaphase, when two sister chromatids (the original and its shiny new copy) are joined together at the centromere, a region of highly repetitive DNA sequence where proteins bind to pull sister chromatids apart.

Because the DNA replication machinery can't copy all the way to the end of the molecule, chromosomes also have special structures at each end called *telomeres*. These are stretches of a six-letter sequence (TTAGGG in humans) repeated over and over again. They're essentially disposable bases, and they have to be, because a DNA strand gets progressively shorter every time a cell divides. The telomere-shortening process is so uniform that, by counting their size, it's possible to estimate the number of times a cell has divided, and from that, the approximate age of the person.

GENES AND FUNCTIONAL ELEMENTS

There are about twenty thousand known genes in our genome that encode proteins (i.e., make messenger RNA that's translated into protein). The fraction of bases that eventually encode protein sequences is exceedingly small (about 1.5 percent). The rest of the genome, the non-coding genome, nevertheless contains many other types of elements that can regulate things happening in a cell. Many of the other elements—promoters, untranslated regions, splice sites, exons, and introns—are structures that help govern transcription (making messenger RNA) and translation (making proteins). We've discovered, however, that there are many other kinds of noncoding elements that help regulate when and how proteins are made:

- **TRANSCRIPTION FACTOR BINDING SITES** are short, specific base sequences that are recognized and bound by the proteins that drive transcription. For example, the sequence TATAAA is usually found in the gene promoter (upstream of the gene) and likely helps position RNA polymerase II—the enzyme that makes messenger RNA from DNA—to start in the right place.
- **ENHANCERS** are big stretches of noncoding DNA that help drive the activity of certain genes. These regions are believed to have binding sites for transcription factors and other proteins. Often, they are near the genes whose activity they enhance, but they can also be located thousands of base pairs away.
- **REPRESSORS** are elements that do the opposite of enhancers: They prevent genes from being transcribed. Usually this is accomplished by recruiting proteins that either bind or make chemical modifications to DNA so it's inaccessible to the transcription machinery. For example, since females are born with two copies of

the X chromosome, one of them is repressed (inactivated) in each cell. This ensures that the cell doesn't get a "double dose" of the genes on the X chromosome.

- **NONCODING RNA GENES** are transcribed into various kinds of functional RNA, such as transfer RNA (tRNA, which matches amino acids to specific codons) and ribosomal RNA (rRNA, which aids in translation). There are also about eight hundred genes that encode micro-RNA, which are very short sequences (eighteen to twenty-four nucleotides long) that can block messenger RNA from being translated into proteins. They do this by binding complementary sequences in the untranslated region of the target micro-RNA.

If you counted the bases in all of the genes and other functional elements I've described so far, you'd come well short of 3.2 billion. Even if we understood all of these elements perfectly well (which we don't), it begs the question: What the heck does the rest of the genome do?

Honestly, we don't know. I think that a lot of it will probably turn out to have no function whatsoever. Other parts might have a function that we simply don't know about.

THE GENOME AND GENETIC DISEASES

Get ready, because I'm about to make this relevant to speculative fiction.

When people hear the phrase "genetic disease," the examples that often come to mind are severe inherited disorders, like sickle cell disease, cystic fibrosis, and Huntington's disease. Most of these are caused by very rare mutations in the coding region of a gene. This makes sense, because a mutation that disrupts or alters protein sequence is understandably capable of having a severe, immediate effect. Yet the vast majority of human traits that are "heritable" (i.e., have a genetic factor) are not so simply explained.

Many researchers, myself included, think that the genetic variation behind these is outside of the known coding regions. Think about it: A subtle change to a regulatory element could easily have an effect on a human being. For this mental exercise, let's use the low-density lipoprotein receptor (LDLR) gene. It makes a protein that transports LDL (the carrier of most cholesterol) out of the blood. Severe mutations in the coding region of LDLR cause autosomal dominant hypercholesterolemia, a severe lipid disease. Instead, picture a subtle change in a regulatory element that influences the LDLR gene activity. It might not cause a severe, obvious effect. Over the seventy-plus years of the average human lifespan, however, even a very minor change can have long-term ramifications.

Now, picture the same scenario, but change "transports LDL" to "prevents magic use" or "protects against becoming a zombie." There's your SF/F story.

CHAPTER 10

EYE-BASED PATERNITY TESTING AND OTHER HUMAN GENETICS MYTHS

by Dan Koboldt

In 2001, scientists announced an incredible accomplishment: They had completed the sequence of the human genome. The complete instruction book for making a human being spans 24 chromosomes and is 3.2 billion letters long. That's about one thousand times the length of the first ten The Wheel of Time books put together. Sequencing the whole thing had taken ten years and something like eight billion dollars.

That's a considerable investment for taxpayers, but the scientists made incredible promises. They said it would be the scientific breakthrough of the century. With the sequence of the genome in hand, they promised to dramatically improve the prevention, diagnosis, and treatment of disease. They told us the completion of the human genome would mark a new era for human health.

They lied.

Well, that's not entirely fair. Finishing the genome was the starting point in a long journey to understanding how our genes make us who we are. The more they study it, the more scientists have found that the genome is incredibly complex. I know, because I'm one of them. I work as a human geneticist at a major children's hospital.

Unfortunately, few things about genetics and inheritance are straightforward. They're certainly not as simple as we often see them portrayed in books, movies, and other media. As a scientist who also enjoys science fiction, I often encounter popular misconceptions about how genetics actually works. Here are a few of the more common (and inaccurate) tropes.

TROPE #1: THE EYE-BASED PATERNITY TEST

Oh, if I had a dime for every time a character recognized a long-lost parent or sibling based on eye color, a widow's peak, a peanut allergy, or some other physical quirk. Sure, first-degree relatives do tend to look alike, and many visible traits tend to run in families. Yet they should not be used to establish (or disprove) kinship because it's not that simple.

Eye color, despite the common wisdom suggesting otherwise, is a complex inherited trait. While it's true that blue eyes tend to be recessive and brown eyes tend to be dominant, eye color is a spectrum, not a multiple-choice test. The color of the iris is determined by the amount of melanin in it, and that can be influenced by as many as ten different genes. Brown-eyed parents can have blue-eyed children, and vice versa. Also, eye color can change: Many newborns have blue eyes that become brown or green during early childhood.

Please, don't rely on physical characteristics to tell who's related to whom. The inheritance of such traits does not always follow a predictable pattern. Even when it does, in real life, these kinds of tests might uncover secrets that were better left buried.

When we do genetics studies of families, we verify the expected relationships as a quality control step. About 4 percent of the time, there's a discrepancy (most often, the reported father is not the biological father). This observation holds true across racial groups and socioeconomic strata, and has been consistently reported by many researchers for over a decade.

We call these *non-paternity events* and, generally speaking, we don't report them back to the study participants.

TROPE #2: DIFFERENT PEOPLE HAVE DIFFERENT GENES

Often I hear people discussing how someone has "the gene" for some trait or ability. Alternatively, an elderly person in good health is often said to have "good genes." In truth, we all have the same set of about twenty thousand genes. In very rare cases, large segments of the genome can be deleted (which removes genes), and usually that's a very bad thing. So the concept of people having "different genes" is not accurate. We all basically have the same set of genes. However, the base pairs in those genes can differ from one person to the next, resulting in slight differences in when and how those genes work. That's what makes us all slightly different from one another.

That being said, I recognize that most people use the term *genes* colloquially. I don't expect people to start saying, "So you're ninety-five years old? You must have a really good set of genetic variants in and around your genes." Even if that would make me happy.

While we're on the topic, I should tell you that traditionally defined genes—that is, things that code for proteins—occupy only about 1.5 percent of the human genome. Non-coding sequences make up the rest of it. Some of them may regulate when or how much certain genes are turned on, or help organize the genome inside the cell. Still others provide physical structures that serve another purpose, such as the repetitive sequences that make up the telomeres (ends) of chromosomes.

But much of the genome either has no specific function or serves a purpose that we haven't yet uncovered.

TROPE #3: YOUR GENETIC DESTINY IS WRITTEN

Gattaca became one of my favorite science fiction movies long before I entered the field of genetics. It portrays a near-future dystopian society in which the worth and future potential of an individual are determined, at birth, with a genetic analysis. As a result, most parents take advantage of genetic selection/enhancement of embryos to get the ideal combination in their future child. These designer babies get the cool jobs, whereas babies born without such intervention are basically treated as invalids.

On the bright side, the idea of sequencing every person's genome at birth is rapidly becoming more plausible. Thanks to the advent of next-generation DNA sequencing technologies, we can now sequence a human genome in less than a week, for a little over a thousand dollars. We can use that information to infer a lot about a person, such as ancestry, risk for certain diseases, and likely physical appearance. But we're a long way off from predicting the lifetime risk for common diseases, like heart disease, diabetes, and psychiatric disorders.

Most of these result from complex interplay between genetic, lifestyle, and environmental factors. The vast majority of genetic variants associated with disease risk have a very small effect and may only increase your risk by 5 percent. There could be thousands of such genetic factors for any given disease, so predicting someone's health at birth, even if we knew everything about the genome, would be a very complex problem.

One thing I particularly admired about *Gattaca* was how the protagonist's genetic future was described in probabilities: neurological disorder, 60 percent; attention-deficit disorder, 89 percent; heart failure, 89 percent. There are few certainties in human genetics, and the movie did well to acknowledge this.

TROPE #4: MUTATIONS ARE AWESOME

Mutations, or acquired changes in DNA, are one of the most misunderstood topics in genetics. Too often in science fiction, I see mutations treated as good or advantageous things. A telling example comes from the 2002 movie *Resident Evil*, in which the Red Queen (a malicious artificial intelligence in control of things) releases a genetically engineered monster that attacks the group of heroes. After

PUTTING THE SCIENCE IN FICTION

it makes a kill, the Red Queen says that after it feeds, it will mutate, then become something new. Presumably an even stronger, deadlier monster.

The reality is that mutation, for humans at least, is uncommon. Most of the genetic variation that we have, we inherited from our parents. New mutations that arise in a child but are absent from both parents are extremely rare. We're talking about forty or fifty throughout the entire genome, compared to three to five million inherited genetic variants.

Generally speaking, new mutations are not beneficial. The human genome has been under natural selection for thousands of years. Think of it like a Formula One racecar. Mutations are like metal screws that you add (or remove) at random. More than likely, this won't have any effect on the racecar, but if it does, you're far more likely to break something than make it better.

The body's cells also acquire mutations over time, sometimes by chance as cells divide, but also through DNA damage induced by radiation or carcinogens. Most cells that suffer damaging mutations will die. Occasionally, however, a cell gets the right set of mutations that allow it to grow and divide uncontrollably. When this happens, cancer is the result.

TROPE #5: MOST GENETIC TRAITS ARE INEVITABLE

I think that the most common myth about human genetics is that most traits are inherited in simple and/or inevitable fashion. The genetics taught in most high school biology classes—like dominant, recessive, and X-linked inheritance patterns—may be partially to blame for this. Mendel's laws and the Punnett square (remember those square diagrams that you used to work out genetic crosses in biology?) only work for rare genetic conditions that are due to mutations in a single gene. Cystic fibrosis and sickle cell disease, for example, are recessive disorders caused by mutations in the *CFTR* and *HBB* genes, respectively.

Although Mendel's laws offer a useful introduction to genetic inheritance, they become problematic when we try to apply them to more complex traits. In fiction, I often meet characters living under a specter of a disease that killed their grandparents and/or parents. It seems inevitable that they, too, will fall victim to it.

Alcoholism, for example, is a complex disorder that's often treated simplistically: "My dad was an alcoholic, so I became one."

I'm sorry to have to tell you this, but most of the traits that make for interesting characters—intelligence, attractiveness, physical/mental health, etc.—do not follow simple laws of inheritance. They might not be passed from parent to child, or shared by siblings. The genetics underlying these characteristics will undoubtedly be complicated.

Just like we are.

CHAPTER II

THE NEAR FUTURE OF HUMAN GENOME ENGINEERING

By Dan Koboldt

Altering the genetic code in humans has long been a staple of science fiction, just as it's represented an important goal for biomedicine. Until recently, making targeted changes to the genomes of living cells was not really feasible, at least on a large scale. The available techniques for genome editing required custom-engineered proteins that were laborious and time-consuming to produce. That changed with the development of the CRISPR/Cas9 system, which allows targeted, precise changes to the DNA of living cells.

HOW IT WORKS

Like many tools for DNA manipulation, this one originated in bacteria. In 1987, researchers studying *Escherichia coli* noticed a strange pattern near the end of one of the bacteria's genes. It was a DNA sequence immediately followed by its mirror image (the same sequence in reverse), then about thirty non-repetitive bases, and then the palindromic structure again. Over the next two decades, this pattern—called *clustered, regularly interspaced, short palindromic repeats,* or CRISPRs—was observed in many other types of bacteria (more than 40 percent of all species).

The function of CRISPRs remained a mystery until 2005, when three independent research groups noticed that the thirty bases of "spacers" between palindromic repeats matched the sequence of certain bacteria-invading viruses called *phages.* CRISPRs encode RNA molecules that help guide DNA-cleaving enzymes called CRISPR-associated (Cas) proteins. Together, they form a sort of adaptive immune system. When a phage invades, the bacteria incorporate small portions of the invading DNA as spacers in CRISPR structures. The entire sequence is "transcribed" into a strand of ribonucleic acid (RNA) that's complementary to the invaders' DNA. This RNA acts as a guide that partners up with Cas enzymes to identify and destroy the invader's genome.

One such enzyme, the Cas9 protein of *Streptococcus pyogenes,* can be paired with a synthetic (manufactured) guide RNA to seek out and cleave specific stretches of DNA. The power of this system is in its simplicity: By modifying the sequence of the guide RNA—which is much, much easier than modifying a protein structure—

we can alter the genome of living cells with surgical precision. And those cells don't need to be bacteria: CRISPR/Cas9 works just as well in plants and animals.

POSSIBLE APPLICATIONS

Simple and precise genome engineering with CRISPR/Cas9 opens a realm of possibilities. Animal models of human disease are perhaps the best place to start. Every person has about three million genetic variants compared with the human genome reference, so it's often difficult to identify which ones contribute to disease. With this system, we can introduce a candidate mutation into a laboratory animal, such as a mouse, to see if it develops a similar disease. Once we identify the disease-causing mutation(s), such lab animals can become the front line for testing possible treatments. And because Cas9 can be given many different editing "targets" at the same time, we could even introduce several genetic changes at once to model complex diseases like diabetes and heart disease.

Another application of CRISPR/Cas9, and one that I'm personally very excited about, is functional screens of genetic changes in living cells. It's a simple fact that while we know the location and sequence of most of the approximately twenty thousand genes in the human genome, we have no idea what many of them do. One way to study gene function is to disrupt or alter its sequence in cell lines or model organisms. CRISPR/Cas9 offers a way to do that with some precision. In essence, we can learn about how the genome works by inducing specific changes and measuring the effect they have on a cell.

The potential applications go well beyond research. Genome editing should make it easier to develop better crops and healthier animal stock, and probably even customized pets (no, it won't make your cat pay more attention to you … some things are just too ingrained).

That's all good news for the research community, but let's be honest: The truly exciting applications for this technology involve editing *human* genomes. First up: correcting the underlying defect in severe genetic disorders like cystic fibrosis, sickle cell disease, and Huntington's disease. The appeal here is that such diseases are typically caused by defects in a single gene. Correcting that defect in a patient might offer a permanent cure for many such diseases.

Another way CRISPR/Cas9 might improve human health is in the defense against infectious diseases. Researchers have already demonstrated that it can be used to protect human cells from infection by viruses like hepatitis C, which implies that we might be able to use it to boost immunity to dangerous pathogens. It's not yet an immediate cure for human viral infections, but it still offers a glimmer of hope for patients suffering from chronic viral infections by herpesvirus (fever blisters), HIV (AIDS), varicella zoster (shingles), and other nasty bugs.

ETHICAL, MORAL, AND SAFETY CONCERNS

By the time we're born, our body comprises millions of individual cells, each with their own copy of the genome. Correcting a genetic defect in all of them is bound to be a difficult and inefficient process. But if the CRISPR/Cas9 system were paired with another technology—*in vitro* fertilization—we could theoretically make changes to germ cells (sperm and eggs) or human embryos prior to implantation.

Most people would agree that using genome editing to correct the underlying defect in patients with severe genetic diseases is a good thing. But as our knowledge of the human genome grows, the possibilities go far beyond that. Right now, we know mutations that lower cholesterol, protect against HIV infection, and reduce the risk of Alzheimer's disease. We also know mutations that affect hair color and eye color. There's even one that boosts your chances of making it as a world-class sprinter. As long as we're addressing health risks, is it all right to confer some of those traits as well?

The 1997 science fiction movie *Gattaca* portrays a society in which most parents employ genetic manipulation technologies to conceive children with the best possible hereditary traits. These designer babies grow up and get all the cool jobs because they're genetically "superior" in nearly every possible way. The children conceived without such manipulations are considered inferior and are basically destined to live out their lives as janitors or trash collectors. *Gattaca* portrays a future that seems both distant and unlikely, but a technology that allows us to edit the genomes of human embryos brings it into the realm of possibility.

As appealing as it may be to think about all of the good things we might do with CRISPR/Cas9, we still don't know enough about the potential long-term risks of human genome engineering. In the past, technologies developed to correct genetic defects have had off-target effects. Early clinical trials of gene therapy with recombinant viruses, for example, were halted after some participants developed leukemia. And changes made to a human embryo can be passed on to children, which means that they could have unforeseen effects in future generations.

The beta hemoglobin gene (*HBB*) offers a useful example. Severe mutations in *HBB* cause sickle cell disease in autosomal-recessive fashion, meaning that a person must inherit two mutated copies of the gene to get the disease. It would be tempting, therefore, to use CRISPR/Cas9 to reverse the disruptive mutation in the germ cells of known mutation carriers. Yet individuals with just a single mutated copy of *HBB* are naturally resistant to malaria, a major cause of morbidity and death in Africa. This "carrier advantage" helps explain why severe disease-causing mutations persist in African populations at frequencies higher than we'd expect. If we used CRISPR/Cas9 to systematically remove *HBB* mutations, we could almost certainly reduce or eliminate sickle cell disease … but future generations might be more susceptible to malaria.

THE GENETIC FUTURE

Thus, there are both ethical and safety considerations that must be addressed before we plunge whole-hog into human genome engineering. Mindful of this, an international group of scientists proposed a moratorium against conducting "genome surgery" on human cells. But a voluntary moratorium is not enough to prevent this research from happening, especially in countries that haven't agreed to it. That became apparent when a research team in China used the technique to modify the genomes of human embryos. They used "nonviable" embryos from a local fertility clinic and hoped to employ CRISPR/Cas9 to alter the gene for beta thalassaemia, a severe blood disorder. The results of the study were disappointing and the journal that published it is rather obscure, but that's the smaller problem. The larger one is that scientists were able to do this and get it published, with virtually no oversight from any outside authority.

The only positive outcome from the study is that it sounded an alarm bell for the medical and research communities. Human genome engineering is coming, whether we like it or not. As a science-fiction author, I think it's exciting. As a scientist, I also think it's a little terrifying. We have only begun to debate the ethics and morality of altering our own genetic code. With great power comes great responsibility, and we've never had more genetic power than we do right now.

●

CHAPTER 12

THE SCIENCE OF *JURASSIC PARK*
By Mike Hays

When I read Michael Crichton's *Jurassic Park* (Knopf, 1990) for the very first time shortly after its release, as the small *Procompsognathu* appeared on the Costa Rican beach, I jumped out of my chair with excitement and hit my head on the hanging light fixture in my living room. By the time I settled back down with the book in one hand and a towel pressed against the cut on my scalp with the other, I was hooked. After the revelation of the cloning of dinosaurs and the science involved, I was firmly in "can't-put-this-book-down-or-even-talk-to-my-wife" mode.

This is what good science fiction does. It brings together plausible science elements to build a story world that the reader can easily enter and be completely convinced this is a place worth spending time in. I still re-read the book about every five years and that magic is always there, a magic grounded in the book's science and technology. And, of course, there are the dinosaurs.

I was a fledgling molecular microbiologist when the book first came out. I was learning the technology of molecular cloning and the revolutionary new technique of polymerase chain reaction in order to study infectious diseases. I remember the science of *Jurassic Park*, both the fictional and the actual science, created an uproar within the science community and led to the big question:

Could we really clone dinosaurs?

Scientists thought about it.

Scientists argued about it.

Scientists wrote about it.

There was much debate about cloning, sequencing, embryology, and paleontological theories on dinosaur behavior. What was perhaps overlooked in the discussion was the fact that *Jurassic Park* was a science *fiction* thriller. Michael Crichton did such an exceptional job building the world that I think we all got caught up in the possibilities he presented.

In science fiction, the science need not be 100 percent accurate; the science needs to be plausible and logical within the world built. In my opinion, Crichton does that rather well in *Jurassic Park*. He lines up the scientific details, everything from large cobra-venom-like protein toxins to genomic space-filling frog DNA, and ticks them off like a timer on a bomb counting down the seconds to disaster.

THE GOOD SCIENCE

Here are some of the accurate science things in *Jurassic Park*.

Dinosaurs!

Michael Crichton brought the most cutting-edge theories in paleontology to life within the framework of the most exciting new molecular technology ever discovered. He reinvigorated dinosaur mania for a whole new generation.

Chaos Theory

To me, the most impressive science facet of *Jurassic Park* was the integration of chaos theory into the story. Chaos theory is when small changes in the initial conditions of a complex system lead to drastic changes in the results.

I like the double pendulum system as a nice and simple model to illustrate the basics of chaos theory. We've all seen a single pendulum swing back and forth with precision and beauty. As the single pendulum moves back and forth, its path and speed stay fairly stable. Back and forth. Back and forth. Back and forth. Predictable and ordered.

In the double pendulum system, a hinge is introduced in the center of the pendulum's arm to provide one small change in the system. As the double pendulum swings, it pretty much holds to an orderly swing pattern for about five trips. After the fifth trip, though, the order breaks down and the arm goes haywire. That small initial change manifests into a totally chaotic pattern later on.

Now, think back to *Jurassic Park*. The first part of the visit to the park is relatively ordered, just like our pendulum model. Then one by one, the compounding small mistakes inherent in the system, which existed in the park's plan from its inception, begin to crumble the perceived order of the entire park system.

Every facet of the *Jurassic Park* vision tumbles into chaos. Small initial changes have a tremendous effect upon the entire system.

Molecular Biology

Jurassic Park pushed the limits of the fledgling molecular biology knowledge base in the late 1980s. Crichton did the best with the technology he had available and did his best to be accurate. In areas where he was weak in his knowledge base in *Jurassic Park*, such as the sequence database information errors in some of the representative GenBank sequences, he brought in bioinformatics experts as consultants for his sequel, *The Lost World* (Knopf, 1995).

THE STRETCHES IN SCIENCE

Here's where Michael Crichton took more creative license and less hard science.

The Genome Factor

Cloning basically means to copy, so if you want to clone something that is or once was living, what do you need, first and foremost? An intact genome.

But finding a genome template from ancient samples with enough intact information in the blueprint to produce more than a few genes is very difficult. The quality and amount of ancient DNA depends on the sample preservation and natural degradation of the genomic DNA. DNA, the chemical strands that contain the genetic instructions for the development and function of living things, is a fairly stable biological molecule. DNA is stable enough that LIFE trusts it with its past, present, and future. But DNA degrades over time. It is difficult to find intact pieces in ancient DNA, especially in amber-trapped insects found in South American rainforest environments, as laid out in *Jurassic Park*. The extraction of the blueprint DNA from this source would probably not produce enough viable genetic information to clone even one deadly claw.

Recent advances in extraction technologies, enrichment of target DNA, and incredible jumps in genome and whole organism sequencing science have increased the prospect of someday being able to cloned prehistoric animals.

Researchers have reported the successful sequencing of woolly mammoths (ten thousand years old), Neanderthals (thirty-eight thousand years old), the genome of a girl belonging to an early species of Homo sapiens called the Denisovans— a close relation to the Neanderthals—who lived about eighty thousand years ago (the study even reports she had brown eyes, hair, and skin!). To push the envelope even further, the entire genetic sequence of a 700,000-year-old extinct species of horse was published in the journal *Nature*.

Interesting to note, all these ancient samples were discovered in a frozen state. Having probably been frozen for millennia, the DNA was better preserved than anything found in a rainforest environment, like amber-trapped insects. The result was a better genomic template, and better templates = better sequence.

These advances in genome sequencing have stretched the ability of scientists to gather genetic information from extinct organisms almost a million years old. Not quite to the age of dinosaurs yet, but I hold out hope we may someday find a sixty-five-million-year-old frozen dino-popsicle containing a solid genome.

Embryo Availability

Another scientific criticism from back in 1991 was the limited available choices for embryo development once a clone was established. The synthetic eggshell technology in the book was an easy out in this regard, but really wasn't an applicable real-life method to hatch a dinosaur clone. Cloning dinosaur embryos may be one thing, but actually hatching and raising viable progeny is a whole different ball of wax.

With recent advances in stem cell technologies and the ability to reprogram a blank cell with a new set of DNA instructions through gene editing, perhaps this hurdle could be overcome if we can learn to piggyback on existing natural reptilian systems.

Time Scale

As a professional scientist, I am pretty certain the discovery, development (especially on a scale of cloning dinosaurs!), and building a secret theme park on Isla Nublar would have easily taken more than a decade. Even with a well-funded army of scientists, cutting-edge laboratories, and all the Cray supercomputers one could get one's greedy hands on, it would have been a long process. Plus, how did they sneak all this technology and equipment past the regulatory agencies?

THAT'S WHAT SCIENCE FICTION DOES

So, from a pure scientific standpoint and within the science knowledge base of the late 1980s, Michael Crichton did a pretty darn good job with the genetics and molecular biology in *Jurassic Park*. He took these cutting-edge technologies and crafted a very entertaining and thought-provoking story world. Sure, there were reaches, but the reaches in science were plausible and logical within his story world.

Besides, can't we give Michael Crichton a pass on some of the science flaws? He cloned dinosaurs! He lit a fire under the imagination of science and technology and raised the bar on the possibilities of new fantastical projects that could actually happen. He sowed a seed in young scientists for future discovery.

That, my friends, is successful science fiction.

And that is enough for me.

(Just keep me away from Steven Spielberg and that cartoon DNA-strand narrated animation ride he used to explain the background science of *Jurassic Park* to visitors in the movie. *Grrrr...*)

Now, where did I put that tattered paperback copy of *Jurassic Park*? I'm ready for a re-read.

CHAPTER 13

ZOMBIE MICROBIOLOGY 101

By Mike Hays

Everybody loves zombies. Okay, maybe not everybody, but zombies have been a source of frightful entertainment for years and their popularity appears to be at an all-time high in today's media market. Why are we so drawn to them? Robert Kirkman, creator of *The Walking Dead* comics, believes it is our innate fear of death that draws us in. And, like the relentless nature of death, he says, "Zombies are out to get you, no matter how hard you try."

Mira Grant, author of the Newsflesh series, thinks zombies hit the human fear chord toward infectious diseases and the potential loss of self and identity caused by a serious infection. The answer probably lies in a little of both fear theories. I lean toward the infectious disease fear side of the fence, though. Maybe the fear of being chased by a relentless and seemingly endless mass of reanimated corpses hell-bent on eating my brain is enough to draw me in, but the fear of losing myself to an unseen microbial Zombie Factor that strikes without warning is what brings me back craving more.

THE ZOMBIE APOCALYPSE

The world turned to chaos as flesh-eating reanimated corpses shuffled across the planet seeking human brains for a snack, caused by a zombie virus. The zombie virus is a very popular causative agent in today's zombie media culture. Books, movies, and TV shows feature the zombie-caused-by-virus story. But is it plausible? Maybe, maybe not. Let's take a look past the decaying flesh, the characteristic zombified gait, and the insatiable drive to consume human flesh, and delve deeper into the potential causative agent of the Zombie Factor.

Viral

Figure 13.1: Cowpea mosaic virus (Getty Images)

Probably the most popular microbial agent for Zombie Factor is a virus. Viruses are a logical choice. They carry the fear stigma we've come to associate with massive outbreaks of diseases, like smallpox, influenza, Ebola, HIV, and rabies. Perfect for the Zombie Factor, right? Well ... maybe not. The most dangerous viruses, the ones that spread rapidly, are usually spread by airborne contact. Other modes of transmission like infected animal bites, insect bites, and ingestion or contact with infected body fluids are slower methods of viral transmission, which in turn, slow the spread of the disease.

The Zombie Apocalypse would require a high-velocity transmission virus to be effective against the intelligent, always-prepared human populace. Viruses have limited genome size and complexity. They infect cells and may hijack some cellular processes, but I don't believe they actually have the genomic power for a massive transformation from human to zombie. It's a sexy, simple agent on which to base a Zombie Factor, but in my opinion, it just doesn't have the muster to get the job done alone.

Bacterial

Ten years ago, I would have said "No way" to bacteria as a causative agent of zombification. Back in my scientific youth, bacteria were thought to attach to the target cells, dump their various toxins, and cause the disease. Now we are discovering that bacteria are much more complex than simple toxin dumpers; they secrete proteins that enter the host cell and modulate host gene expression. What does that mean? It means the bacteria can reprogram normal cellular responses. The bacteria can create host mediated changes that help its survival. Now things are getting interesting, huh? Especially when we add another layer of complexity and consider the effects of a whole population of bacteria, called a *microbiome*.

Figure 13.2: Escherichia coli under the microscope (Getty Images)

A microbiome is the collection of microorganisms that exist in a particular environment. Part of what we research in the laboratory where I work involves study of the intestinal microbiota and the interactions these microbes have with the host gut in the prevention of infection with enteric pathogens. It is an intricate system where the microbes modulate the cells of the intestine to benefit both the host and the microorganisms of the gut biome. Frankly, I did not put zombification and microbiome together until I received a research alert for an article describing the human death microbiome that the authors called the *thanatomicrobiome*. The researchers report a characteristic, time-dependent, postmortem shift of the bacteria in human tissues from a predominantly aerobic (oxygen-loving) bacterial population to an anaerobic population (oxygen-hating).

Perhaps a single bacterial pathogen may not have the bang to induce zombification, but how about a unique zombie microbiome signature that triggers a transformation in a nearly dead human host to a member of the walking dead? The zombie bite introduces a zombie bacterial microbiome, which sits resident in the host until the host faces death and then triggers the transformation from deathbed human to walking dead. Sweet, huh?

Parasites

Parasites are potential contributors to the Zombie Factor. Fungus, yeasts, molds, and worms all have the genomic complexity that could potentially cause such a massive transformation. There are documented cases of parasites affecting host behavior, with many of these discoveries rising from the relatively new field of neuroparasitology. *Toxoplasma gondii* infection in rats makes them less scared of cats and more likely to be eaten by these cats, where the parasite multiplies and is released in the cat's feces.

Figure 13.3: Schistosoma mansoni parasite (Getty Images)

The flatworm *Euhaplorchis californiensis* changes its fish host's behavior to make it easier to be captured and eaten by birds, which are the reproductive host. Perhaps the most interesting example is of the *Ophiocordyceps* fungus, coined the *zombie-ant fungus*. The fungal spore lands on a specific variety of carpenter ants. The spore secretes enzymes that allow entry into the body of the ant where the fungus grows. The fungus releases chemicals to hijack the ant's neural control

PUTTING THE SCIENCE IN FICTION

and forces it to wander until it finds the perfect leaf. The ant then bites into the leaf, dies, and the fungus grows out of the dead ant's head. The fungal shoot matures to produce and release more spores that infect more ants. Zombie ants. As you can see, parasites really begin to reveal a microorganism with the potential to be a cause of the behavioral changes associated with zombification and become a potential candidate for the elusive Zombie Factor.

Prions

Prions can be another potential Zombie Factor agent. These infectious proteins are often described as virus-like particles without any nucleic acid (DNA or RNA). In general, these prion proteins appear to be similar to native host proteins, except with slight conformational changes that cause them to spontaneously aggregate, form crystals, and kill host cells. Prion diseases are associated with the degenerative brain disorders, Creutzfeldt-Jakob disease and Kuru in humans, bovine spongiform encephalitis ("mad cow") disease in cattle, chronic wasting disease in deer or elk, and scrapie in sheep.

The degenerative neurological effects of prion-induced, spongiform encephalitis affect brain function and could potentially induce the characteristics of a zombie: wonky motor skills, speech, and eating disorders. The problem with prions is they are slow moving. It may take years for enough prion protein crystals to aggregate to the point of causing brain damage.

Epidemiology

Can the Zombie Factor move fast enough, be infectious enough, and (this should be a big AND) spread without some sort of intervention through immunity or vaccination, to actually produce an effective army of the living dead hellbent on live, healthy, human brain consumption?

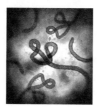

Figure 13.4: Ebola virus virion (Getty Images)

Well, it would have to have a high reproduction number (R_0 value), which is a calculation used by epidemiologists to enumerate how many new individuals become infected per one original infected individual. A more contagious infectious agent would have a higher R_0 value (measles with an R_0 of 18) than a less contagious infectious agent (Ebola virus with an R_0 of 2).

Airborne transmission of the infectious agent also makes it a more contagious agent, which makes it more likely to be spread rapidly and widely. The Zombie Factor would have to be more easily transmittable than through the accepted model of a bite. Infectious agents transmitted through bites are usually slow spreading. Rabies, for example, a virus often associated as the basis for a zombie virus, is a rare disease with an R_0 value barely over 1. Another thing to consider is the level of care and monitoring of the established public health care system. The rapid recognition, diagnosis, and appropriate isolation of those infected can lower the R_0 value to almost 0. An infectious Zombie Factor would have to spread very quickly before containment of those infected could be completed in order to be effective.

THE ZOMBIE FACTOR

In a nutshell, although there are some intriguing, existing microbial agents that have some potential to be the infectious Zombie Factor, they all fall short. Zombie populace, the odds are *not* in your favor for a global takeover. It doesn't matter if you are a classic voodoo zombie fan (that's a whole separate essay on toxins!) or are drawn to the brain-eating side of the zombie fence either by your fear of death or your fear of infectious disease—keep your walking dead fandom going strong. Keep reading, keep watching, and keep writing. And keep those awesome zombie stories coming.

●

CHAPTER 14

ROGUE VIRUSES AND PATHOGENS

by Lee A. Everett

I recently watched a friend play a popular video game. His character was an assassin, and one of his missions involved stealing a virus from a laboratory—a relatively common trope, right? But as the character manhandled his way into the lab, charged by the bewildered scientists, grabbed the vial, and left by a side door straight onto a busy street, the most memorable part of the gameplay—to me— was how *unfeasible* it was.

We've all witnessed the heist of a biologic agent in some form or another. (And when I refer to an *agent*, I mean the bacteria, virus, protein, alien technology, or compound of interest.) It's fun to write and it's fun to read, but two things these scenarios usually have in common are the seeming ignorance of the types of places these agents are kept, and the mechanisms put in place to keep people and the environment safe from the agent.

When handled wrong, any reader with a small amount of experience in the area is likely to doubt the credibility of your plot for the duration of the book. I don't think that's the sort of notable mention most of us are going for when setting out to write a novel.

Unless you're going to pull a "many Bothans died" and sweep the getting of the agent under the rug (it doesn't matter how we got it, we just got it!), you're going to need to break your character in and out of the lab in a believable way.

ALL ABOUT THE AGENT

So what are the top three things you should consider when brainstorming the agent for your "virus gone rogue" novel?

1. **WHAT THE AGENT DOES**

    How does it affect the target? Is it contagious to humans only, or animals as well? Most important: How is it spread and how long can it live outside the host? An agent that can be aerosolized—spread through the air (like influenza), especially one that can survive outside of the host for a long time—is a lot more dangerous than one only spread by direct contact, sexual contact, or ingestion. The way you'd try to contain a flu-like agent would be a bit different from how you'd try to contain an Ebola-like agent, and they'd have different epidemiologic impacts. With the flu, preventing respiratory spread is key. People working with pathogenic flus will wear various types of respirators to protect themselves and lab-dedicated clothing to keep from carrying the virus outside the lab. But with Ebola and its ability to spread through direct contact, researchers need to protect themselves even more strenuously. They wear "space suit"-like positive air pressure suits hooked to an air supply coming from outside the lab so no part of their body or the air they're breathing can come in contact with the agent.

Get creative! There are a lot of dastardly agents out there that are quirkier than a highly pathogenic flu or a hemorrhagic disease. For example, prions aren't even alive—they're misfolded proteins—yet they are one of the hardest agents to destroy, are highly contagious, and diseases caused by them are incurable (as well as invariably fatal).

2. **AGENT CREATION AND STORAGE**

What the agent can do and how stable it is are going to impact how scientists create and store it. Additionally, how hardy an agent is will determine how mobile it is and how long your characters will be able to handle and keep it without some pretty specialized equipment. Does the agent need to be inoculated into a carrier host to keep it viable, or will a splash of it still be infective on the ground a decade later?

The *Mycobacterium* that causes leprosy, for example, can only be grown within live tissue, while other bacteria like *Clostridium* can form spores that persist in the environment for years before infecting a host. Viruses, which hijack host cells for replication, may have capsids that protect the viral genetic material like a shield, allowing them to live outside a host longer than viruses without capsids. In general, viruses and bacteria can be "cultured" (kept alive in nutritional broth or media in refrigerators or incubators) but very high or low temperatures will kill them. Yet body tissues containing prions can still be infective after being stored at -80° C.

Theoretically, rogue pathogens created on Earth may have more constraints and limitations than something like an alien pathogen. Foreign to the planet, these would likely be able to survive temperature fluctuations and levels of radiation that Earth-borne pathogens have never been exposed to—and may be a lot harder to contain.

3. BIOSECURITY AND BIOCONTAINMENT

Now here's the part that will likely impact your plot the most: How do the characters handle the biosecurity and biocontainment of the facility they're breaking into? These are the procedures designed to keep a "rogue virus event" from ever happening (without nefarious interference, anyway). Most facilities have primary and secondary means of containment: the ways they keep people and the environment safe from the agent.

CONTAINMENT: YOUR CHARACTER'S MAIN ADVERSARY

There are four biosafety level (BSL) designations created by the Centers for Disease Control and Prevention. The riskier an agent is to work with, the more facilities/ controls are necessary to keep people and the environment safe, and thus the agent should be contained in a higher BSL lab. BSL-1 facilities house agents that typically don't cause human disease (like non-pathogenic *Escherichia coli*); at BSL-2, the agents pose moderate hazards to humans and may be found normally in the population (like *Salmonella*). At BSL-3, the agents can cause severe or lethal disease and are often spread by aerosolization (like tuberculosis); security and personnel clearance thresholds need to be increased because some diseases worked with at BSL-3 facilities could be potential agents in biological terrorism (like anthrax or the plague). At the potentially deadly BSL-4 (something really risky to work with, something that can infect humans but for which we have no cure—an alien virus, for example), there is going to be a *lot* of security within the building. After going through suitability assessments and background checks to get access to the building, there are lots of locked layers to get through before you reach the lab, likely involving keys or swipe cards—even biometric scanning.

Infiltrating the Lab

And of course, there will be security personnel and security cameras to thwart. Blackmailing or otherwise manipulating someone who already is cleared to enter these spaces might be the simplest way of infiltrating the lab, or perhaps technology can be used to circumvent the surveillance. But what happens once you get inside?

If you're sneaking in or trying to blend in with the staff, then step one, you're going to head to the locker room and get naked. Yup, nothing that goes into a lab containing such a deadly agent is going to be able to come out without some serious decontamination. That includes people.

Personal Protective Equipment (PPE)

So you strip completely and put on facility PPE: often long-sleeved scrubs, socks, shoes (probably Crocs), hairnet, special respirator that you've been approved to use, and two layers of gloves. To get back out of the lab once you've done your thing, there is a careful order of removing PPE so it can be autoclaved, decontaminated with chemicals, or destroyed. Then you shower before you're allowed to go back to the locker room.

Chances are, if you are trying to steal an agent, you don't really care if you expose the outside world to it—so perhaps you skip the shower. But putting on the proper PPE is the best way to blend in and decrease the chances that the staff or scientists notice you don't belong there.

Once you leave the locker room and head toward the lab, if you want to prevent yourself from getting sick from the agent, you're going to pull on a Tyvek suit with a powered air-purifying respirator at BSL-3; or at the BSL-4, one of those positive pressure ventilated space suits where you're hooked into a wall air supply. The goal of these is to blow clean air to you, while also pushing potential contaminate away from you. (It's uncomfortable, hot, and loud under all those layers! If your character has any sort of communication device—or fear of enclosed spaces—you're going to need to handle that additional conflict.)

Lab Containment Measures

Now you're inside the lab, and your PPE is keeping you safe from the agent. What's keeping the lab space and rest of the environment safe? Ideally, the agent should be so contained that the lab itself remains clean. If you're following proper procedure (ahem, *not* breaking it out of the lab), agents will always be worked with under some sort of hood or biosafety cabinet. These are special working spaces that use a wall of air to keep the agent inside the cabinet and contaminants outside, and are ventilated so the air passing over the agent is HEPA-filtered before being vented outside or recirculated.

Or, at the BSL-4, the agent may be kept in a completely sealed cabinet and can only be manipulated using thick, unwieldy gloves attached to the unit. To reach the agent, a character is going to have to bust the agent out of that containment cabinet somehow and keep herself safe from it as she heads back out of the locker room—if someone doesn't catch her first.

Contamination Shutdowns

We could talk for a while about airflow back in these facilities, but suffice it to say, if the all-important airflow is ever messed up, or if there is a biological spill, all workers must immediately leave and the whole lab gets shut down until everything is back to normal. The distraction of that sort of chaos might be ideal cover for the theft. In the event of emergency (power loss, natural disaster), you're going to have to quickly be able to leave the lab, yet do so in a manner that won't contaminate the outside world. Usually this involves putting extra, clean PPE on top of what you're already wearing to trap any contaminant inside with you as you head to an emergency meeting point—which will be separate from where the rest of the building is meeting.

Often, local fire departments and hospitals are kept aware of the type of work going on in the labs and receive extra training on what to do and where to go in medical emergencies. If some sort of emergency was staged and your character had allies among the paramedics or fire department, that might be another unobtrusive way to slip an agent out.

IN SUMMARY

Understandably, including all these detailed layers in your narrative could start to feel a little bulky. But I think it's important that, as a writer, you've thought about these aspects—at least in terms of setting and world building—so the characters can subvert them in a believable way. How a character handles biosecurity measures can really impact the plot—especially when things start to go wrong—because stealing a deadly, world-altering virus shouldn't be easy, right?

●

CHAPTER 15

PLAGUES AND PANDEMICS

By Gabriel Vidrine

Plagues are a common science fiction plot trope, either as a main source of tension and plot or as backdrop. They can range from Michael Crichton's alien *la linea verde de muerte* (also known as the Andromeda Strain) to George R.R. Martin's greyscale to J.K. Rowling's somewhat amusingly named Spattergroit. The range of symptoms, like real plagues, can vary from deadly and horrid to merely annoying.

The problem comes in when these plagues reach too far into science fiction and become merely fiction (i.e., have no basis in science). Of course, magical (and possibly alien) plagues will have their own rules, but if you want your science fiction to be more than merely fiction, keep reading.

MYTH #1: A PLAGUE NEEDS TO BE A VIRUS TO BE DEADLY

While browsing through a list of fictional plagues for some background research for this article, I noticed something interesting: Most fictional plagues are viral. While it is true that science has yet to come up with completely effective treatments for viral diseases, not all deadly diseases are viral. Influenza probably holds the record for deadliest disease in history, but one of the most horrifying diseases we have is the Black Death, and that was caused by the lowly bacterium *Yersinia pestis*. Ebola (a virus) isn't a picnic, either, but Ebola has killed less than fifteen thousand people.

The Black Death killed roughly twenty-five *million* people. That's a lot of people, and it was nearly a third of Europe's population at the time. Imagine what it would be like to live through a time where one out of every three people you know succumbs to a terrible plague that has no cure. And the Black Death *still* kills people, even in this age of antibiotics, though typically from lack of treatment. And with the way antibiotic resistance is going, bacteria are poised to make a comeback as a force to be reckoned with, so don't rule out bacteria as a source for your plague.

MYTH #2: PLAGUES WILL ONLY INFECT OR KILL A CERTAIN POPULATION

A lot of fictional plagues only kill off certain "undesirables" in the fictional world, like Jim Hendee's Codon Zero (which itself has other problems) that only infects Arabs and Jews, or kills only adults (Karel Čapek's White Disease), or kills only women (Frank Herbert's White Plague). I've got news for you: If a disease can infect one part of a human population, it can infect *all* of the human population. Variation in lethality could be caused by variations in immunity (caused by genetics) or by exposure, but generally speaking, any deadly virus can infect and kill any human.

There are diseases that some people have a natural immunity to, but this is usually due to exposure over generations or exposure to a similar virus (like cowpox) and the passing of immunity on to babies from mother's milk, not by any magical ability of the virus. Bacteria are also not picky about whom they infect.

There *are* diseases that affect certain populations, but these are genetically linked (like sickle cell anemia, beta thalassemia, and Tay-Sachs, to name a few) not viral or bacterial. Besides, it's a documented fact that women have stronger immune systems than men (sorry, Frank).

MYTH #3: SCIENTISTS ARE ALWAYS GENETICALLY ENGINEERING DEADLY VIRUSES

As I talked about in chapter 2 of this book, we already have a lot of scary, deadly diseases; we certainly don't need more of them. There are few reasons for scientists to engineer deadly viruses, though the viruses and bacteria we do have are researched for possible weaponization (I once heard a scientist claim that some Russian scientists mixed smallpox and Ebola, but the veracity of that is questionable).

When scientists genetically tinker with viruses it's usually to put them to good use, as with lentivirus (like HIV), which is used in cancer research and gene therapy. The disease-causing portion of the virus has been removed or inactivated, and the National Institutes of Health monitors lentivirus research *very carefully* to ensure that no HIV-like disease develops with lentivirus treatments.

GETTING PLAGUES RIGHT IN FICTION

Here are a few tips for writing realistic plagues and pandemics into your fiction.

Vectors and Transmission

If you want a plague, you need a way to get that plague to spread among your population. Thus, you need a means of transmission. Bacteria and viruses (and even parasites that cause spreadable, plague-like diseases like malaria) have hosts and a way to infect others to continue the life cycle. The way that diseases spread will completely depend on the type of virus, bacteria, or parasite you're working with.

Viruses often have reservoirs, hosts that carry the virus but rarely get sick from it, that can spread the virus through contact with other species, though viruses don't need to go through reservoirs to spread from human to human. Viruses are actually fairly fragile and don't last long outside of their host or reservoir (think minutes to hours, not days), so they must be spread by close contact or by a short time in the air.

Oh, and since the Ebola outbreak has everyone confused about what airborne transmission means, let's go over that. *Airborne* means a disease can be spread just by breathing in the same air as someone who has the disease. He breathes out particles, you breathe them in. Boom, you have the flu. Ebola is not airborne. It can, however, be *aerosolized*, which means that when someone coughs, she sprays droplets of blood or saliva into the air, which surrounds the virus and keeps it alive long enough to get into someone else's eyes, nose, or mouth. Just being in the same airspace as her does not mean you will get it (unless she coughs). Airborne viruses, like the flu and tuberculosis, are more easily spread than aerosolized viruses.

Parasites, like malaria, often need an intermediary, like a mosquito, to spread from human to human. Bacteria live everywhere and will happily live on a surface for hours and, in some cases, longer than that. Some bacterial species can form endospores, which can last for *centuries*.

Killing in Hours Is Not Useful to a Disease

Exceptionally lethal diseases that kill quickly are not, evolutionarily speaking, very useful. A parasite that kills off its host too quickly isn't a very successful parasite because it kills its host before it has a chance to spread. One of the reasons Ebola hasn't been as much of a problem as it could be is its high mortality rate, the speed at which it can kill, and the difficulty in spreading it. Smallpox was so horrible because it had a lower mortality rate, spread more easily, and didn't kill as quickly.

Viruses typically do not take hours to incubate, either. It takes time for the virus to enter a cell, hijack its machinery, produce more virus, and get enough viral particles in the blood for the immune system to take notice and start the defense. That takes time—usually a few days, not hours.

PICK YOUR POISON CORRECTLY

Keep everything you have read in mind when creating your virus. There's nothing really wrong with coming up with a whole new plague that your characters must struggle through. But make it follow the rules (unless it's a magical or alien plague). It needs a method of transmission that is suitable for the type of organism. It shouldn't kill off the host in hours. Also consider another type of organism, like a bacterium that is resistant to all of our antibiotics, if you want something truly terrifying. Or, for even more fun, try a fungus (look up valley fever if you're interested).

PART THREE

THE BRAIN IS WIDER
THAN THE SKY

CHAPTER 16

●

WRITING MENTAL HEALTH
IN FICTION

By Kathleen S. Allen, RN, DNP

Like you, I am a writer. I'm also a mental health professional, and I often cringe when I come across mental illness depicted in fiction because it's usually either not quite right or half-right or completely off track.

It's fine to use search engines to do research, but there is so much misinformation on the Internet it's often difficult to discern what is correct and what is downright wrong. It can be damaging to a reader who has a psychiatric disorder when a book writes mental illness poorly. I'm going to dispel myths about several psychiatric disorders in order to help you write mental illness to empower your readers.

During my stint as a psychiatric nurse practitioner I diagnosed patients/clients, wrote orders for patients in a locked psychiatric unit, did admissions and discharges, and prescribed medications and did therapy for adolescents and adults who had depression, anxiety, post-traumatic stress disorder (PTSD), bipolar disorder, obsessive-compulsive disorder, and schizophrenia. I've worked with patients/clients who have attempted suicide, were suicidal, or were getting electroconvulsive therapy (ECT), and no, it's not like *One Flew Over the Cuckoo's Nest*. Think of it more like a computer reboot.

I've also seen people suffering from a mental disorder due to their medical condition, and that's why it's important for psychiatric patients, especially those with first-time symptoms, to be medically cleared before a psychiatric diagnosis can be given to them.

So what does this mean for you, a writer? If you are able to speak to a mental health professional, great! If not, invest in the *Diagnostic and Statistical Manual of Mental Disorders*, Fifth Edition (DSM-5), a manual that mental health professionals use to diagnose their patients/clients. Each category in the DSM-5 lists criteria for a certain disorder and how many of those criteria need to be met to make a diagnosis.

I believe it is important to write characters who have been diagnosed (or will be diagnosed in your story) with a mental illness to help remove the stigma of mental illness. Stigma can be one of the major reasons why people don't get help for mental illness along with not knowing resources that may be available to them, having a low (or no) income, homelessness (although not all homeless individuals have a mental illness), and unavailable child care or transportation to treatment.

So, let's get started with writing a character who has a mental illness in your story.

FACTS ABOUT MENTAL ILLNESS

Depression

Depression can be diagnosed at any age, including as a child. According to the National Alliance on Mental Illness, one in five children will have or has a serious mental illness. Anxiety disorders often accompany depression. This can include generalized anxiety disorder, social anxiety disorder, and panic disorder (with panic attacks).

The most vulnerable groups are adolescents and women. Vulnerable populations are adolescents who are bullied, who identify as being LGBT, who have a history of family with depression or suicide, and who are involved in violence. According to the World Health Organization, suicide is the third leading cause of death for adolescents between the ages of fifteen and nineteen and the second leading cause of death for adolescents and adults between the ages of fifteen and twenty-nine.

Symptoms

Characters with depression can oversleep, not sleep enough, overeat, not eat much, feel suicidal, be irritable, be angry, feel sad, cry too much, or feel numb. They no longer enjoy doing the activities they used to enjoy. Their depression can be mild, moderate, or severe (unable to function in their daily lives). In a severe depression they can also have psychosis and experience hallucinations or hear voices that aren't there. Characters with depression (moderate or severe) may also be suicidal.

Treatment

Treatment for depression is a combination of talk therapy with a social worker or psychologist who has been trained in cognitive behavioral therapy or interpersonal therapy and medications such as selective serotonin reuptake inhibitors that help balance the neurotransmitters that regulate mood in the brain.

When writing about medications for characters, I find it easier to make up a name of a medication rather than have the fictional character taking the wrong medication for his disorder.

If your character is suicidal, she needs to be hospitalized if she has a plan and intent. If she is feeling suicidal with no exact plan or intent, others need to be vigilant about the degree to which the character is experiencing suicidal thoughts.

Busting Myths About Depression

Please don't use the word *depressed* when your character is feeling sad or blue. Being depressed is not the same as feeling down. If your character has depression, it's not uncommon for him to laugh, smile, or appear happy even when he is in the midst of a depressive episode.

Characters who ask others if they are suicidal will not put the idea in their head. It's already there, and asking about suicidal thoughts will not force someone to commit suicide if the thought with plan and intent wasn't already there.

If a character is a cutter (cuts on self to relieve stress or extreme emotional anxiety), it doesn't mean she is suicidal. Does this mean anyone who cuts isn't suicidal? No, of course not, but again, ask.

Bipolar Disorder

Bipolar disorder means a person with this mental illness experiences both depression and elation during different times. There is a spectrum of bipolar disorders and not everyone experiences extreme lows or extreme highs, although some can. Some have rapid cycling, meaning their periods of ups and downs can occur like a rollercoaster over several days or weeks, and some can have depression for months before they have an upswing.

A character with bipolar disorder can be diagnosed as an adolescent and sometimes as a child. At risk are those with an immediate family member also diagnosed with it.

Symptoms

A character with bipolar disorder can exhibit manic signs such as not needing sleep, having increased energy, eating less, having grandiose thoughts or ideas, talking too fast, or talking nonsense. He may engage in high-risk activities such as spending too much money or other risky behaviors. When he is not in a manic state he can experience signs of depression including being suicidal. He can also experience psychosis.

Treatment

Bipolar disorder is treated with medications called *mood stabilizers* and therapy. It is a myth that everyone who has been diagnosed with bipolar disorder will have extreme highs and lows. It isn't uncommon for some to have extreme highs and lows, of course, but not everyone does. Some only have a slight spike in the high end; some might experience a low mood. It all depends on their baseline, which is why a good history is so important.

Schizophrenia

Schizophrenia is usually diagnosed between the ages of eighteen and twenty-five when someone has a "first break" and exhibits signs of psychosis. That's not to say older people can't have a first break, but it's not as common.

This mental illness is characterized by having auditory, visual and/or olfactory hallucinations. People with schizophrenia can also be delusional and have thought disorders.

Treatment

Schizophrenia is treated with antipsychotic drugs. Other medications such as those for depression may also be used if the patient is also depressed. There is no cure for schizophrenia, but symptoms can be minimized with the right combination of medications.

Busting Myths About Schizophrenia

A character with schizophrenia will not stop hearing voices or having hallucinations overnight. It takes weeks for antipsychotics to work and sometimes months to find the right combination of medications. Delusions are difficult to dispel and may not respond to medication.

A character with schizophrenia is no more violent than a character without it. She may be delusional if she is untreated and be hard to reason with, but a character with schizophrenia is not more violent than one without schizophrenia.

Post-Traumatic Stress Disorder (PTSD)

PTSD can happen after a traumatic event occurs where the person believes his life is in immediate danger. Soldiers in combat often are diagnosed with PTSD, but it can happen with any trauma such as surviving a sexual assault, surviving a disaster such as a plane crash, or from being in an armed robbery situation.

Symptoms

A character with PTSD can have flashbacks of the trauma, nightmares, be hypervigilant, be startled easily, avoid loud noises such as fireworks, and experience signs of depression such as not eating or sleeping enough. She may also avoid the area/situation of the trauma, such as avoiding being in a car after a car accident.

Treatment

PTSD is treated with therapy and medications to treat the symptoms. PTSD can happen after a trauma, so getting psychological help immediately after a trauma is imperative. The symptoms vary by individual, but not everyone who has been through a trauma will experience PTSD.

Dissociative Identity Disorder (DID)

People with DID may experience symptoms such as losing time, waking up in a different outfit or in a different place, experiencing memory loss or a gap in memory, or feeling like they are out of their body. They may also have an awareness of two or more personalities. An extensive history by a psychiatric professional should be done. Treatment for DID is usually psychotherapy and although medications can be used if someone is experiencing depression or anxiety, there is no medication specifically for DID.

This psychiatric disorder is rarer than it is shown in novels, on TV, or in movies. If your character has DID, a mention about how rare it is should be part of the narrative. A character with DID will not kill when he isn't in his core personality state. In other words, if he kills when he is using an alternative personality, he would also kill when he was in his core personality. He will not have amnesia after killing someone, so it wouldn't be a surprise or something to be revealed.

There you have some common mental health disorders you might want to have your characters experience. The most important takeaway is *DO YOUR RESEARCH*. There are other mental health disorders I didn't discuss (such as eating disorders, attention-deficit hyperactivity disorder, or anxiety disorders) but again, do your research and speak with a mental health professional to get your story right so you don't lose readers or perpetuate damaging stereotypes.

RESOURCES FOR LEARNING ABOUT MENTAL ILLNESS

National Alliance on Mental Illness: www.nami.org
World Health Organization: www.who.int
National Institute of Mental Health: www.nimh.nih.gov
University of Michigan Depression Center: www.depressioncenter.org
WebMD: www.webmd.com
Mayo Clinic: www.mayoclinic.org

CHAPTER 17

BIPOLAR DISORDER

By Jonathan Peeples

As a psychiatrist, I treat all types of mental illness. There are plenty of popular misconceptions about what mental illness looks like, but there seems to be more confusion surrounding bipolar disorder than any other condition. I work in the emergency department of a hospital, and nearly half the patients I see tell me they've been diagnosed with bipolar disorder by a provider in the past, but most of the time the patient is suffering from something else entirely.

Since I started writing, I've become more interested in how psychiatric conditions are portrayed in fiction. I went to a local bookstore recently and asked for recommendations of young adult novels that contain elements of mental illness. An employee suggested Rainbow Rowell's *Fangirl* (St. Martin's Press, 2013), which turned out to be the highlight of my Thanksgiving season. I loved it. I sat down and devoured it like it was my mom's green bean casserole. The main character's father suffers from bipolar disorder, and Rowell does a wonderful job showing what this can look like. She accurately describes manic symptoms and demonstrates a solid understanding of how the illness can impact friends and family members. The only problem is that I wasn't expecting to read about a character with bipolar disorder because the bookstore employee thought the father was suffering from obsessive-compulsive disorder.

Let's take a closer look at bipolar disorder.

IS BIPOLAR DISORDER THE SAME THING AS MOOD SWINGS?

Nope. This seems to be one of the most common misconceptions. Patients often come in and tell me that they have bipolar disorder because their mood can change from one minute to the next and the smallest thing can set them off. True bipolar spectrum disorders involve manic, hypomanic, and depressive episodes (see next section) that last for days at a time.

What most patients with these minute-to-minute "mood swings" are actually experiencing is mood dysregulation associated with their personality structure and primitive defense mechanisms. This doesn't mean that these patients are any less sick, but making the correct diagnosis has tremendous implications for treatment. Patients with bipolar disorder almost always need medications to control their symptoms over time, whereas for patients suffering from the mood dysregulation described earlier, therapy is the mainstay of treatment.

Mood dysregulation isn't an actual diagnosis, though it's a symptom commonly seen in personality disorders such as borderline personality disorder. It'd take years to fully discuss all the theories of personality structure, but I'll give an example of how it might develop.

Imagine a child living in an abusive household. He's new to the world, and his life has been chaotic since birth. Whenever he feels threatened, he'll fight back or scream or run away—whatever it takes to protect himself. Sometimes these primitive defenses work, and the behaviors are reinforced. Eventually, he grows up and moves out of his childhood home. He's no longer being abused, but when he faces the stressors of everyday life, he doesn't know how to respond except to use the same defenses he developed as a child. Screaming and fighting over minor insults leads to a pervasive instability in his adult relationships and often contributes to feelings of depression or dissatisfaction.

If you're going to write a character who has mood swings like those described, call it borderline personality disorder, not bipolar disorder.

MANIC, HYPOMANIC, AND MAJOR DEPRESSIVE EPISODES

Now we're getting to the heart of it. What's important to point out is that to qualify for any of the following episodes, the collection of the symptoms must be associated with a change in previous functioning and can't be due to substance use or another medical condition.

Manic Episodes

To have a manic episode, a person must have either elevated, expansive, or irritable mood AND increased goal-directed activity or energy. There's a great example of this behavior in *Fangirl*. The main character's father calls her in the middle of the night because he's not sleeping and has plans to install a fireman's pole to connect the upstairs bathroom to her bedroom. People may also experience grandiosity, pressured speech, a decreased need for sleep, distractibility, and engaging in harmful activities. A manic episode must last at least seven days unless the person experiencing it has psychosis or needs hospitalization during the first week of symptom onset. A manic episode must be severe enough to cause impairment in social or occupational functioning.

Hypomanic Episodes

A hypomanic episode has similar symptoms to a manic episode, but the symptoms only need to last for four days. Other people are going to notice changes in the person's behavior, but unlike manic episodes, hypomanic episodes aren't severe enough to cause a serious impairment in social or occupational function.

Major Depressive Episodes

A major depressive episode must have depressed mood AND loss of interest and pleasure for two weeks in a row. You also may see fluctuations in weight (more often weight loss), insomnia or hypersomnia, fatigue, guilt, feelings of worthlessness, and thoughts about death. The symptoms need to be severe enough to cause impairment.

TYPES OF BIPOLAR DISORDER

There are several variations of bipolar disorder, but the two major ones are bipolar I and bipolar II. *To be diagnosed with bipolar I, you must have had a manic episode.* Patients with bipolar I often have hypomanic and major depressive episodes as well, but these aren't required for the diagnosis. *To be diagnosed with bipolar II, you cannot have had a manic episode, but you must have had both a hypomanic episode and a major depressive episode.*

Other diagnoses on the bipolar spectrum include cyclothymic disorder and substance/medication-induced bipolar and related disorders. Manic and hypomanic episodes can be mimicked by illicit substances such as cocaine and methamphetamines. Sometimes, prescribed medications such as steroids or stimulants (e.g., Vyvanse, Adderall) can lead to manic behavior.

Who Gets Bipolar Disorder?

Bipolar disorder is present in about 1 percent of the general population worldwide, but it's more common in high-income countries. It's slightly more prevalent in men. There's a strong genetic component, and relatives of people with either schizophrenia or bipolar disorder have an increased chance of developing bipolar disorder.

The onset of bipolar I is about age eighteen, and the onset for bipolar II is in the mid-twenties. Bipolar disorder often isn't diagnosed until years after its onset because it can look like major depressive disorder or other conditions. Most people spend more time in a depressed state than a manic state, but the amount of time varies widely from person to person. There are also periods when people don't qualify for any type of mood episode and are relatively stable. There are many commonly co-occurring mental disorders including anxiety disorder, conduct disorder, and substance use disorders.

Treatments for Bipolar Disorder

There are many agents available to treat bipolar disorder, and it often comes down to the doctor discussing the risks and benefits of each agent with the patient and reaching a mutual decision.

Lithium and valproic acid are two agents that control mania well. It's important to periodically check blood levels of these medications to ensure the patient is receiving enough of the medication without causing toxicity. Lithium also has an antidepressant effect and has been shown to decrease suicidality in certain populations. Valproic acid is thought to have an antidepressant effect as well, though the data for this aren't as robust.

Giving someone with bipolar disorder an antidepressant increases the risk of developing a manic episode, even if the person is on a therapeutic dose of lithium or valproic acid. That said, since many people with bipolar disorder spend significant time in a depressed state, antidepressant use in patients with bipolar disorder is a common practice. Some people agree with this practice while others don't, but it's worth knowing it's out there.

Antipsychotics are often used in acute manic episodes, but some can also be used long-term or for depression. The three drugs approved by the U.S. Food and Drug Administration for bipolar depression are Latuda, Seroquel, and Symbyax. Lamictal is a mood stabilizer that doesn't control mania as well as lithium or valproic acid but is commonly used for bipolar depression.

HOW TO APPLY THIS TO WRITING

If you've considered creating a character with bipolar disorder, I hope this information is helpful in guiding you through that process. The most important thing to recognize is that the "mood swings" seen in bipolar disorder are sustained periods of elevated or depressed mood, not something that changes from one minute to the next. Your character will probably have other family members with mental health diagnoses such as bipolar disorder or schizophrenia, and the character will usually develop the condition in her late teens or early twenties. Medications can be helpful in controlling symptoms, but people often don't like taking them because of the side effects or "feeling numb." Unfortunately, many people decompensate without medication.

Toward the end of *Fangirl*, I was worried that the main character was going to develop bipolar disorder like her father. She was the right age, and there was occasional decreased need for sleep and increase in goal directed activity. I don't know if Rowell wrote it that way on purpose, but it certainly added to the tension when I read it. By describing mental illness accurately, she made it much easier for me to buy into her story and to enjoy it from beginning to end. A little bit of research can go a long way in making your story believable.

CHAPTER 18

SCHIZOPHRENIA

By Jonathan Peeples

Schizophrenia is probably the most difficult psychiatric condition to write about because there's so much we don't understand. Though we've made tremendous strides in recent years, we still don't know exactly what causes it or why it may affect one person and not another. Genetic studies have suggested that what we call *schizophrenia* probably represents several distinct disorders, each with its own set of symptoms that may respond very differently to medication. In addition to the numerous uncertainties, it's also incredibly challenging for a writer to accurately present the thought process of someone who has the disease.

There's no way for me to capture all of the complexities of schizophrenia in this chapter. Research studies often yield conflicting findings, and leading academics may disagree on anything from causative factors (e.g., adolescent marijuana use) to treatment efficacy (e.g., whether clozapine *really* statistically separates from the rest of the antipsychotics).

The condition is further confused by its portrayal in film and literature. Sometimes a work may explicitly state that a person has schizophrenia (Sylvia Nasar's *A Beautiful Mind* [Simon & Schuster, 1998]), but often the viewer assumes that any time a character is a psychotic murderer with seven personalities, he has schizophrenia. That's just not the case.

I want to use this chapter to describe what schizophrenia may *look* like, rather than talking about its biological basis (which is imperfectly understood). The most important thing that I want to convey is that the patients I've worked with are not "schizophrenics." One patient wanted to become a great tennis player. Another spent eight hours a day writing books. I've met with a business owner, a thrift store worker, a college student, a musician, a custodian at Wendy's, and a sculptor. Schizophrenia is a tough illness, and they were all fighters. Don't use schizophrenia as a cheap plot device. People with schizophrenia are complex—with hopes, dreams, goals, and desires. Whatever you do, please don't lose sight of that.

IS SCHIZOPHRENIA HAVING MULTIPLE PERSONALITIES?

Definitely not. I've heard many people use the two interchangeably, but they're totally different disorders. The idea of "multiple personalities" is most similar to a condition called *dissociative identity disorder* (DID) in which a person has two or more distinct personality states. DID is much rarer than schizophrenia.

IS PSYCHOSIS ALWAYS SCHIZOPHRENIA?

No. In fact, "psychosis" can be seen in a number of different situations. Severe depression or mania can have psychotic features. Hallucinations are present in a variety of conditions. Sudden-onset hallucinations and behavioral changes are more suggestive of substance use or medical problems (e.g., delirium, brain tumors) than primary psychotic disorders. You can also see hallucinations in alcohol withdrawal, various dementias, and as side effects to some medications. It's important to rule out medical causes of psychosis before giving a diagnosis of schizophrenia.

Hallucinations are often reported by people with personality disorders and can be a manifestation of primitive coping mechanisms. There are also various internal and external incentives to having a diagnosis of schizophrenia such as disability payments, seeking inpatient hospitalization to avoid being homeless, and taking on a "sick" role. There are probably hundreds of thousands of people in the United States who are unnecessarily subjected to the damaging side effects of antipsychotics due to inaccurate diagnoses.

WHO GETS SCHIZOPHRENIA?

A commonly cited number for the prevalence of schizophrenia is 1 percent, though there's some variation across countries. It's not entirely clear what causes this variation, but some of it may be due to inconsistent diagnostic procedures and different exposures to risk factors.

Schizophrenia has a usual onset of early twenties in men and late twenties in women. Late-onset schizophrenia (over age forty) is much more common in women than men, though its features are different than typical schizophrenia and may have a different biological basis.

There are definite genetic links to schizophrenia, though many people with the illness have no family history. If a person with schizophrenia has an identical twin, that twin has about a 50 percent likelihood of having schizophrenia as well. This shows that while there's certainly a genetic component, other factors are at play. Increased paternal age, hypoxia (lack of oxygen) during birth, and early marijuana use are thought to be contributing factors.

WHAT DOES SCHIZOPHRENIA LOOK LIKE?

As mentioned earlier, schizophrenia likely represents several distinct disorders that we group together based on clusters of symptoms such as delusions, hallucinations, disorganized thinking, disorganized motor behavior, and negative symptoms. Not everyone with schizophrenia has all of these symptoms, but they must have some of them to get the diagnosis.

Delusions

Delusions are fixed beliefs that don't change even when someone is presented with conflicting evidence. There are many types of delusions. I've seen patients who were convinced that certain criminal organizations were trying to kill them. One patient was severely distressed because she believed she'd given a little boy AIDS through a blood transfusion. Patients may believe that famous people are in love with them. I've seen two instances of a rare condition called a Cotard delusion where the patients believed they were dead, though neither had schizophrenia (one had bipolar disorder and the other had major depressive disorder).

Hallucinations

Hallucinations are perception-like experiences that occur without an external cause. As I've mentioned earlier, hallucinations can be seen in a variety of mental and physical conditions. Hallucinations during alcohol withdrawal, substance intoxication, and medical illness are often visual, but auditory hallucinations are more common in psychotic disorders, like schizophrenia. Though auditory and visual are the most common types of hallucinations, hallucinations can occur in any sensory modality (e.g., tactile, olfactory).

Disorganized Thinking

Disorganized thinking really stands out during the diagnostic interview. The patient may jump from one subject to the next without any clear connection between the two topics. Sometimes the patient is so disorganized that even his words don't fit together to make a coherent sentence. It's important to check for substance use because people who are intoxicated on certain drugs can present very similarly.

Disorganized or Abnormal Motor Behavior

Abnormal motor behavior can present in different ways, but I want to focus on something called *catatonia*. Catatonia can be seen in a number of medical and mental disorders, including schizophrenia. Presentations of catatonia can be very different, but you may see catalepsy (rigid, fixed posturing held against gravity), waxy flexibility (slight, even resistance to positioning by the examiner), mutism, posturing, echolalia (mimicking another's speech), and echopraxia (mimicking another's movements). Though catatonia is often thought of as having a lack of motor activity, people can also be in a state of over-activity with repetitive, purposeless movements. Treatment usually involves benzodiazepines, though electroconvulsive therapy can be used for resistant cases. It's also important to identify and treat the underlying cause.

Negative Symptoms

Negative symptoms are especially prominent in schizophrenia and can manifest in a number of ways. People with schizophrenia often show diminished emotional expression on their faces, which can be described as a "flat" or "blunted" affect. They may also seem less motivated and display decreased engagement in self-initiated purposeful activities. Negative symptoms are some of the most difficult features to treat.

SCHIZOPHRENIA SPECTRUM TIMELINES AND DIAGNOSTICS

There are several psychotic disorders that fall under the schizophrenia spectrum, but the ones I want to discuss are brief psychotic disorder, schizophreniform disorder, schizophrenia, and schizoaffective disorder. These disorders are organized by different timelines of symptoms because chronicity of psychosis has implications for long-term prognosis. The longer a person is psychotic, the lower the chance is that she will have a complete recovery.

- **BRIEF PSYCHOTIC DISORDER** occurs when someone experiences one of the psychotic symptoms described earlier for longer than one day but less than one month.
- **SCHIZOPHRENIFORM DISORDER** is diagnosed when someone experiences two (or more) of the psychotic symptoms described earlier for at least one month but less than six months. If a person is only experiencing delusions and no other psychotic symptoms, she can be diagnosed with delusional disorder instead.

- **SCHIZOPHRENIA** is similar to schizophreniform disorder, but the symptoms must have been present for at least six months. Sometimes a person may have only had full-blown psychosis for one month, but if he's shown a gradual decline in functioning for more than six months, he can still be diagnosed with schizophrenia.
- **SCHIZOAFFECTIVE DISORDER** is diagnosed when someone meets the criteria for schizophrenia but also has a major mood episode (e.g., major depressive episode, manic episode). It's important for the delusions or hallucinations to exist outside of the mood episode, otherwise the person may be experiencing psychotic features related to severe depression or mania, not schizophrenia. I have patients who come in all the time saying they have "bipolar schizophrenia." Though it's a commonly used phrase, it's not a diagnosis. The correct term is schizoaffective disorder, bipolar type.

WRAPPING UP

Above all else, I encourage writers to respect the individual with the illness and to create characters who are real people with real hopes and dreams. People who have schizophrenia often feel that they're alone or not heard, and authors should do whatever it takes to retain their humanity.

●

CHAPTER 19

MISCONCEPTIONS ABOUT MEMORY

By Anne M. Lipton, M.D., Ph.D.

Memory is crucial to a sense of self, and memory loss can be devastating to a person in real life—or a character in a story. Thus, remembering and forgetting make for good plot points and have given rise to a number of writing tropes. Popular culture has thereby colored our perceptions about the nature of memory, and not always accurately. On the one hand, a person is unlikely to have total recall. On the other hand, someone is unlikely to forget his life completely. Reality lies somewhere between these extremes. To help writers lend authenticity to their character and story arcs, this chapter addresses some common misconceptions about memory via neuroscientific principles and clinically based perspectives.

MYTH #1: MEMORY = ATTENTION (OR LANGUAGE OR VISUOSPATIAL SKILLS OR ALL OF THE ABOVE)

Memory refers to specific cognitive processes for the encoding (processing), storage, and recall (retrieval) of information. These functions are analogous to writing, filing, and later reading a message.

Neuroscientists refer to mental processing as *cognition*. Besides memory, the other main areas of cognition are attention/concentration, executive functioning, language, and visuospatial skills. Executive functions are higher-order thought processes such as insight, judgment, planning, and organization, mediated by the brain's frontal lobes.

Sometimes people conflate memory with another cognitive domain—or all of them. For example, a person may have difficulty recognizing faces (*prosopagnosia*). This type of perceptual difficulty, or agnosia, may be misinterpreted as a problem with recalling names. "Memory" is also sometimes incorrectly applied as shorthand for all aspects of cognition. However, in writing and in real life, it's best to be specific.

Memory may be divided into declarative (explicit) memory, which can be tested verbally, and non-declarative (implicit-procedural) memory, involving perception and motor skills, such as riding a bike or playing an instrument. Episodic memory (recall of events) and semantic memory (one's "encyclopedia" of learned facts) are types of declarative memory.

Anatomically, different brain regions mediate different aspects of memory. Key among these are areas in the brain's frontal lobes and temporal lobes. The hippocampus and its associated entorhinal cortex are essential structures for explicit memory. Named for its seahorse-shape, the hippocampus is part of the limbic system, which includes the amygdala, a structure underlying basic drives and emotions.

MYTH #2: MEMORY IS A STATIC, STAND-ALONE FUNCTION

Memory doesn't operate in isolation. It works in concert with sensory input to the brain and is intertwined with other cognitive domains.

Numerous examples of what I call "made-for-TV amnesia" abound in movies and books like Robert Ludlum's *The Bourne Identity* (Richard Marek Publishers, 1980). Jason Bourne finds himself in a strange place or situation and can't remember his name. He is otherwise healthy and alert, walking, talking, and in fighting shape. Somehow, he can recall the names of things like phones, boats, or passports (words that one usually learns well after one's name). He can learn new information and also remembers how to drive, etc. Memory doesn't work like this.

People often see memory as operating independently of these other cognitive processes, but the system is interdependent. Language and memory are so tied together in terms of how we humans communicate and remember that memory is often classified in terms of verbal and nonverbal recall.

Visual memory tends to be the nonverbal type of most clinical interest. But other types of nonverbal memory can be just as important, if not more so, in daily life—and writing. Marcel Proust's madeleine in *Remembrance of Things Past* is a sweet example of gustatory (taste) memory:

> "And suddenly the memory revealed itself. The taste was that of the little piece of madeleine which on Sunday mornings at Combray (because on those mornings I did not go out before mass), when I went to say good morning to her in her bedroom, my aunt Léonie used to give me, dipping it first in her own cup of tea ..."

Memory also has temporal patterns. Most laypeople use the terms *short-term* and *long-term memory*, but neuroscientists generally refer to working memory and reference memory or immediate (short-term), recent (e.g., current events), and remote (long-term) recall.

If a head injury (or similar insult) is severe enough, one may have retrograde amnesia (memory loss for recent events), particularly if there is altered consciousness. But this would be most profound for events around the time of the trauma. Jason Bourne could have such amnesia, but this would be unlikely to extend only to longstanding aspects of his identity while sparing more recent information. It should be the other way around. Ribot's law of retrograde amnesia refers to the common phenomenon in which more recent memories are forgotten to a greater degree than more remote ones.

Someone with a traumatic brain injury (TBI) may also experience anterograde amnesia (difficulty learning and remembering *new* information). Jason Bourne doesn't seem to have a problem with "new learning," which also makes his selectively impaired recall less credulous: The more severe a trauma that caused amnesia, the more likely that anterograde amnesia (problems with learning and remembering new information) will occur. There's no singular or centralized memory center that can be obliterated to erase all of someone's memories. However, destruction of the bilateral hippocampi (each hippocampus on either side of the brain) can produce severe anterograde amnesia. Both hippocampi may be damaged after trauma or during a hypoxic (oxygen-depleting) event such as cardiopulmonary arrest.

A person who has completely forgotten her identity and journeys to find it again makes for a great story, which is probably why this plot point is so popular, even if it is so improbable. But our oldest and most-often used memories (e.g., our names) are what we memory specialists sometimes like to call *overlearned* information or what laypeople sometimes call *hardwired*. To suddenly forget one's name, other identifying traits, and all the major players in one's life, while otherwise functioning normally, is not easily explained by a head injury or other neurological insult. Because of the interconnectedness of cognitive processes, sudden and severe memory loss is likely to be associated with other medical issues.

For example, TBI can cause concussions with forgetfulness, but usually in the context of accompanying problems such as inattentiveness, headaches, and dizziness.

Transient global amnesia is a condition often linked to an underlying medical condition, such as blood vessel (vascular) disease or migraines. "Global" overstates the case, as the amnesia is often not total. Symptoms usually resolve within twenty-four hours.

Drugs may cause amnesia but are unlikely to cause someone to forget his identity unless he becomes delirious (a delirium = an acute confusional state).

Forgetting one's identity while functioning normally in all other realms doesn't fit with the anatomy or temporal patterns of memory and suggests a possible psychogenic amnesia (memory loss related to mental illness or psychological issues). After extreme physical and/or psychological trauma, such as severe abuse or another situation someone wishes to escape, a person may enter a profound "dissociative fugue" state (e.g., the man who washes up on the beach and can't recall his name but can play the piano and learn the names of new people he meets). Such patients typically exhibit significant mood and/or behavioral symptoms. Psychogenic amnesia is distinct from "malingering" (deliberately faking memory loss or other illness in order to escape criminal proceedings or for some other personal gain).

Even in the case of a dementia such as Alzheimer's disease, where memory loss is prominent (albeit gradual), a person's name is likely to be the last thing she forgets.

MYTH #3: THE PERFECT MEMORY

Memory is rather imperfect. Which is not necessarily a bad thing, although it can be if one's fate depends on the testimony of eyewitnesses, who are notoriously unreliable. The perfect memory is right up there with the perfect murder and the unsinkable ship. But writers can leverage an unreliable character or narrator to great advantage.

Memory has its limits. Memories often fade with time or become reworked. Events associated with profound emotion (e.g., the death of a parent, September 11) sear memories into our consciousness. Retrieving a memory using cues (recognition memory) is easier than spontaneous (or free) recall. Repetition can aid memory—or alter it. The human penchant for pattern recognition may likewise help or bias our memory. Roast, roast, roast, roast. What do you put in a toaster? (Hint: not toast). This is an example of anchoring bias or focalism, in which the first piece of information biases decision-making.

Certainly, some people have better memory abilities than others, memory can improve with practice, and certain techniques (referred to as *mnemonics*) can aid memory. However, anyone who remembered everything would have a difficult time making it through everyday life (beautifully illustrated in the classic short story "Funes the Memorious" by Jorge Luis Borges). Besides, flawed characters are much more interesting. So are flawed, repressed, or unshakable memories. Every Superman should have his kryptonite.

●

CHAPTER 20

DEMENTIA MYTHS, PART I

By Anne M. Lipton, M.D., Ph.D.

Dementia is an all too frequent—and much too often misunderstood—disorder. Of course, every writer of fiction can build a novel brain, hatch new illnesses, or invent cool neurotechnology. But an understanding of dementia in this neck of the universe may help a writer dealing with similar themes to portray a fictional character or scenario with greater authenticity. This chapter provides an introduction to dementia and presents scientific and clinical perspectives to clear up some common misconceptions, which persist both in fiction and in real life.

WHAT IS DEMENTIA?

Dementia is a neurodegenerative disorder or progressive brain illness. (In clinical terms, *progressive* is synonymous with *progressively worsening*.) Rather than referring to a specific disease, however, dementia is a general or "umbrella" term for a constellation of symptoms. There are many different types (and subtypes) of dementia and diverse etiologies (causes), which vary by individual. Dementia may occur as a result of primary neurodegenerative disease (such as Alzheimer's disease). Or it may be a secondary disorder, brought about by another illness or injury affecting the brain (e.g., strokes).

Dementia is regarded as a clinical diagnosis, which may be confirmed pathologically. To meet clinical criteria for diagnosis, dementia must adversely affect a person's thinking (cognition) and/or behavior enough to interfere with everyday functioning. (For more information on cognition, see Chapter 19, Misconceptions About Memory.) A diagnosis of dementia is based on the symptoms an individual experiences as well as signs found on clinical evaluation. However, a diagnosis of dementia can only be definitively proven by specific findings on brain autopsy (performed by a pathologist or neuropathologist).

MYTH #1: SENILITY = DEMENTIA

Senility simply refers to old age. Hence, "senile dementia" = "old-age" dementia. Medical professionals usually define *old age* to be age sixty-five or older, and *geriatric* is the currently preferred clinical term used to refer to this population. Colloquially, both in conversation and in published works, the phrase "getting senile" is frequently misused to refer to someone having memory problems. It behooves everyone, especially writers, to understand and respect the power of words: Don't confuse senility with dementia.

Age is certainly one of the most significant risk factors in developing dementia. But memory problems interfering with daily function are not a part of normal aging. An individual who is "senile" (age sixty-five or older) does not necessarily have dementia. On the other hand, a person who is younger than sixty-five may develop dementia. Hence, someone who has dementia isn't necessarily "senile" and may be much younger than sixty-five. Such an individual would be said to have early-onset dementia. It is important to note that early onset dementia is not the same as early-stage dementia.

Early-onset dementia = dementia occurring in an individual younger than sixty-five.

Early-stage dementia = the initial stage (typically, a few years) of dementia, regardless of a person's age.

While these terms are distinct, they are not mutually exclusive (i.e., someone may have early onset dementia and also be in the early stage of dementia).

MYTH #2: "DEMENTED" MEANS PSYCHOTIC

Dementia may include psychosis but the terms are not equivalent. Psychosis refers to a mental break with reality, which may include hallucinations (sensory misperceptions), delusions (false beliefs), and agitation. People with dementia may develop psychosis, which may or may not be related to their dementia. For example, psychosis may occur secondary to delirium, which is an acute confusional state. Delirium may result from a variety of factors, including infection and/or medications. But *dementia* is distinct from *psychosis*, and vice versa. A person with dementia may be competent to make decisions on his own behalf, as opposed to someone who is psychotic (i.e., has lost touch with reality and experiences hallucinations and/or delusions).

To be respectful—and to avoid confusion—it is usually best to say someone "has a dementia or dementing illness," rather than that the individual "is demented." The same is true of "psychosis" instead of "psychotic." A person may have a disease, but a person is not the disease.

So don't let the disease define a person—at least not in real life. In fiction, illness may provide a rich vein of internal goals, obstacles, and stakes for a character and story. Although when it comes to fiction, a writer should be mindful of the usage of such words and consider a sensitivity or expert reader as needed.

MYTH #3: ALZHEIMER'S DISEASE AND DEMENTIA ARE THE SAME THING

All Alzheimer's disease is dementia, but not all dementia is Alzheimer's disease. Alzheimer's disease is a common and well-known type of dementia, but there are many others, including (but not limited to) vascular dementia, mixed dementia (specifically, Alzheimer's disease plus vascular dementia), Parkinson's disease dementia, dementia with Lewy bodies (DLB), and frontotemporal dementia (FTD). Each type of dementia differs in terms of signs and symptoms (particularly in onset), disease course and duration, and other associated factors.

In Alzheimer's disease, memory is typically the first and worst problem: "Memory leads the way," the saying goes. For example, a person with Alzheimer's disease may have difficulty recalling recent events. However, changes in mood, insight, or language may also herald Alzheimer's disease.

Vascular dementia is associated with strokes, and symptoms depend on the location of the strokes in the brain. Mood symptoms such as agitation, apathy, depression, and irritability are commonly seen. But memory is usually not as impaired in an individual with vascular dementia as it is in Alzheimer's disease. The progression of vascular dementia tends to have a stair-step progression with worsening after a stroke, followed by a plateau of symptoms until the next stroke. Thus, stroke prevention is a mainstay of treatment.

Parkinson's disease has a typical duration of decades and motor symptoms (parkinsonism) that persist long before the onset of dementia symptoms. The cardinal motor symptoms of Parkinson's disease are rest tremor (usually beginning on one side), slowness of movement (bradykinesia), postural instability (tendency to fall, especially backwards), and rigidity. A good response to antiparkinsonian medication helps validate the diagnosis.

DLB is characterized by vivid hallucinations and parkinsonism, as well as dementia with cognitive fluctuations, all initially occurring within two to three years. Patients with DLB typically do not respond as well to antiparkinsonian medication as those who have Parkinson's disease.

FTD often affects people under age sixty-five and has speech/language variants and behavioral variants. Memory may be intact in initial stages. FTD may be associated with amyotrophic lateral sclerosis (ALS, or Lou Gehrig's disease) and/

or parkinsonism. A number of genetic mutations have been identified in families affected by FTD.

MYTH #4: DEMENTIA BEGINS WITH MEMORY LOSS

As noted in the previous section, memory loss is typically the presenting symptom for Alzheimer's disease but not for many other types of dementia. If a person has dementia, and memory is NOT the initial symptom, this may suggest a type of dementia other than Alzheimer's disease.

MYTH #5: DEMENTIA IS A FAST-MOVING PROCESS

Dementia usually results in the gradual decline of cognition, behavior, and functioning over a period of years or even a decade or more. Even a "rapidly progressive dementia" typically occurs over a duration of many months to a few years.

In *Harry Potter and the Prisoner of Azkaban* (Arthur A. Levine Books, 1999), J.K. Rowling coined the term *dementors* for demonic tormentors who suck memories (and other cognitive abilities) from someone's brain. Although the name *dementor* may conjure up the term *dementia*, the sudden and precipitous amnesia and other cognitive loss that dementors inflict is not typical of the insidious onset and gradual decline seen in dementia.

Dementia sometimes appears to occur suddenly when a hospitalization or other crisis brings it to light (e.g., police escorting home someone who has become lost). But a good medical history (described in the next chapter) can often uncover previous problems.

●

CHAPTER 21

DEMENTIA MYTHS, PART II

By Anne M. Lipton, M.D., Ph.D.

This chapter focuses on the evaluation, diagnosis, and treatment of dementia and common misconceptions regarding these aspects of dementia in writing and popular culture.

MYTH #1: DEMENTIA CAN BE DIAGNOSED QUICKLY AND EASILY

Dementia is a hard diagnosis to receive, a hard diagnosis to give, and often requires hard work to diagnose. An adequate evaluation for dementia can require painstaking time and effort, especially for those with milder symptoms and/or unusual features, such as age of onset under sixty-five or behavioral problems early in the course of disease. A medical professional (doctor or similar) makes a diagnosis of dementia based on several factors:

1. **MEDICAL HISTORY:** A patient with dementia may not be able to provide necessary information due to memory loss or other cognitive problems. Therefore, medical history is also gathered from a family member or another individual close to the patient.

2. **HISTORY OF PRESENT ILLNESS:** This encompasses initial symptom (problems with memory, language, mood, or behavior), associated symptoms (problems with gait [walking]), onset (When did symptoms start?), duration (length of symptoms), and disease course/progression (gradual, stair-step, rapid, or fluctuating). It is important to ascertain the impact of these symptoms on daily functioning. The patient's medical history, medications, and social history (use of alcohol and other substances, sexual history, and education/occupation) may also be relevant.

3. **EXAMINATION OF THE PATIENT:** This includes mental status (cognition, such as memory, language, visuospatial skills, and executive functioning). The diagnosis may require up to a full day of neuropsychological testing (which includes thorough cognitive assessment). The history and examination may be enough to diagnose dementia and even the type of dementia based on certain clinical criteria and guidelines. In medical school, doctors are taught to listen

carefully as "the patient gives the diagnosis." Specialists who care for people with dementia learn that the family gives the diagnosis.

MYTH #2: A BLOOD TEST IS THE BEST WAY TO DIAGNOSE DEMENTIA

Dementia is a clinical diagnosis. Generally speaking, the history is more important than any test in diagnosing dementia. Laboratory and other tests may aid in clarifying the type of dementia and are useful in evaluating for treatable conditions. However, no individual test or medical procedure (or combination thereof) is sufficient for a diagnosis of dementia.

A biomarker is a substance, such as a protein in blood or spinal fluid, which may serve as an objective measure of disease. Researchers have identified a number of potential biomarkers of dementia, but none are definitive. A diagnosis of dementia cannot be made solely on the basis of a lab test, brain scan, lumbar puncture (spinal tap), and/or other medical diagnostic procedure (at least with currently available technology). However, lab tests of blood and urine may help identify or rule out (exclude) reversible types of dementia. In the future, it is more likely that a panel of protein, genetic, or other biomarkers will be used in the diagnosis of dementia rather than a single biomarker.

Genetic testing is a major focus of dementia research. Such testing may inform the diagnosis for certain patients, based on family history, early age of onset, and other factors. It also may help pinpoint a specific type of dementia. However, the genetics for most cases of dementia are not well understood. An analogy may be drawn with heart attacks: While heart attacks seem to run in some families, they are not usually linked to a specific genetic mutation but rather a mix of genetic, environmental, and lifestyle factors.

If a patient has a certain gene or genetic mutation associated with dementia, it may simply confer an increased risk and not necessarily indicate that the individual has dementia or is destined to get it. In many cases where dementia is a concern, genetic testing adds cost without adding benefit. Such testing may even create harm by sowing confusion or have untoward employment or insurance implications for patients and families.

MYTH #3: "THEY SAW DEMENTIA ON THE BRAIN SCAN"

Dementia *per se* can't be seen on a brain scan, however, a brain scan may reveal associated features of dementia. Current clinical guidelines recommend structural neuroimaging with head computed tomography (CT) or brain magnetic resonance imaging (MRI) as part of a medical evaluation for dementia. Associated neuroimaging features include atrophy (brain shrinkage) and cerebrovascular disease (CVD). Such findings may help diagnose a specific type of dementia, as certain patterns of atrophy suggest certain types of dementia.

CVD is blood vessel disease of the brain, such as leukoaraiosis (small-vessel white matter disease) or evidence of strokes (infarcts, or dead brain tissue). A significant amount of CVD may suggest a vascular dementia, but not always. Atrophy and/or CVD may occur in a person with no dementia, in which case these findings are said to be "nonspecific" or "incidental." In keeping with the precept that dementia is a clinical diagnosis, it is imperative to look at the patient, not just the scan.

Another possible finding on neuroimaging is hydrocephalus (increased cerebrospinal fluid in brain ventricles). In cases of dementia, this is commonly hydrocephalus ex vacuo (hydrocephalus occurring secondary to atrophy). Since nature abhors a vacuum, the fluid-filled ventricles expand to account for the loss of brain tissue. But again, this is a nonspecific finding that may occur with aging and is not sufficient for a diagnosis of dementia.

On the other hand, normal pressure hydrocephalus (NPH) is a specific type of hydrocephalus that can cause urinary incontinence, dementia, and gait problems and is treatable via neurosurgical placement of a shunt. This underscores why it's important to do a brain scan: not to "see dementia" but to evaluate for other potentially treatable conditions, such as NPH or tumors, which can cause dementia or dementia-type symptoms.

Dementia can't be diagnosed by brain scan alone. But neuroimaging may provide corroborating evidence for the diagnosis, exclude the diagnosis (e.g., if the scan uncovers a brain tumor or something else that may account for the patient's symptoms), or help identify the type of dementia.

Functional neuroimaging includes functional MRI (fMRI), brain positron emission tomography (PET), and brain single-photon emission computed tomography (SPECT). fMRI is primarily used for research purposes. Lowered brain metabolism (*hypometabolism*) on PET or SPECT scans, as well as radioligand (radioactively labeled probes) studies on PET scans, may help in differentiating dementia types. However, these scans are expensive and not necessary for all patients.

PET offers the closest thing to "seeing dementia" in a living person. Radioligands may make visible some of the proteins that collect abnormally in the brain in dementia. PET scans are mainly done for research (e.g., studies investigating medications to treat these abnormal proteins) or in difficult-to-diagnose clinical cases, especially in patients under age sixty-five.

MYTH #4: "YOU CAN'T DIAGNOSE ALZHEIMER'S DISEASE WHILE SOMEONE IS ALIVE"

Dementia, including Alzheimer's disease, can be diagnosed during life—at least possible and probable Alzheimer's disease. However, a diagnosis of definite Alzheimer's disease requires postmortem confirmation by a brain autopsy (neuropathological evaluation).

MYTH #5: DEMENTIA IS NOT TREATABLE

Most dementias are treatable, although usually not curable or reversible. Current medications for dementia treat day-to-day symptoms and may slow cognitive, behavioral, and functional decline. In addition, behavioral and environmental interventions, brain therapy (adult day programs), planning, participation in research studies, support groups, and understanding the specific diagnosis and prognosis may make a world of difference for people with dementia and their families.

Some dementias are considered as potentially reversible (i.e., possibly curable). These are far and few between in real life but may make for a rich plot point in fiction. The mnemonic (memory prompt) that doctors sometimes use to remember the reversible dementias is

DEMENTIA:
Drugs (including certain medications and alcohol)
Endocrine (e.g., certain thyroid conditions) or metabolic (e.g., Wilson's disease, which involves an overaccumulation of copper)
Mental illness (e.g., severe depression)
Eyes and ears declining
Normal pressure hydrocephalus or tumor or other "space-occupying" brain lesion
Toxins (e.g., excessive manganese in miners or bismuth overdose)
Infection (e.g., neurosyphilis)
Anemia (vitamin B12 or folate deficiency)

Timely medical evaluation is key in identifying any potentially reversible cause of dementia. Cognitive, behavioral, and functional symptoms can progress to a point of no return, even in a so-called "reversible" dementia. In fiction, this can serve as an important pacing device (the so-called "ticking time bomb").

●

CHAPTER 22

CHILDREN WITH BEHAVIORAL, EMOTIONAL, & SOCIAL DIFFICULTIES

By Rachel Heaps-Page

K was eleven years old and was always smiling, but his anxiety showed in the raw red marks all the way round his mouth. The skin was always dry, cracked, and bleeding because he licked almost constantly and nothing could make him stop. The other children tried not to notice, but most days someone upset him with their stare.

As his designated adult, it was my job to make sure K didn't react, protect his learning and the other children from his problems, and prevent the triggers that would set him off. I wrenched chairs from K's hands and taught him under tables. I cajoled him through work that seemed impossible, helping him navigate through overwhelming losses he was struggling to handle so he could learn how to read, or do math, or speak a little French.

After two years, we had grown quite familiar. I had my tactics and resources to help K attempt an education. I recognized the signs that warned of tantrums or tears and I knew by the way K took off his coat in the morning if we were going to have a bad day: K would unzip his coat extra carefully on those mornings and leave it in the middle of the floor, a small and innocuous gesture that was his way of saying, *I am in pain and today is going to hurt.*

I had my purse stolen on a bad day, and my car keys. I stood for hours in the rain while he screamed personal slurs against me and watched him climb over fences or onto the roof. Once, a bad day got me sent to the hospital, pouring blood after I fell trying to retrieve my fleeing charge, the icy ground taking a chunk of my leg and leaving a scar to this day.

K was just one of many children with behavioral, emotional, and social difficulties (BESD) I have met on my journey as an educator, broadening my understanding of the term attributed to them and deepening my insight into their world. These are some of the lessons they have taught me that may assist you when writing characters who share their title or traits.

LESSON #1: BESD DOESN'T REQUIRE EXTREME BEHAVIOR

K was extreme, but I am glad to say that in six years of classrooms I only met one child like him. Though children experiencing BESD have issues that run very deep, I have met very few who showed it through overtly negative behavior.

Through our time together, K taught me a valuable lesson: that children with BESD have choices. K's destructive, visceral responses were understandable but they weren't always justified. There were times he couldn't control himself, but far more often he indulged violence because a provocative streak urged him to. Meanwhile J, a pleasant boy I once supported, only revealed his crippling social anxiety through his catchphrase. He would mutter "potato" under his breath, picked up from a popular comedian he watched obsessively and who made him feel safe. This was a minor disruption at best and taught me that no matter how severe a child's condition, there is no "typical" reaction or guarantee of extreme responses.

BESD is typically only diagnosed when it is severe, but the characters you will write will have the same question facing them: Though things may be difficult, how will they respond?

I have witnessed a wide range of reactions to BESD, from an eyebrow raising to self-harm and violence. There is no "right" or typical behavior, so develop your character's coping strategies while staying true to the personality you are forging in him.

LESSON #2: BESD AND LEARNING DISABILITIES ARE NOT THE SAME THING

BESD is the umbrella term we use to explain a child's consistent exhibition of disruptive behaviors or issues regarding their social skills, relationship skills, and emotional health. These behaviors and issues *can* stem from a developmental or intellectual disability such as Down syndrome, but they do not occur exclusively.

It is true that a child dealing with other issues is likely to suffer academically, but not because she has no capacity to excel. In many cases, a child with BESD will suffer academically simply because she faced much greater obstacles when she came to learn. This can be overcome by educators with insight who obtain the right resources and offer the best support to the struggling child. Unfortunately, many children miss out on this help as they are overlooked or remain undiagnosed, or their teachers are simply too pressed by other responsibilities to do any more. So, you should feel free to retain your character's title of "genius'" even if he hates the classroom or to allow "troubled" souls to achieve greatness in the end.

LESSON #3: NOT EVERY CASE STARTS WITH ABUSE

Though it is common for tragedy and trauma to be a root cause of BESD, it is not a precursor. Children can be born with problems: genetic issues that undermine a child's ability to cope or to learn or diseases/conditions that prevent full mental or physical development. These can be at the heart of your character's issue and a contributing factor or real reason behind his BESD, just as legitimately as a murdered parent or infliction of abuse.

It may help to think of this disorder as being, ultimately, about obstruction. There is *something* that causes the child to act out or fail to connect with the world or others around her. There is a reason he struggles to moderate his behavior or constantly misunderstands his friends, why he can't express himself healthily or at all. It is your place as the author to decide what this is. The options are limitless and a true test of your creative skill when it comes to their creation.

Many writers advise asking questions to get to the heart of each character, and I would advise the same in this case. If you are compelled to bestow BESD to your character I would urge you to consider, why? What is the obscure or significant element of your character's nature, physiology, or experience that first set her on this developmental path? That first act to light her behavioral fuse?

You may decide this won't be revealed to your readers, but I believe such insight helps to understand your character and lends depth to his behavior as you write.

LESSON #4: CHARACTERS WITH BESD DON'T HAVE TO BE VILLAINS OR VICTIMS

There is an old adage I like to apply in this instance: Hate the sin, not the sinner. As a teacher, I was trained to look beyond a child's behavior to who he was as a person: a child who could be encouraged to learn and make better choices, even if he acted terribly. This was particularly challenging when working with troubled children, as their behavior was often a veil for the person inside. Many gentle souls I worked with had terrible reputations because violent outbursts, even when caused by exceptional circumstances, aren't easily forgotten and are even less easily forgiven.

There is a tendency to look at a child with BESD and try to predict his life as an adult based on that short window of time. It is hard to imagine a healthy marriage or successful career for the child who stands on a table to urinate during lessons.

PUTTING THE SCIENCE IN FICTION

But childhood is only a part of our life journey, and damaged children can recover from, or at least control, their dysfunction as they enter adulthood.

Every damaged child in your fictional world does not have to become the helpless damsel or cruel tyrant. An author has the privileged opportunity to play out the whole story, so consider offering your wounded character a chance to heal or to redeem herself for past mistakes.

LESSON #5: YOU DON'T HAVE TO GET EVERYTHING RIGHT

What I learned as a teacher I retained as a writer, and I suspect some of my personal insights inform the characters I create. However, I don't allow facts to constrain me.

I find that the more I worry about technical accuracy, the more soulless my character (and indeed my writing) becomes. Unless you are hoping to create the quintessential BESD child and set him forth as a case study, do not feel restricted when creating your character.

With the right research and a sensitive approach any topic can be masterfully explored in your writing, but bear in mind that "expert" and author is a rare combination and readers won't expect it of you. Fiction writers in particular can take liberties and are expected to fabricate, so let your creative juices flow! After all, it is one of the great joys of our craft.

My last thought is to urge you to forge a character with depth and complexity in mind and less concern for "ticking the boxes" of her label. She may have severe BESD, but don't feel obliged to mold her from that singular definition or try too hard to justify the label in your work. Your characters can wrestle with issues beyond your experience, or respond in a way some might consider unconventional, but if they are "real"—if they are complex and human—they will still ring true.

CHAPTER 23

●

CHARACTER DEVELOPMENT BEYOND PERSONALITY QUIRKS

By Maria Grace

Characters are foundational to any story, and much discussion revolves around getting them right. We create interviews and dossiers, yet oftentimes they still fall flat. All the focus on their appearance and personality misses a crucial element: development.

Psychological development is a key component in how people and characters differ from one another beyond simple temperament differences. It can explain how people who are fundamentally dissimilar may share a common way of interacting with their world, and how characters who might possess many similarities can be very different. Moreover, developmental issues can provide motivations and establish a realistic pathway for growth and guidance for convincing character arcs.

DIMENSIONS OF GROWTH

Development occurs on a number of interrelated axes including physical, psychosocial, cognitive, and emotional/personality. The physical aspects are the most obvious and the ones we tend to be most aware of. However, development along the other axes has greater potential for influencing behaviors.

Briefly, psychosocial development encompasses the changes in an individual as they manage various distinct societal expectations across the lifespan. Cognitive development refers to changes in mental processes over the lifecycle. Not only does how much an individual knows change, but the way in which they know that information and how it may be used progresses along a predictable developmental path. More globally, individuals progress in their self-perceptions and how those perceptions influence the way they see others and make choices.

PSYCHOSOCIAL DEVELOPMENT

Psychosocial development considers the way in which a person interacts with their society/culture and the role they play in it. These effects are cumulative, and earlier experiences influence the way later development occurs. These aspects of growth generalize across different cultures, although gender may affect the order in which developmental challenges are faced and what a healthy resolution to the challenge might look like. Both physical maturation and changing social expectations of people as they progress through the lifespan fuel development.

Individuals who do not successfully navigate early developmental hurdles may appear "stalled" at earlier stages of the lifespan. Under stress, adult characters may revert to immature, even childlike means of dealing with situations, acting far "younger" than they actually are.

Although childhood spans several distinct stages, they all revolve around the theme of acquiring important fundamental skills—whatever is necessary for the culture, whether reading and writing or hunting and gathering. Successful individuals enter adolescence with:

1. The ability to form healthy attachments to others
2. A sense of autonomy and ability to do things for themselves
3. Willingness to take appropriate risks and initiate activities
4. A belief in their own competence and ability to be a contributing member of their society

Unsuccessful resolutions to childhood developmental challenges are most likely when children are faced with abusive or unstable caregivers; are unable to interact with the world around them, such as trying new things and exploring new capabilities; are denied opportunities to initiate activities of their own choosing and impact the environment around them; or lack age-and culture-appropriate skills training.

Adolescence and early adulthood are concerned with establishing identity and meaningful relationships that often lead to procreation. Usually, this transition is marked by the development of secondary sexual characteristics. In some cultures, elaborate rites of passage mark the move from childhood to adulthood and sexual maturity. Gender may play a role in the order in which these challenges are resolved. Females in particular may define their identities out of the connections (such as marriage) they form.

Establishing identity requires a balance between the need for individual uniqueness and group solidarity. This is often achieved through experimentation where the person "tries on" various "characters" or "identities" available in the culture. If the individual fails to find a sense of self that fits, the result may be an individual who drifts from situation to situation, apathetic, with few goals, little commitment, and no declared values.

The capacity to form lasting relationships and navigate other adult challenges may be seriously compromised without a strong sense of identity. Cultural institutions like education and military service can provide safe grounds in the search for identity, although some cultures allow for very limited exploration and tolerate little deviance from defined norms.

Deep meaningful relationships, romantic/love/sexual as well as platonic connections, form major structural components of society. The ability or inability to create and maintain such affiliations impacts the roles an individual might occupy in society (e.g., parenting, mentoring, or leading) and how they might impact future generations. Successful marriage and procreation may or may not be requisite for positive resolution to this challenge, depending on the cultural context. In either case, resolutions to earlier developmental challenges strongly influence the way an individual navigates this developmental hurdle.

Early adulthood development figures highly in fiction, but middle and later adulthood transitions are often overlooked. Middle adulthood presents the challenge of caring for other generations, older (parents) and younger (children), or turning away from those responsibilities and focusing on the individual's needs and wants. Ideally a person balances both of those needs.

Many times in fiction, the former responsibilities are explained away so the character can focus on the conflict that is core to the plot. Writers ignore the opportunity to create complex and nuanced plots and character arcs to avoid dealing with the multifaceted challenges potentially faced by characters at this point in the lifespan.

In addition to the tasks of preparing older progeny for launch into the world and managing the increasing needs of older parents, individuals at this stage of the lifespan are also expected to step into social leadership roles. On a more personal level, maintaining long-term relationships (both marriages and friendships) becomes a growing concern. A commitment to lifelong learning and growth marks a positive resolution to this stage, whereas Ebenezer Scrooge-like preoccupation with self and comfort mark an unsuccessful one.

As the lifespan draws to an end, the issues of late adulthood come into play. Individuals must adjust to physical changes, including chronic illness and accumulated injuries, which may figure highly in an individual's day-to-day experience. Individuals may retire or reduce their involvement in society, though this is not a given in all circumstances. Cultural attitudes toward the aged play a significant role in an individual's adjustment during this stage. Societies

PUTTING THE SCIENCE IN FICTION

that venerate their older members might invite their participation in civic responsibilities while societies that honor youth might push older individuals out.

Finally, individuals must deal with the loss of their friends, spouses, and cohort members, which may result in increasing isolation. Ultimately, the reality of impending death must be confronted as well. Those who manage this transition successfully do so by recognizing the worth of their previous and continued contributions to their society and future generations. Depression, despair, and giving up mark unsuccessful transitions.

HOW TO USE PSYCHOSOCIAL DEVELOPMENT IN FICTION

While understanding the typical path of human growth and development offers many opportunities for writers to deepen their characters, authors can really go to town applying these concepts of development to alien creatures and societies. At a high level, authors need to consider what development might look like in cultures different from "Earth norm." Physical development plays a huge role here. How quickly or slowly does a race mature? Is development a continuous progression, or does it happen in huge leaps—think insect development with larval, pupal, and adult stages. What might a failed larval stage look like?

Other considerations include: When do gender differentiation and sexual maturity occur? Are the young integrated into society at large or segregated and if the latter, how does integration occur? Are physical skills acquired slowly or by abrupt transition? What role do mentors and teachers play in the acquisition of these skills? Answers to these questions will set the stage for early developmental pathways.

Differential paths for the genders or for classes or castes might be considerations. Consider the "classes" presented in Aldous Huxley's *Brave New World*. How might the developmental path for Alphas differ from Epsilons? In a culture analogous to a beehive or ant hill where individuals are bred for certain roles, how might developmental issues influence characters and plots?

Rites of passage often mark specific transitions between periods of development. What do those look like in an alien culture, and what role do they play in a character's development and sense of self? How do they translate cross-culturally? For an example, consider Orson Scott Card's *Speaker for the Dead* (Tor, 1986).

In a completely alien culture, developmental tasks might be very different altogether. In this case, the author should consider carefully the interaction between the individual and their society and how that might change through the lifespan the author has imagined. Major transitions are good indicators of developmental milestones that can be utilized for dramatic effects. Another interesting consideration: What happens to an individual whose physical being sets up one developmental path when raised in a setting where a very different developmental path is prescribed?

Successes and struggles during the developmental process offer an ideal structure for creating essential character backstory, informing who the character is and who that character will become. Moreover, they offer a strong framework for building character arcs, subplots, and even main storylines.

CHAPTER 24

---•---

THE HORIZONS OF NEUROSCIENCE

By Paul Regier

Neuroscience research has made a lot of progress in understanding the brain and how it works. Even so, there is still much we do not know. Mysteries, like black boxes, tend to get filled with ideas. Some of these ideas get tested as hypotheses that, after plenty of evidence is gathered, may become scientific theories. Often, however, they devolve into myths and falsehoods driven by incomplete data or anecdotal evidence.

One persistent myth is that humans only use 10 percent of our brains. Essentially, the idea is that if humans only use 10 percent of their brains—and do a lot with it—there remains 90 percent of unused brain potential that conceivably could mean untapped superpowers. It is a particularly attractive myth in fiction, and many stories in movies, books, video games, and comics have used the 10 percent fallacy as a foundation. Stories use various devices, such as drugs, science, or training, to "unlock" the 90 percent, thereby facilitating various special abilities: telekinesis, ultra-fast learning and planning, a perfect memory, or even magic.

The truth is the whole brain is active most of the time. Consider a relatively simple task such as reading this book. To provide a broad overview, areas of activation and not the complexities that occur at each area to process information, each of which would require an entire chapter, will be the focus. While reading, visual information enters the eyes and is relayed by the optic nerve through the optic chiasm, where information from the left side of the visual field viewed with the left eye crosses over to the right hemisphere; the same thing happens with the right. After the optic chiasm, the visual information is carried by the optic tract to the visual part of the thalamus, called the *lateral geniculate nucleus*, which relays the signal via the optic radiation to the visual cortex. In order to understand the visual information received, the signal is processed by the visual cortex and passed on to the angular gyrus of the left interior parietal lobe. This area does some higher-level processing (e.g., categorization, conceptualization) before sending the information to Wernicke's area, which finally recognizes the visual information as words on a page. Finally, if you speak aloud as you are reading, Broca's area and the motor cortex also get involved.

In order to make sense of each sentence and the chapter as a whole, you need to keep track of everything you have read. Memory is governed by areas of the brain such as the hippocampus and prefrontal cortex. Then several other cortical areas get involved as you imagine the mental and physical representations these words represent. Thus, the result of a basic action like reading activates a large portion of the brain: areas involved with vision, word recognition, language comprehension, memory, and executive function.

Brain regions important for reading text are more active functions, requiring conscious attention, but there are also subconscious processes that either support some action or are required just to exist. For example, if you are reading while sitting in a chair, the cerebellum and motor cortex work together to maintain balance and coordinate little muscle movements to keep the book in your hands. Even if you haven't been paying attention, your ears have been receiving sounds, which are interpreted by the auditory cortex. To top it all off, your heart and breathing and other autonomous actions that you rarely think of are being controlled by the brain stem.

It is remarkable: Just by performing a simple task, most, if not all, of the brain is active in a matter of minutes, processing specific stimuli and information, important for both conscious and subconscious processes.

NEUROSCIENCE IN FICTION

I mentioned that the 10 percent myth is particularly attractive in fiction, and it makes sense if a potential future version of our reality might allow a protagonist to have superpowers. Often, however, stories based on the 10 percent myth do not present a potential future vision; instead they offer an alternative universe, wherein human brains have untapped powers ready to be unlocked, but that's not fiction, that's fantasy. In fantasy writing, there could be a whole world of beings with brains ready to be unlocked, but fiction about humans should present the possible, at least on some level, even if extreme cases must rely on time and technology to change enough for something fantastical to occur.

Even without having to reach into the far future, neuroscience research has shown that deviations from normal brain structure can lead to interesting and advantageous behavioral abnormalities. For instance, evidence suggests that, compared with the average person, Albert Einstein had a thicker corpus callosum, which is basically an information highway between the two brain hemispheres, and this may have contributed to some of his genius. Recently, scientists have discovered a handful of people with an extraordinary ability to recall the events of their lives, a condition called highly superior autobiographical memory (HSAM). Simply prompted with a date, people with HSAM can recall what day of the week it was and what they were doing. It works the other way as well. Ask them when they first heard a song, for example, and they can tell you the exact date, the day of the week, and what they were doing. On average, people with HSAM are 87 percent accurate with their recall of these types of personal memories. This extraordinary memory recall might appear to resemble the idea behind the 10 percent myth, but the ability seems to be specific to autobiographical memory, as initial tests indicate that individuals with HSAM do not have better cognitive or memory abilities—other than autobiographical—compared with the average person. The underlying neurobiology that drives HSAM is just beginning to be understood, but initial evidence points to structural abnormalities in the brain. In other words, their brains probably developed differently, and their brains might even resemble those of people with obsessive-compulsive disorder.

Current technology, such as transcranial magnetic stimulation, which noninvasively stimulates parts of the brain, offers hints of potential exploitation of HSAM. If this ability's neurobiological underpinnings could be isolated, future technology might hypothetically induce it. Taking it a step further, the hypothetical technique to create HSAM might be applied to other parts of the brain, creating superior processing of other types of memory, cognition, or even vision. Technology offers potential ways to augment parts of the brain. External hard drives or SD cards might be connected to memory centers in the brain, allowing for extra storage and quicker and more accurate retrieval of information. A fully external visual system, like a digital version of the pathway described earlier, might allow for a greater visual field and for generally enhanced visual perception.

On the flip side, there are numerous examples of losing brain function or structures that result in behavioral changes. The literature on animal research is full of examples, wherein scientists deactivate certain parts of a brain to better understand the function of a brain region. However, this damage can occur naturally in humans, as well. One poignant example is a true story about a railroad construction foreman, Phineas Gage, in the early 1800s. While setting a charge in a rock with a tamping rod, a spark ignited the blasting powder and shot the rod through Gage's head, entering at the cheek, destroying his left eye, going through the frontal part of the brain, and coming out the top of his head, landing many yards away. Remarkably, he didn't die. The doctor who saw him after the accident reported that Gage was talkative, though a bit tired, as Gage told the doctor about the accident. The doctor was skeptical of the story until Gage threw up, and the doctor noticed bits of brain in the mess. Gage lived for twelve more years, and some people might use this story as evidence that the 10 percent myth is at least partially true. But losing part of his frontal lobe changed Gage. He became childish, impulsive, and profane to the point where friends and acquaintances reported him as being "no longer Gage."

The 10 percent myth may not be true, but neuroscientific research has numerous examples of deviations in behavior driven by changes in the brain: damage to the brain, developmentally different brains, and structural and functional changes caused by disorders and disease. Results from scientific studies can be just as interesting for the basis of a story, and a solid scientific foundation allows for a more believable fiction world and shows that the writer has taken the time to understand the mechanisms that affect those living in that environment. Thus, whether hindering or enhancing a character's neural abilities, the neuroscientific literature offers plenty of validated information to help with the creation process.

PART FOUR

FROM ZERO TO SIXTY
(LEGS, THAT IS)

●

CHAPTER 25

WILDLIFE BIOLOGY

By Rebecca Mowry

As a wildlife biologist, I notice a lot of wildlife-related errors in books, film, and television that irritate me to no end. In many cases, even a little bit of research could clear these things up. The pool of examples is endless, so here are just a few broad topics that come to mind.

MYTH #1: CACTUS WRENS LIVE IN MAINE

This remark stems from one of my favorite films, *The Shawshank Redemption*. You know that scene where Red finds Andy's money under a rock wall in Maine? The bird singing in the background is a cactus wren. Cactus wrens live in the Southwest. You know, near cacti.

Another classic example is the Coca-Cola advertising campaign featuring polar bears interacting with emperor penguins, which I'm fairly certain drove every zoologist bonkers. What's the problem? Never mind the image of one of the most aggressive carnivores on the planet sitting happily next to a family of flightless birds, which I'll grudgingly accept as a little cute anthropomorphism between charismatic megafauna. Hopefully nobody thinks that actually happens. What I can't stand is that Coke ignored the fact that polar bears live only in the Arctic, and penguins live only in the Antarctic. Fun fact: The root of the word Arctic, *arctos*, means *bear*.

It's really not that hard to look up a species' habitat and geographic range before you put it in your story. People love animals—which is a great thing—but with the rise of citizen science and species identification apps for your smartphone, especially when it comes to bird-watching, your readers may know a lot more than you expect them to, increasing the odds that your lack of research will be noticed and scorned.

Oh, and to add to the confusion, lots of animals migrate. So don't tell me about the turkey vultures circling your hero lost in Montana in the winter, because they're only there in the summertime.

MYTH #2: THE GEOGRAPHIC RANGE AND HABITATS OF SPECIES NEVER CHANGE

If you're writing any kind of historical fiction, you should be aware that the range, habitats, and even appearance of a species can change over time. For example:

- Prior to the red/gray wolf's extirpation from the eastern United States, there were no coyotes there.
- Until a few hundred years ago, jaguars lived throughout most of Arizona, New Mexico, Texas, and even Louisiana.
- Horses were brought to North America in the 1400s, but they actually evolved here before being wiped out ten to twelve thousand years ago.
- Recent climate change is causing all kinds of shifts in animal behavior (read on!).

Just like any other facet of historical fiction, it's worth researching what the wildlife community would have looked like back when your story takes place. In North America, most habitats have changed drastically since the advent of Europeans (and even since the advent of the first humans, period). You can probably get away with a lot of stuff, but you want your novel to be authentic, don't you?

MYTH #3: WILDLIFE BIOLOGISTS ARE ALL PARK RANGERS, ZOOKEEPERS, OR TV SHOW HOSTS

My friends and I all got tired of that comment in college. I was just watching an episode of *The West Wing* where C.J. Cregg gets a visit from a park ranger. This park ranger proceeds to tell Cregg's assistant that he studied shrub/range ecosystems, and that it was a good thing the Park Service hired him, because he wouldn't have had anything else to do. Headdesk.

I'll admit that I felt this way for my entire childhood. Steve Irwin was my hero (may he rest in peace), but I was seventeen before I discovered that wildlife biology was a thing. Now, of course, I know that the field is incredibly rich and varied, and not just because of the variety of species we have to work with. There aren't many of us in stories, which is a shame, because there sure are a lot of us in the world!

Wildlife biologists do lead tours in natural areas, arrest poachers, and educate the public on television. But they also trek into remote jungles to document rare and unknown species. They survey deer and turkeys to set hunting quotas. University professors research wildlife behavior, evolution, habitat, and threats to conservation. Each state has an agency dedicated to wildlife research and management, and there are several federal entities that do this as well (like the U.S. Fish and Wildlife Service, U.S. Forest Service, and U.S. Geological Survey). Then there are nonprofit organizations that do their own work for species and habitat conservation, like the Sierra Club, the Nature Conservancy, and the World Wildlife Fund. They all employ wildlife biologists.

And we're also not all tree-hugging, granola-eating hippies. Some biologists love game animals and hate predators. Some biologists love predators and hate hunters. Some biologists love everything. And some biologists are tree-hugging, granola-eating hippies.

MYTH #4: WE KNOW ALL THERE IS TO KNOW ABOUT WILDLIFE AND ECOSYSTEMS

We're still learning. Constantly.

For one, scientists are continuing to unravel the evolutionary history of wildlife species. Advances in genetic analysis have a lot to do with this. That's why taxonomists (the people who classify animals) are always changing the scientific names of stuff, much to the dismay of people like me who had to memorize them in college.

More pressing, however, is the fact that the world is always changing, especially over the last century. Thanks to urban sprawl, climate change, and other contemporary challenges, a growing segment of wildlife research focuses on how these big changes will affect animals and their habitats.

Birds are altering the timing of reproduction and migration. Grizzly and polar bears may be hybridizing more often. Wildfire suppression prevents naturally occurring fire cycles to which plants and wildlife had evolved. Emerging diseases like white-nose syndrome and chytridiomycosis are wiping out entire populations of bats and amphibians, respectively. Overfishing may be causing trophic cascades running all the way down the food chain; seals and sea lions decline due to lack of food, orca then run out of seals and switch to sea otters, sea otter declines result in an overpopulation of sea urchins, which damage kelp forests, which are an important habitat for many marine organisms. And those are just a few examples. I haven't even mentioned the epic loss of coral reefs. Okay, now I have.

We're still learning just how important these issues are and what we can do about them.

MYTH #5: THERE WILL BE NO ANIMALS IN THE FUTURE

Yikes, now that's depressing! Sorry about that doom-and-gloom stuff. Yes, we will likely witness many species extinctions in the coming centuries, but I find the prospect of a wildlife-free Earth highly improbable.

Certain animals and plants can survive in any number of tough situations; that's part of the beauty of mutation and evolution. I'm simplifying this a lot, but consider the Cretaceous-Paleogene mass extinction sixty-six million years ago that killed off the then-predominant terrestrial vertebrates, the dinosaurs. Many small mammals were able to survive the extreme environmental conditions that the very large reptiles couldn't. That ushered in the explosion of mammalian diversity, which allowed mammals to eventually evolve into many of their current forms (including humans).

Humans may be one of the most devastating forces of nature when it comes to species extinction, but don't forget that many species thrive in human-dominated landscapes. Pigeons, feral dogs, rats, and cockroaches come to mind. There are even some that aren't quite as cliché, like white-winged doves, peregrine falcons, red foxes, raccoons, and coyotes; in fact, I worked on a project in urban Orange County, California where we observed bobcats and coyotes making themselves at home in culverts under office parks and freeways, often denning up in people's backyards. Granted, getting hit by cars was the primary source of mortality, but if the smartest survive—that's evolution!

Animals adapt, and evolution is still occurring. We may not be able to predict exactly what this will mean for the future, but what an opening for creativity!

HOW TO HANDLE WILDLIFE BIOLOGY IN YOUR NOVELS

Do Your Research

If you want to make your story as authentic as possible, make sure you're describing the appropriate ecosystems and animal communities. There are tons of resources on the Internet for this: eBird.com for birds, iNaturalist.org for everything, and even Wikipedia gets things right most of the time. If only eBird had been around for Frank Darabont when he directed *The Shawshank Redemption*!

And for a classic example of a well-researched novel that manages to be biologically accurate without sacrificing awesomeness, read Richard Adams' *Watership Down* (Rex Collings, 1972).

Have Fun With It!

Because we're always learning, there's a lot of wiggle room for using wildlife in fiction. For example, George R.R. Martin decided to use ravens as messengers in his fictional world, and while I've never heard of them being used as such, corvids (the taxonomic group of which ravens are a member and includes crows, jays, and magpies) are famously intelligent. Scientists have observed crows not only using tools but using sequences of tools and showing the ability to reason. Crows have been observed using passing cars as tools to crack nuts. In Washington, researchers demonstrated that crows can recognize human faces.

I don't expect things to be 100 percent ecologically accurate all the time, but I'd at least like your details to be believable. In *The Hunger Games* (Scholastic, 2008), Suzanne Collins bred genetically altered jays with wild mockingbirds to create the mockingjay. Jays and mockingbirds are classified into different taxonomic families (which makes hybridization less likely), but I still find this to be an excellent incorporation of wildlife behavior into a futuristic story. Use your research on species' habitats, evolution, and behavior to come up with a mind-blowing prediction of futuristic animal communities.

Contact a Wildlife Biologist If You Have Any Questions

Seriously. There are so many of us, and we'll probably be very happy to help you and even give you fun ideas for ways to incorporate wildlife into your story. How about some chronic wasting disease deer zombies? Too soon?

CHAPTER 26

WRITING OUTSIDE THE HUMAN BOX

By Brie Paddock

We are surrounded by representations of humans at the pinnacle of society, communication, and technology, with little room left for the other thousands of species that share our planet. Leonardo da Vinci's *The Vitruvian Man*, a beautiful piece of art that relates architecture to the proportions of a human man, shows just how self-centered we are, despite being only one of nearly nine million species on this planet.

But speculative fiction goes beyond the limitations of the mundane and human and into the realm of the fantastic. Elves, dragons, vampires. J.R.R. Tolkien, Anne McCaffrey, Bram Stoker. Love them. But it's been done. You can dust off these supernatural beings, reinvent an aspect, tweak a trope. Or you can invent your own monsters and aliens. Give them their own form, their own behaviors, their own motivations, thoughts, and strangeness. Make them *real*.

THE TRUTH ABOUT FLIES

I spent many years putting electrodes into the nerves of fruit flies to see, exactly, how they work. This (among some other things) earned me a Ph.D. with a focus in neuroscience. You probably know that they can smell bananas better than we can. But fruit flies also:

- Flirt with each other
- Can get jet-lagged
- Learn and remember things that happen to them

I'm not trying to get you to write about fruit flies as your next alien or fantasy villain or mount for your hero in plate mail. But think about this: Our brains are not fundamentally different from those of other animals.

WHAT MAKES US HUMAN?

Most people are shocked to discover that flies show other complex behaviors over which we feel possessive. Our job as writers of fiction is to support those ideas with words that resonate with readers and make them question and assess their own humanity.

Humanity is defined in many ways, and most of us feel fairly comfortable that we are the dominant species on the planet. But what measurable thing makes us human? Tool use? Warfare? Monogamy? Love? Depression? Enjoyment of the society of like-minded individuals (with apologies to Jane Austen)?

When Jane Goodall revealed that chimpanzees waged war on one another, many were shocked to have another species invade a sphere thought strictly the purview of humans.

HUMANS ARE ANIMALS

The idea that humans are different or special is a myth I want to dispel. Humans aren't different from animals. We *are* animals. Each character you write about is an animal. Humanity is a nebulous ideal and can be represented by characters other than humans.

So, let's get to some nitty-gritty science ideas that can help you break out of the human box when designing characters. How can you make a new species that's interesting and different but understandable and relatable to your readers? Let's talk differences.

ANIMAL SENSES

Many animals have senses—sight, smell, hearing, touch—that outstrip our own. Most people are familiar with the idea that dogs have a sense of smell that far outstrips ours, but many don't realize the diversity of animals that have sensory systems far superior to ours. Much like children unaware of the double meanings of words used by our parents, we sense only a portion of the world around us.

Sight

Most animals have the ability to see. Light enters our bodies, and we have specialized cells and tissues that change when that light hits those cells. That is the basis of all sight, from jellyfish that float in the ocean, to a hawk circling above a field and searching for a tasty mouse in the grass.

Light is a type of energy; we perceive it as having color and brightness. Our eyes have two types of cells that allow us to see color: rods and cones. Rods are active at low levels of light, so they allow us to see in the dark. Cones, which are active at brighter light levels, provide color vision. Special proteins in rods and cones, called opsins, help us distinguish between different colors. People who are red-green color-blind, for example, lack the opsin that distinguishes these two colors.

What if an animal had different opsins in their rods? Could they see color at night? What if an animal had another opsin? Could they see colors we can't?

The answer to that last question is yes. Birds have additional opsins that allow them to see beyond the wavelengths of light that humans get to enjoy. Other animals that can see ultraviolet light include butterflies, bees, salmon, and reindeer.

Hearing

Sound provides a different realm. Relatively few animals can actually sense sound, a fact that surprises most humans partially because we use sound to communicate so thoroughly, constantly, and urbanely. Why?

In part, because we live on land.

Anyone who has been to a loud beach or swimming pool has experienced the apparent decrease in volume when you dunk your head (with your accompanying ears) under the surface of the water. Sound waves don't travel as effectively through water, and many animals live underwater. Some fish use bones along their spine to hear sounds otherwise rendered too faint by traveling through the deep ocean.

Other Senses

Some voracious aquatic predators, including sharks and rays, use a sense that is completely foreign to us as they hunt their prey. They have pits along their lower body that allow them to sense bioelectricity. Their prey can remain utterly immobile, invisible under the sand, but the prey can't stop their own brains from working or hearts from beating. So the rays and sharks prey upon that weakness.

Sharks aren't very nice. But the chubby, pollinating, bumbling honey bee uses electroreception, too. Just like a person shuffling his feet on a thick carpet, bees accumulate static electricity when their wings rub during flight. Some of that charge is transferred when they visit flowers. Bees use electroreception to determine which flowers have recently been visited by other bees so they don't waste their own time and energy.

DON'T LIMIT YOUR CREATIONS

There's more to this world that we can see or hear, smell, or sense. But that doesn't mean our characters have to be similarly limited.

Evolution begins every animal with a mistake, an aberration in the genetic code. Most of these mutations condemn their owners to certain death, but a powerful few have created all the terrifying squid and fluffy bunnies of our planet. Next time you design a monster or an alien, make a mistake. Make a thousand. Then see which one survives the natural selection of your story.

CHAPTER 27

WHAT BUGS ME ABOUT INSECTS

By Robinne Weiss

Arthropods (insects, spiders, centipedes, etc.) show up regularly in fiction. I love a good science fiction or fantasy story, but as an entomologist, I often cringe at the way arthropods are portrayed in books and movies. Here are a few of the common portrayals that "bug" me.

HUGE ARTHROPODS

There's no doubt that increasing the size of an arthropod to that of a bus makes it a more terrifying antagonist (let's face it, Shelob in *The Lord of the Rings* would have been nothing but a nuisance if Frodo could have squashed her with his heel), but unless your giant insects live on some other planet with different physical laws and gravitational conditions, it's simply not possible.

As an animal increases in size, its surface area increases in proportion to the square of the length of the animal (because surface area is measured in two dimensions), but the animal's volume increases in proportion to the cube of the length (because volume is measured in three dimensions). So as an arthropod's size increases, its volume-to-surface ratio goes up. This relationship has important implications for the behavior of a hypothetical giant arthropod.

Ants seem incredibly strong because their muscles are moving a very small mass compared to the muscles' cross-sectional area. But if we increase the size of an ant to that of a human, the ratio of mass-to-muscle cross-section rises dramatically. So an ant the size of a human would have about the same physical prowess as a human.

Okay, so maybe huge arthropods wouldn't have superhuman abilities, but they'd still be impressive, right?

Except they couldn't possibly grow that big in the first place.

Arthropods have an exoskeleton—the rigid structure of their bodies is on the outside. An exoskeleton is great if you're small because it provides both structure and protection. Unfortunately, an exoskeleton has some major disadvantages at larger sizes.

Exoskeletons don't grow with the animal's body. In order to get larger, an arthropod must shed its old exoskeleton and grow a new one. When the old exoskeleton is shed, the new one is soft and pliable. It takes time for the new exoskeleton to harden. That's fine for a small arthropod because the pull of gravity is not great on a small body. Enlarge an arthropod to the size of a human, however, and it will be crushed by its own weight before its new exoskeleton can harden.

INSECTS AS BAD GUYS

Books and movies love to demonize insects and other arthropods. It's always the spiders, ants, bees, or whatever that threaten humanity. But the truth of the matter is that we couldn't survive without insects.

Everybody can name insects that can harm us or our crops. We are familiar with these pests because they seek us out as a source of food. But fewer than 1 percent of insect species are pests, and those that are considered pests are often only a problem in particular times and places, not all the time. Most insects are beneficial or neutral as far as humans are concerned.

Insects provide food for wildlife, control pests, and help break down dead plant and animal material. They are used in scientific research and medicine. They pollinate 35 percent of the world's crop production. Without them, there would be no coffee, no chocolate, no fruits or vegetables. Insects also provide honey, wax, silk, shellac, and food coloring.

Far from being our worst enemies, arthropods are essential to our existence. I would like to see them appear as the good guys in fiction now and again.

TRUTH IS STRANGER THAN FICTION

What bothers me most about insects portrayed in fiction is authors often don't know the facts about insects, so they miss out on a deep well of creative opportunity. The truth about insects can be so outrageous it hardly needs fictionalization. Here are some inspiring true stories of insects that I would love to see worked into fiction.

Chemical Warfare

Insects and other arthropods are masters of chemical defense. Some collect toxins from the plants they eat; others manufacture their own poisonous arsenal. Some inject their toxins with stingers or fangs, but many more exude or spray noxious chemicals from glands on various parts of their bodies. Thousands of species of vinegaroons, cockroaches, earwigs, stick insects, beetles, and other arthropods can eject irritating chemicals with surprising accuracy and range when threatened.

Some of these chemicals are the most concentrated acids occurring in nature, and it's a wonder the insects themselves can tolerate them.

Blister beetles are an extreme example of chemical protection. They contain the chemical cantharidin, which has been considered an aphrodisiac in the past because, when taken orally by men, it causes erections. Unfortunately, it does so by destroying the man's renal and reproductive systems. Half a dozen blister beetles contain enough cantharidin to kill a person.

An example close to home is the friendly ladybug, beloved by gardeners and school children. But ladybugs' cheerful appearance is deceiving. Their bright coloration warns predators they are toxic. Their blood is packed with bitter alkaloids. When they are attacked, they bleed from their knee joints, giving the predator a nasty mouthful. Some scientists speculate that poison dart frogs may eat ladybugs, stealing the ladybug poison for their own protection.

Pavlov's Bees

Most insects are highly sensitive to smell. The chemoreceptors on their antennae can detect chemicals in concentrations much lower than humans can.

Researchers have taken advantage of these abilities. Honey bees and moths have been trained to detect land mines. Parasitic wasps have been trained to sense explosives, illegal drugs, plant diseases, and buried bodies. Researchers train insects by feeding them treats laced with the chemicals until the insects associate the chemicals with food—a bit like Pavlov's dogs.

Parasitoid Wasps

The most well-known use of parasitoids in science fiction has to be in the *Alien* movies. Parasitoids lay their eggs inside other organisms. The eggs hatch out, and the baby parasitoids eat their host from the inside out, keeping their host alive by saving the critical organs for last. This type of parasitism is common in the insect world. Some of the most spectacular examples of parasitoids are the giant ichneumon wasps in the genus *Megarhyssa*. Some species of *Megarhyssa* have ovipositors (egg-laying tubes) 4 inches (100mm) long. Their ovipositors, stiffened by blood pressure, can drill deep into wood. Sensors on the tip of the ovipositor can taste horntail larvae—the wasps' prey—that live inside tree trunks.

Aerial Maneuvers

Fantasy and science fiction often involve spectacular flying fantasy creatures— dragons, enormous birds, griffins, and the like. But if you're looking for feats of aerial agility, insects beat fantasy creatures every time. Insects can steer accurately at speed, hover, and fly sideways or backward. They need no runway, starting and stopping their flight from a standstill. Some predatory insects, like dragonflies, tiger beetles, and robber flies catch other insects on the wing. Many moths can outmaneuver even a hunting bat. Insect flight can seem to defy gravity and physics, and scientists are still trying to work out exactly how insects manage what they do in the air.

Biblical Plagues

Plagues of locusts appear occasionally in fiction, but the astonishing biology and ecology of locust plagues is rarely seen.

Plague-forming locusts generally live in arid regions where food is sparse. Most of the time, locusts are solitary. They're well camouflaged by their green or brown color, and they actively avoid other locusts. Locust numbers rise rapidly during periods of wet weather. When it dries out again and food becomes scarce, the locusts are forced to congregate in the remaining patches of food. When this happens, they undergo a tremendous shift. The parts of their brains associated with learning and processing complex information grow. Their bodies turn from cryptic greens and browns to bright orange and black. They switch from a purely vegetarian diet to a diet that includes cannibalism. Their flight muscles grow. They actively seek out other locusts and start moving in huge numbers across the landscape. They essentially transform into an entirely different insect, all in the course of a few weeks.

Entomological Warfare

Arthropod-borne diseases such as malaria, yellow fever, encephalitis, and dozens more kill millions of people every year. It's no surprise that military powers have tried to put these diseases to work during wartime. The most developed of these endeavors took place in Japan during World War II. Using Chinese prisoners as guinea pigs and blood sources, the Japanese military weaponized plague-infested fleas and cholera-infected flies, releasing them in China and killing tens of thousands of people. The program was effectively hushed up by the U.S. military after the war in a rather morally suspect deal in which the Japanese mastermind behind the entomological warfare program, General Ishii Shiro, was given immunity from prosecution in exchange for his data.

If I were to give advice to authors writing insects into their stories, it would be to get to know the real-life versions of your many-legged characters—they may not be who you think they are, and they may be much more interesting.

CHAPTER 28

PORTRAYING WOLVES FAIRLY AND ACCURATELY

By William Huggins

"Demand evidence, and think critically."

—NEIL DEGRASSE TYSON

Of all nonhuman animals used, abused, misused, misrepresented, mistreated, and turned into poor clichés of their actual selves over the course of literary history, few have been so wrongly written about as wolves (*Canis lupus*). Such poor representation has consequences in realms both literary and temporal. Consider that wolves have been exterminated from over 90 percent of their historic range. A systematic elimination of a keystone species, essential to planetary ecological health, emerges from a cultural history built on poor storytelling—that the wolf is a threat to human pastoral land management, not a benefit. Misrepresenting the wolf in story has led to blaming the species for more than its share of damage done, primarily economic, such as preying on cattle and sheep—which more often than not is the fault of domesticated dogs gone feral.

Putting a nonhuman animal in a story means we, as writers and readers, must be honest about how that four-legged sentient being might behave in its real life, which means we must be scientifically literate enough to give agency to the nonhuman animals about whom we write. Or, as S.K. Robisch notes, "All of the components used in framing an argument are both proactively and retroactively affected by the argument, including any ecological components. This means when we put a wolf in a story, the story at that point must be responsible to the wolf."[1]

DEMONIZATION OF THE WOLF

For the most part, from the earliest religious literature the wolf has been demonized for its purely natural proclivities. Most of the world's major religions portrayed wolves in a particularly unkind light. In Tablet VI of the *Epic of Gilgamesh*, Ishtar returns a shepherd's love for her by turning him into a wolf, the very bane of his

---

[1] *Wolves and the Wolf Myth in American Literature*, 11, (University of Nevada Press, 2009)

profession. In the *Kaushitaki Upanishad*, Indra delivers Arunmukhas to wolves. The Christian Bible is replete with negative connotations for wolves, in line with Matthew 7:15's "Beware of the false prophets, who come to you in sheep's clothing but inwardly are ravenous wolves." Not to be left out, the Koran's sole mention of wolves, chapter 12, has them responsible for Joseph's death. St. Francis and the Wolf of Gubbio stand as an extremely rare example of wolf tolerance, only because St. Francis convinces the wolf to leave the village alone. So the dichotomy of one vision of the wolf stems from our earliest writings: civilization versus the wild.

Children's stories have been no less unkind. One exception might be *Aesop's Fables*, which are almost evenly balanced; the pithy morals that close each fable don't wholly make wolves evil but give them some leniency for natural actions. In most children's stories, wolves are a convenient foil for the heroes or heroines: think Red Riding Hood or the Three Little Pigs, obvious examples of a comforting civility threatened by a wild world. First impressions are important because children form biases at an early age.

Medieval bestiaries often compared the wolf to the devil, hunting sheep with cunning and guile—which is, of course, true, at least in the case of the wolf. In Europe, Portugal, Spain, and Italy contain the only wolf packs considered sustainable at this writing, though wolves have slowly been migrating back into areas they once occupied hundreds of years ago, like Poland and Germany. The British Isles are entirely devoid of wolves. Even great poets such as Geoffrey Chaucer borrowed from the bestiaries and noted wolves negatively in "The Nun's Priest's Tale" and the nearly unreadable *The Parson's Tale*.

This same medieval mind with all its unfair cultural biases crossed the Atlantic with early Euro-American settlers. With better guns and ammunition than their European forebears, the settlers of America and Canada declared an unnecessary war on wolves that removed the species almost entirely from the entire North American continent—and continues today.

Recent young adult books, possibly because of better scientific understanding of wolves' role in nature or a more forceful conservation movement, have turned the tide a bit: Kathryn Lasky's Wolves of the Beyond series and Michelle Paver's Wolf Brother series both do a fair job of showing wolves as they more naturally behave, especially in their devotion and dedication to their young, in which the entire pack plays a role. Though these books do not represent wolves scientifically, they at least give young readers the chance to consider other characterizations besides The Big Bad Wolf.

WOLVES IN GENRE FICTION

Science fiction and fantasy have not been entirely accurate in representations of wolves, either. *The Lord of the Rings* takes a staunchly medievalist approach, turning them into agents of the dark forces. Whitley Strieber, in *The Wolfen* (William Morrow & Co., 1977), presents wolves as intelligent actors in their revenge strategy but the story goes a bit off the rails—*The Wolfen* is one of those rare moments where the movie might have done a better job representing wolves as they naturally act than the book. Many other examples exist, perhaps most recently the relationship of the Starks to their direwolves in *Game of Thrones*. Yet while an opportunity may have existed to show wolves in a more natural light, *Game of Thrones'* direwolves function more as devoted pets. Though Arya does release Nymeria, the possibility of warging with direwolves takes some of their potential wildness away. Even the ever-amazing C.J. Cherryh falls into cliché in *Chernevog* (Del Rey, 1990) with the traditional Russian fable of wolves at the door, which has never been backed up by science, though, is prevalent in the Russian folktales from which Cherryh draws.

One noteworthy positive exception exists in how wolves get represented in story, both orally and textually: indigenous writers. James Welch's *Fools Crow* (Bison Books, 1994) portrays wolves as they might exist in a natural setting, fictional or not. The lone wolf attack in the book comes from a rabid wolf, which is consistent with the scientific literature. Welch's other wolf scenes feature *Canis lupus* as it lives. Unlike the feral attackers in James Fenimore Cooper (see *The Oak Openings*) and Jack London (take your pick) or Nicholas Evans' facile *The Loop* (Delacorte Press, 1998), wolves do not like being around human beings very much and will avoid us if possible. Welch establishes this fact perfectly.

Louise Erdrich, a member of the indigenous people group the Anishinaabe, aptly portrays wolves in her Turtle Mountain cycle of novels, perhaps nowhere better than *The Painted Drum* (Harper, 2005) where an Anishinaabe elder actually hears a nearby wolf speaking to him and converses with it, though "not in words." The connection of wolf and elder is defined through shared trauma, and the wolf's "response" gives the elder a reason to continue living. Erdrich's wolves also play with ravens, a connection seen throughout nature but rarely on the pages of fiction involving wolves.

Writers of non-indigenous descent can learn a great deal from indigenous writers, not only in matters of technique but also in perceiving the world in a way to make not only a story but connecting other nonhuman sentient beings realistically into a story. Perhaps this is because of John Wayne-style Western films or the 1990 film *Dances With Wolves*—the indigenous peoples of our planet know what it is like to be misrepresented in literature and cinema.

There are examples of wolves well done outside indigenous literatures, but they are few and far between. Mostly this issue evolved from culture: Euro-Americans were not taught to respect the wolf and its role in nature as were indigenous peoples. The wolf was seen as either a harbinger of doom, a wild beast possessed of supernatural powers, or simply a pest that stole and killed stock. Many even today envision wolves as sharks with four legs, continuously eating. In reality, wolves often go days without food. "Being a predator is only one aspect of being a wolf. While eating is essential, predation is but a method."[2] So it is that writers like Rick Bass (*Where the Sea Used to Be* [Houghton Mifflin, 1998]), Renee Askins (*Shadow Mountain* [Doubleday, 2002]), Seth Kantner (*Ordinary Wolves* [Milkweed Editions, 2004]), and Cormac McCarthy (*The Crossing* [Alfred A. Knopf, 1994]) and others have a lot more work to do to balance out negative portrayals of wolves. Yet there may be some hope: BK Loren's debut novel *Theft* (Counterpoint, 2012) realistically extrapolates the character of a wild wolf and may be a harbinger of better things to come.

Authors, especially in the fields of science fiction and fantasy, where some writers literally inhabit and recreate the minds of alien beings, including nonhuman animals, can and should do better. If one can write about aliens, one should be able to write about the other intelligences with which we share our own planet. Wolves predate humans by millions of years and have just as much right to be here as we do. In a world where science—especially wildlife biology and the emerging field of ethology—has shown us the ecological importance of wolves in properly managed wilderness systems (think of Yellowstone National Park since the reintroduction of wolves there in 1994, how the renewed presence of wolves brought a cascade effect of health, including the revitalization of the Park's forests), one would think that science would translate into better writing and storytelling.

Wolves deserve better, both on the ground and on the page. Writers, it's time to be honest and tell stories that are not only good but true to the nonhuman characters on the page, as well. As the wolf makes a comeback across its historic range, reviving itself and the landscapes that absolutely had to miss it, stories matter. If we are to reverse the destruction and mismanagement the human occupation of the planet has caused, rewriting our stories with respect to science and the rights of nonhuman animals would not be the worst place to start. In a world of ever-diminishing biodiversity, we need to recognize the power of our words: otiose writing, flawed legends, and no science took wolves to the brink of extinction; good writing and good science could keep them where they belong, right here, with us, on the page and in person.

Neither in our actions nor our literatures have we been responsible to the wolf. It is high time we should be.

---

2 *Wolves and the Wolf Myth in American Literature*, 94

CHAPTER 29

GENDER DETERMINATION
IN ANIMALS

By Robinne Weiss

Hordes of mutant insects, alien creatures, dragons, unicorns, and all the other weird and wonderful creatures that appear in fiction have to reproduce. Otherwise they wouldn't exist, right? It's tempting to ignore the reproduction of our fantastical creatures, though—they hatch, or land on Earth, or whatever, and *then* the excitement starts.

But the world of reproductive biology is full of juicy facts, ripe for exploitation by fiction writers. Take the matter of gender, for instance. For many animals, gender is a relatively simple matter determined by genetics, but in other animals, gender is far more complex.

WHY DOES IT TAKE TWO TO TANGO?

Gender determination has evolved many times in different animals, but it has almost always led to two genders. Why two? Why not three or four? To understand, we have to look back to the evolution of sex cells (*gametes*). When sexual reproduction evolved, the first gametes were all the same size—there were no sperm or eggs. But selective pressures pushed gametes into two directions. Small gametes were better at moving around and finding other gametes to fertilize. Larger gametes were better provisioned and better able to develop into an embryo once fertilized. These competing pressures led to small, mobile sperm (and the males to produce them) and large, immobile eggs (and the females to produce them).

SOME LIKE IT HOT

Some species of reptile have temperature-determined genders. The incubation temperature of the egg determines whether the embryo develops as female or male. Unlike warm-blooded birds that sit on their eggs to keep them warm, reptiles are largely at the mercy of their environment when it comes to incubation. They generally lay their eggs in clutches, buried in sand or soil in a sunny location, and hope for the best.

In many turtles, eggs incubated at lower temperatures develop as males, and those incubated at higher temperatures become females. In American alligators, extreme temperatures (high or low) produce females and moderate ones produce males. With this system of gender determination, entire clutches of eggs may emerge as one gender or the other. A storm that buries eggs more deeply in sand or soil or exposes eggs more directly to the sun can change the gender of a whole clutch of eggs.

Some fish are also affected by incubation temperature, with extreme temperatures leading to more males, though studies suggest that fish also have a genetic component to gender determination and temperature only affects gender at extreme conditions. The same is true for some insects, where cool temperatures cause the chromosomes to behave differently during meiosis, resulting in more male offspring.

Marie Brennan used this idea beautifully in *Voyage of the Basilisk: A Memoir by Lady Trent* (Tor, 2015). In the story, a nation tries to breed dragons to defend their borders, but the dragons all develop as small males, useless for defense. The intrepid naturalist, Lady Trent, conjectures it is because incubation conditions were wrong for the production of the much larger females.

GOING BOTH WAYS

Some fish and snails actually switch genders throughout their lives. The switches may be triggered by social or environmental cues. Clown anemonefish (think Nemo) all begin life as males. In a group, only the two largest fish are sexually mature—one female and one male. If the group's dominant female dies, the dominant male becomes female and takes her place.

Indo-Pacific cleaner wrasses do it the opposite, with groups of one male and many smaller females. When the male dies, the largest female becomes male and takes his place.

Parrotfish and hawkfish can begin life as either gender, and switch throughout their lives.

Imagine how *Finding Nemo* could have been wildly different with this little bit of biology included, considering that Nemo's mother is killed, and he and his father are the only two clownfish left …

HAVE YOUR CAKE AND EAT IT, TOO

Some animals don't really have different genders because each individual possesses both male and female sex organs. We call these animals *hermaphrodites*, after Hermaphroditus, the son of Hermes and Aphrodite who became both male and female after being united with a water nymph. Hermaphroditism is a useful adaptation for slow-moving animals that may have difficulty finding a member of the opposite sex. If all members of the species are both male and female, any individual will do as a mate. Earthworms are an example of hermaphroditic animals. Every earthworm has testes near the rear of its body and ovaries near the head. During mating, earthworms lie head to tail, and each worm acts as male and female, passing sperm to the other worm. Many species of snail and slug are also hermaphroditic and practice the same sort of mutual fertilization that worms do.

Sea squirts and other tunicates are also hermaphrodites. As adults, these animals are sessile—they are attached to a surface and can't move around to find mates. They release sperm and/or eggs into the water to be fertilized. Many of these organisms are self-sterile, meaning that if sperm and eggs from the same individual should encounter each other, the sperm cannot fertilize the egg.

All this may sound familiar because plants do exactly the same thing. Most plants are hermaphrodites—within each flower are male parts (anthers, producing pollen, the equivalent of sperm) and female parts (ovaries, producing ovules, the equivalent of eggs). Only rarely are plants gendered in a genetic system similar to our own, with X and Y chromosomes. Ginkgo is one example. Male ginkgo trees are prized for urban landscaping, but the females are reviled for their foul-smelling fruit.

HE'S HALF THE WOMAN SHE IS

In many bees, wasps, and ants, males develop from unfertilized eggs (haploid—with genes from the mother only), and females from fertilized eggs (diploid—with a set of genes from each parent). Usually the adult female controls the process, choosing when to produce males and when to produce females by controlling the release of sperm she has stored from mating. Sometimes, as in some scale insects, the males originate from fertilized eggs in which the father's genome is destroyed during development, becoming haploid.

INVASION OF THE GENDER SNATCHERS

The strangest (and perhaps most interesting for fiction) gender determination oddity is that found in many insects and other arthropods.

A wide variety of insects produce only females or produce males only rarely. There are insect species for which no males have ever been found—females simply clone themselves or lay unfertilized eggs.

The elimination of the male gender appears to be caused almost entirely by strains of bacteria in the genus *Wolbachia*, which infects arthropods and some nematodes and is considered a reproductive parasite. The relationships between

Wolbachia and its hosts range from parasitic to mutualistic, but almost always involve a modification of genders and reproduction.

Infected females pass *Wolbachia* to their offspring but males don't, so it is in the bacteria's interest to eliminate males. *Wolbachia* accomplishes this in one of several ways (different among *Wolbachia* strains and hosts): by killing males before maturity, causing males to develop as females, giving female hosts the ability to reproduce parthenogenically (without males), or causing cytoplasmic incompatibility between infected males and uninfected females so only infected females can reproduce.

The relationship between *Wolbachia* and arthropods is a long one and has shaped the evolution of both hosts and parasites. In some cases, the relationship has evolved into an obligate one—the host cannot survive or reproduce at all without the bacteria. In some cases, insect species under the influence of the bacteria have evolved to be single-gendered, so even if the bacteria are removed, only females are produced.

Whether obligate or not, *Wolbachia* gives many infected insects a reproductive advantage over uninfected ones. It also often gives the insect a survival advantage, providing the host protection against pathogens and, in some cases, improved nutrient uptake.

So, infection by bacteria produces all-female races of superbugs … now *there's* some cool science fiction!

Because *Wolbachia* does more than simply change insects' gender, its presence and its many and varied strains raise interesting opportunities for us as humans. Mosquitoes that transmit diseases like malaria, chikungunya, West Nile virus, dengue, and Zika virus are less susceptible to infection by these pathogens when they are infected with certain strains of *Wolbachia*. Scientists have been studying the feasibility of using *Wolbachia* in the fight against arthropod-borne diseases, both to decrease their ability to carry the diseases and as a way to limit reproduction (by infecting males with incompatible strains of *Wolbachia*, thus preventing viable offspring).

GENDER IN OTHER LIFE FORMS

Of course, this is just animals. Gender determination becomes even more weird and wonderful when it comes to other organisms. Fungi, for instance, have genetically based gender determination, but may have thousands of genders (*mating types*). This diversity can make it hard for a fungus to find a compatible mate, so many have evolved the ability to change some of their cells to a compatible mating type and mate with themselves.

CHAPTER 30

———●———

OUT IN THE COLD: POLAR ANIMALS

By Brie Paddock

A hearty crew of adventuring space pirates, or gritty interstellar mercenaries, or tatty but idealistic rebels have just landed on a totally new planet. They crack open the airlock, stumble outside and find ... an entirely new world. Jungle? Desert? Savannah?

Or, better yet, ice.

Ever since Hoth in the 1980 movie *The Empire Strikes Back*, ice planets have popped up in popular science fiction films and books to challenge the protagonists with their bitter winds, barren landscapes, and the threat of frostbite. Maybe it's the call of the poles on our own planet—so far, distant, and mysterious—that drives readers and writers to explore these icy extremes of light and dark.

As a kid growing up in Alaska, these frozen literary landscapes appealed to me immensely. But so often, the depictions of these Arctic-like wildernesses were peppered with small inaccuracies that rang false. Mostly, that the Arctic (or Antarctic) is an empty, barren landscape waiting to challenge protagonists. I missed the ravens cackling, massive herds of wandering caribou, tenacious mountain goats, vicious and solitary wolverine. Stunning flocks of migratory tern and geese, showing up as the days stretch to impossible lengths, like tourists wandering off of cruise ships.

Let's face it, folks. There's more to polar landscapes than ice and glaciers. Let's talk about cold-adapted animals. Maybe you can add some of these ideas to your next climate fiction or space opera.

HEAT IS THE NAME OF THE GAME

Most animals that successfully live at the poles are warm-blooded, or *endotherms*. They spend huge amounts of energy keeping their bodies warm, and most adaptations to the polar environment center around the production or conservation of heat: polar bears, musk oxen, walruses, orcas (killer whales), puffins, penguins. Thus, the poles have mostly been colonized by mammals and birds, the two major groups of warm-blooded animals (polar fish being the notable exception). But unless you're working out the next Antarctic mermaid adventure, this may be a little far afield. (Though if you are, message me. We could totally chat.)

BIGGER IS BETTER

Polar animals are big. Bigger than their warmer-adapted cousins, with fewer surface extensions (think ears, fingers, toes). This larger body size helps them hold a lot of body heat inside, as they're constantly surrounded by the challenge of the cold environment. Physiologists call this Bergmann's rule. You can call it whatever you want, as long as you have really, really large animals in your frigid environments.

Polar bears are the biggest of the bears. Arctic hares are larger than other jackrabbits, and their shorter ears and legs give less surface area for losing heat to the cold, cold Arctic winters. Orcas, which most people call killer whales, are actually dolphins. The largest members of the dolphin family, to be precise.

NEVER ENOUGH FLUFF

Insulation provides an important and necessary layer to trap all that body heat inside. Fluffy polar bears, fluffy seals, fluffy Arctic foxes, fluffy and waterproof sea otters. Only mammals have hair, but birds manage fluff with dense layers of feathers that can be extended. Penguins, ptarmigan, and puffins, which are all year-round residents at the poles, can extend their feathers to a thickness that would shame your favorite North Face jacket.

Insulation isn't just fluff. Some marine mammals rely on dense coats of fur (and some have been hunted nearly to extinction for them), but others rely on other insulation. Blubber. Fat is a fantastic insulator, used by walruses, seals, and whales to fantastic effect, as well as woolly bear caterpillars and their fluffy setae (we'll talk more about these lovely guys in just a minute).

COLORATION IS MORE THAN CAMOUFLAGE

White polar bears. White ptarmigan. White Arctic foxes. It's easy to chalk their coloration up to snow camouflage and move on to the next phenotype. But white reflects heat energy, and there's little enough to be had at the poles. So, a white coat reflects back the little heat energy provided by the sun at the poles, rather than absorbing it. But ... this white fur also reflects back heat energy given off by the body of the animal itself. So, white coloration provides good camouflage and also helps to trap body heat next to the skin. Polar bears take this one step further, having black skin that helps absorb that reflected heat energy.

DENS, BURROWS, HOMES

Most successful polar animals don't spend the majority of their lives basking in the snow. Many extend their own insulation by seeking or creating microclimates—burrows or dens in which they sleep, hibernate, and bear young. The dens of polar bears, for example, can be extensive, multi-room dwellings that remain many degrees warmer than the outside environment. Arctic fox dens are similarly extensive, and families pass them down through generations. Some are centuries old and recent evidence suggest that, in the summer, these dens are the sites of fantastic wildflower growth in the tundra.

Including den-building capabilities in the next Arctic animal would give them an air of realism, but the dens themselves provide a wealth of opportunities for adventurers to stumble out of the cold.

COLD-BLOODED SURVIVALISTS

While most polar animals are warm-blooded, let's not forget about the Arctic woolly bear moth. This little bug takes seven to ten years to get through the caterpillar stage, because that's how long it takes to get enough plant food to fuel its transition into adult moth. In between the few weeks of feeding opportunity provided by the brief summer, these caterpillars hibernate in shared cocoons. Travelers through deep space in cryo-freeze could learn a thing or two from the woolly bear moth.

CRYOPROTECTANTS

Antifreeze chemicals. They need them, they've got them. And by them, I mean cold-blooded animals that live near the poles. These chemicals, found in the blood (or other body fluids) of insects, worms, and fish near the poles, protect the organs and tissues of these animals as they freeze. These chemicals can work a little like salt in boiling water for pasta. But, instead of changing the boiling point, they decrease the freezing point so the organs and tissues of the animals freeze at a much lower temperature.

MAPPING AND NAVIGATION CAPABILITIES

Extreme climates shape more than physical features. Many polar animals have excellent mapping and navigation capabilities different from their temperate cousins. Imagine a Weddell seal, spending hours scouring the frozen Antarctic Ocean for

PUTTING THE SCIENCE IN FICTION

food, trying to remember where he left his breathing hole. Rather more dire consequences if he fails than when we wander around the mall parking lot. Similarly, polar bears or Arctic foxes searching for their dens in the white expanse of snow can hardly rely on regular landmarks to find their way home.

Not all polar animals are residents. Many, especially birds and marine mammals, migrate to polar areas to feed in the summers. Migratory animals that find the same tiny island in the middle of the circumpolar seas also use amazing navigation capabilities in their thousand-mile-long journeys.

These evolutionary pressures have resulted in incredible mapping capabilities in the brains of most polar adapted animals, whether they're year-round residents or migratory tourists.

In short, intrepid adventurers trapped on a frozen planet needn't be alone. While Arctic-like landscapes may appear barren at first glance, there are a multitude of well-insulated animals lurking in warm dens just under the surface. Some may be frozen solid, some may have wondrous new antifreeze chemicals in their blood, while others may have thick, warm coats rivaling any man-made insulation. I look forward to seeing what new animals you use to populate your snowy landscapes.

Write well, my friends. Winter is coming.

CHAPTER 31

TENTACLES: FROM OCTOPUS TO ALIEN

by Danna Staaf

Nothing says "alien" like a face full of tentacles. These appendages seem to enjoy perennial popularity in science fiction, from the Martians of H.G. Wells's *The War of the Worlds* to the heptapods in the 2016 film *Arrival*.

The original inspiration for all these boneless limbs comes from our own home ocean. Step into the water off any coast and you'll find it chock-full of tentacles—decorated with suction cups, stinging cells, feather dusters, and more. Writers who leave the depths of tentacular possibility unplumbed run the risk of using them as generic squiggles, slapped on a creature merely to enhance its weirdness. Here's a bit of real-world biology to boost your creativity without getting your feet wet.

THE TRUE TENTACLE MASTERS

Octopuses, squid, and cuttlefish are arguably the closest to intelligent aliens we've got right here on our own planet. They might even be the reason we're prone to imagining tentacled extraterrestrials. But here's a funny bit of trivia: Octopuses do not have tentacles. Technically.

Along with their cousins, squid and cuttlefish, octopuses belong to a group known as *cephalopods*, and scientists find it useful to distinguish between cephalopod "arms" and "tentacles." Arms are shorter; tentacles are longer—and elastic. Arms are lined with suckers; tentacles only have suckers at their tips. According to these definitions, squid and cuttlefish have eight arms and two tentacles. Octopuses have eight arms and zero tentacles. And now you know.

Cephalopods can solve puzzles, use tools, play, and communicate with one another. Individuals even have distinct personalities. Yet all this complex behavior, in some ways so similar to that of our own species, is coordinated by an extremely different nervous system. Instead of one large central brain like ours, cephalopods have both a central brain and a great deal of distributed processing throughout their bodies—especially in the arms and tentacles.

As philosopher of science Peter Godfrey-Smith wrote in his book *Other Minds: The Octopus, the Sea, and the Deep Origins of Consciousness* (Farrar, Straus and Giroux, 2016):

"For an octopus, its arms are partly *self*—they can be directed and used to manipulate things. But from the central brain's perspective, they are partly *non-self* too, partly agents of their own." He goes on to explain that, "If you were an octopus … to some extent you would guide your arms, and to some extent you would just watch them go."

Then Godfrey-Smith offers this careful caveat: "To tell the story this way is to tell it from the vantage point of the 'central octopus.' That might be an error." What a beautiful invitation to a fiction writer! How would *you* write a character whose intelligence resides throughout its limbs? Does its life feel like a continuous out-of-body experience? An *in-someone-else's-body* experience?

Cephalopod arms not only exert control over their own movement, but also take in their own sensory impressions of the surrounding environment. Acting as combination finger-tongues, they are constantly touching and tasting the water, the rocks, their prey, even their fellow octopuses. Gathering sensory input like this is actually quite common for all kinds of tentacles throughout the animal kingdom. Two of the tentacles that wave shyly from the head of a garden snail are equipped with eyes, while the other two perceive chemical data. A tentacle, then, can be far more than an appendage—it can be a way of bringing the senses that, in humans, are limited to a flat face out into the world.

Remember the aliens on the planet Ixchel from Madeleine L'Engle's *A Wrinkle in Time* (Farrar, Straus and Giroux, 1962)? "They had four arms and far more than five fingers to each hand, and the fingers were not fingers, but long waving tentacles … in place of ears and hair there were more tentacles." These tentacles seemed to serve as both sense organs and the aliens' mode of communication, producing a voice for conversation as well as transcendently beautiful song.

L'Engle did not delve into acoustic details, but I always liked to imagine that the fine hairs covering the beasts' tentacles (and the rest of their bodies) contributed to sound production. Which brings me to the rich realm of tentacle accessories …

ACCESSORIZE, ACCESSORIZE!

Cephalopod suction cups may be the best-known tentacle tack-on. In addition to their facility with touching and tasting, they can *grip*. There may be hundreds of suction cups on a single arm and each one can independently attach and release, facilitating delicate manipulation of objects. When acting in concert, their power is impressive. An octopus clinging to a rock is typically stronger than any diver trying to pull it off. (Note: don't try to pull octopuses off rocks. They don't like it. Plus, you'll probably tear their skin. They *really* don't like that.)

However, even the strongest cephalopod tentacle can't squeeze you to death. It may be tempting to deploy a villainous octopus like eight boa constrictors to squeeze the life out of some poor victim, but cephalopod arms just don't work that way. Their job is to stick, not constrict; during a hunt they bring prey to the mouth for killing and carving.

If you'd like to hurt someone (fictional, of course) with actual tentacles, turn from cephalopods to the marvelous world of jellyfish. Jellyfish tentacles carry loads of tiny stinging cells, and inside each one is a coiled thread ending in a minute, harpoon-like barb. When the cell is triggered, the thread inverts explosively and flings the barb into the jelly's prey. Being punctured with a tiny barb doesn't hurt much—the damage is done by the subsequent injection through the barb of mysterious toxins. Scientists are only beginning to understand the enormous diversity of chemicals found in jellyfish venoms, despite their potency. The world's fiercest tentacles belong to the box jelly, whose sting is powerful enough to take down a grown human. Need an obscure or oddly specific poison? Try mining jellyfish.

Similar stinging cells are found in jellyfish relatives like coral and anemones. But if you brush the tentacles of a tide pool anemone, they'll simply feel sticky, even though you're experiencing an explosion of barbs similar to a jellyfish sting. To a little shrimp or fish, it might be quite painful, but to a human the sting is so mild it just feels like touching a glue stick.

Because nature is like that, there *are* tentacles that produce genuine glue—they just don't belong to anemones. They belong instead to animals called comb jellies. Comb jelly tentacles are also lined with tiny cells, but instead of barbs and toxins these cells contain sticky threads that can be flung out to capture prey. They're a bit like spiderwebs, although … maybe you can guess where I'm going with this. Of course there are tentacles that are much *more* like spiderwebs.

If you think you know worms because you've dug up earthworms, think again. Their marine cousins are (dare I say it?) a whole different can of worms. And among these, the spaghetti worm is truly exceptional. It lives in a tube of its own making, hidden in the rocks, exposing only its tentacles—but these can reach up to three feet in length. The slender, sprawling strands collect small particles of food and carry them back to the worm's mouth. Meanwhile, they also make the surrounding reef or tide pool look like the morning after a wild party, with fallen streamers splayed every which way.

Other marine worms use a more orderly array of tentacles to capture edible bits and pieces from the surrounding water. Feather duster worms and Christmas tree worms live in tubes, too, but instead of flopping their tentacles all over the ground, they extend their tentacles upward in graceful crowns and spirals. These delicate frills may be the world's most beautiful tentacles.

If some tentacles are so lovely we name them after holiday decorations, well, others aren't.

THE TENTACLES WE MUST NOT NAME

I can hardly close any discussion of tentacles without mentioning Cthulhu. The Great Old One of H.P. Lovecraft's imagination bore "an octopus-like head whose face was a mass of feelers." It seems that replacing facial features with tentacles is an excellent shortcut to producing horror. Even Meg Murry in *A Wrinkle in Time* was initially repulsed by the aliens of Ixchel, only relaxing when the tentacles themselves began to soothe her.

Whether your tentacled creatures will ultimately prove diabolical or benevolent, it's worth considering what seems to be humanity's gut reaction to these appendages: to freak out. In many stories, the monsters themselves consider it, and use technology, magic, or superpowers to adopt the trope known as "A Form You Are Comfortable With."

Consider the true forms of the Thermians in the 1999 movie *Galaxy Quest*. Having spent considerable screen time as humans (albeit super awkward humans), a few of these aliens abruptly show up as disturbing crosses between Cthulhu and Jabba the Hutt. It turns out they forgot to activate their "appearance generators" and quickly remedy this mistake, to the immense relief of the human protagonists.

The next time you're working on science fiction aliens or fantasy monsters, take a moment to consider the myriad forms of tentacles right here on our own planet. Some are sticky; some are poisonous. Some bear hooks; others have eyes. Many can regenerate, and some might even think for themselves. The more we inspire ourselves with reality, the wilder the products of our own imaginations.

PART FIVE

THINGS TO KNOW FOR WHEN SKYNET TAKES OVER

CHAPTER 32

———————●———————

DEBUNKING MYTHS ABOUT COMPUTERS AND THE INTERNET

By Matt Perkins

Here's a hard truth for anyone writing science fiction, fantasy, or any other form of speculative fiction: A big part of your audience knows a lot more about computers than you do. If you choose to feature computing or the Internet in your work, you run a big risk of stretching credibility for these readers who are, sadly, accustomed to disappointment from portrayals of technology in fiction. Missteps like these take readers out of the story and hurt their suspension of disbelief. With a large percentage of today's populace working in IT, these tech-savvy readers are too numerous to ignore.

Though reality isn't always as exciting as the bad assumptions we've grown accustomed to, there are still plenty of opportunities for excitement and conflict in the digital world that you can use to your advantage. Your techie readers will certainly appreciate your attention to detail, and your respect for the reality of modern computing will make your story stand out in a crowd of tech ignorance.

MYTH #1: THE KNOW-IT-ALL COMPUTER GEEK

You probably wouldn't expect Maytag to make a good car, nor would you expect Volkswagen to make a good dishwasher. And I bet you wouldn't want a psychiatrist doing your liver transplant. The world of computing is as highly specialized as engineering or medicine, if not more so. This is why the trope of the computer geek character who effortlessly masters every piece of technology in existence is so irritating: It's impossible for one person to be that knowledgeable. Computer tech as a whole is, quite literally, beyond the understanding of any one person.

Real IT pros tend to specialize in one small subset of computing, gaining deep knowledge and experience in their chosen discipline. When they encounter a problem outside their area of expertise, they consult with a specialist in that domain, much like a doctor would. Large companies employ dozens, if not hundreds, of diverse specialists, while small organizations typically outsource their most demanding IT tasks to firms that provide these services. Nobody hires an IT generalist—even if such a person existed, the "jack of all trades, master of none" principle would apply.

In any case, having one character who can solve every tech problem imaginable is lazy writing. That doesn't mean your computer geek can't *try* to solve a given problem—there's nothing more enticing than a challenging puzzle—but you must put realistic limits on his abilities. There will be certain things he won't be able to do, no matter how smart he is.

For your reference, some (definitely not all) of the most common areas of IT specialization are:

- **SOFTWARE DEVELOPER/ENGINEERS:** create and update the software that runs on a computer.
- **OS DEVELOPERS:** a subspecialty of the above; work on the underlying operating system of the computer (e.g., Windows, Android).
- **DATABASE ADMINISTRATORS:** build and maintain databases, big and small; database security is typically part of their job.
- **NETWORK ADMINISTRATORS:** build and maintain computer networks and keep everything connected; they often handle network security as well.
- **HARDWARE ENGINEERS:** design, build, or maintain the hardware components of computers and computer accessories; as you can probably guess, this profession has a lot of subspecialties.
- **TECHNICAL SUPPORT:** the unsung heroes who pick up the phone when someone has a problem with their computer; good communication and plenty of patience are the hallmarks of this role; they fix basic issues on their own and triage the more complex problems to other IT people.

MYTH #2: QUICK AND EASY HACKING

We've all seen this one: A hacker sits in front of a hostile computer (or even a keypad on a locked door), types a magical sequence of characters/digits, then smiles and says those two thrilling words: "I'm in." The door opens, the files are downloaded, the missile launch is aborted, and the protagonists have succeeded again, all thanks to the mighty hacker and her arcane computer knowledge.

This is patently absurd, especially the door-and-keypad scenario. Please don't ever write anything like this. It's lazy and unrealistic, and few computer tropes will cause more eye rolls than this one.

Want to know the "magic" secret behind most real-world hacks? Someone was careless with his password, and a hacker got a hold of it. The Sony Pictures hack of 2014 is a perfect example of this: A system administrator's password was used to gain full access to Sony Pictures' network. There's no magic, no secret "open sesame" codes—just stolen network credentials. A hack like this is no more sophisticated than a pickpocket.

So, how do hackers obtain passwords? There are plenty of possibilities. The most common is basic negligence on the part of the account holder. At a previous job, my colleagues and I would always joke that if you flipped over ten of our clients' keyboards, you'd find nine passwords. Worse, a lot of clueless users have passwords that are very easy to guess, like *password* or *letmein* (side note: for your own sake, please come up with a password that's long and complex, but easy for you to remember). Then there's phishing: a technique where a hacker impersonates a trusted party in order to steal login credentials; it is increasingly common and alarmingly successful. In some cases, a software vulnerability in weak or out-of-date software can expose passwords to someone who knows where to look; this is exactly how the Heartbleed bug in OpenSSL worked. And, of course, there's the old-fashioned way: You can give the system administrator a briefcase full of cash or point a gun at his head. There's a saying in information security: Your network is only as secure as your most vulnerable IT employee.

One possibility is to have the hack be an inside job, which is alarmingly common in the real world. In my Winterwakers series, the hacker protagonist is a network support tech whose job grants him legitimate access to plenty of computer networks.

MYTH #3: THE ONE AND ONLY COPY

"I have the last remaining copy of your mom's secret banana pancake recipe," cackled the villain. "Give me the nuclear launch codes, or I delete it forever!"

This one always makes me laugh. Data is everywhere, and it's virtually immortal. This is true now more than ever, with real-time backups and cloud drives being the new normal. Companies and governments know their data is precious and treat it accordingly, employing frequent backups and redundant storage. Even private individuals today have access to strong data protection via home backup drives or with cloud storage services like Dropbox or iCloud. If something ever gets erased, either deliberately or accidentally, it's a trivial matter to bring it back from the dead. Conversely, finding and erasing all traces of a file from all these backups and redundant systems is a complex, laborious task.

Assuming none of your backups or clouds have you covered, there are still ways you can retrieve deleted files. Consumer apps exist that find deleted data and reconstitute it, often with perfect success. Data recovery pros have access to even more advanced tools and can sometimes recover files from fire or flood-damaged computers.

If you want data to be lost or inaccessible to your characters, consider encryption instead of deletion. A properly encrypted file is nearly impossible to crack without the decryption key (the rules in "Quick and Easy Hacking" apply here as well).

MYTH #4: ENHANCE FROM NOTHING

This one has been used and abused countless times in police procedurals and science fiction thrillers alike. Using what appears to be simple computer software, a tech transforms a grainy, indistinct image into a crisp, sharp rendering of a license plate, an address, or a person's face. Fictional techs can zoom in and enhance virtually any image the hard-nosed detective throws at them.

Reality is nowhere near this convenient. A computer image is stored as a grid of pixels: tiny colored squares that combine to create a picture. When you zoom in on an image, all the computer can do is make those pixels larger, which just looks like a blockier version of the same image. The software can't add more pixels—it has no way of knowing what's supposed to be there after the image was created.

That said, if you had a massive, hi-res image, it might in fact be possible to zoom in on it and get better detail, simply because of the sheer number of pixels available. Beware of relying on this possibility, though. A YouTube-quality (i.e., not that great) video weighs in at around 3 GB per hour of footage. Higher resolution uncompressed video files are hundreds of times that size. If your villain's secret compound has dozens of security cameras (as all good secret compounds should), the data storage demands of hi-def video would be cost-prohibitive, if not massively taxing on the hardware. This is why security camera footage is so grainy: If it weren't, you'd only be able to store a few minutes at a time.

Instead of zoom-and-enhance, real police departments use quantity over quality. Cameras are everywhere nowadays, and most positive IDs are made by examining and comparing images from multiple cameras, usually without the aid of software. Learn from the real world and don't lazily rely on this well-worn trope: Make your characters work hard to crack that case. Computers can do many amazing things, but magically enhancing an image to move your plot along isn't one of them.

CHAPTER 33

YOUR SCIENCE FICTION CELL PHONE ISN'T COOL ENOUGH

By Effie Seiberg

From the *Star Trek* communicator to Dick Tracy's two-way wrist radio, science fiction has always imagined new types of portable communication devices. However, recent science fiction hasn't pushed this so far. Go ahead—think of a story from the last fifteen years that gives you an amazing idea for mobile computing. Chances are, real technology has already caught up to it. Usually in fiction, our scientific assumptions are too wild to work. This is the opposite: Your science fiction cell phone isn't cool enough.

Mobile technology has evolved in a number of new directions that have made crazy cool things possible today … which means that the communicators in distant science fiction worlds haven't taken things far enough.

THE CLOUD

Because your phone is always connected, it does more than communicate with other machines. It can outsource to them. Massively distributed computational engines let you get difficult results on cell phones that don't require the phone itself to be able to run the results. The Google Assistant, Siri, Alexa, Cortana … they can all take in what you're saying (which needs to programmatically take into account your accent, the sounds around you, your local slang, etc.) and figure out your actual meaning. Doing this on a phone itself would be quite difficult, but because of the connectivity, your phone is as powerful as the most powerful computer cluster.

Many SF pieces show the phone as able to connect to the (nebulously-defined-yet-nearly-all-encompassing) "database." But the fact that your phone can do more than just pull existing data—it can bring in new data and get it analyzed and returned—makes the phone in your pocket stronger than most fictional phones.

THE CAMERA

Your phone camera is smarter than you think. Because of the connectivity, your phone's vision gets smarter not only with facial recognition (which is improving at a dramatic pace—already you can unlock your phone with a smile or the pattern of blood vessels in your eye on some platforms) but also at recognizing anything else and doing interesting things with that information. This same facial recognition is what lets Snapchat add a rainbow of vomit out of anyone's mouth, or a flower crown to anyone's head in real time—silly features using speedy visual analysis to tell what's a face and where to place things around it.

CamioCam combines computer vision and machine learning to make a smarter home security camera, and all it takes is your old phone, propped up and connected to wi-fi, to do it. The processing on the back end helps figure out which types of motion aren't interesting (moving branches in the breeze shouldn't trigger a motion alert) and it's improving on its ability to give specific insights. For example, in their interface you can search for "brown" to see if the UPS truck has arrived today.

MIT has released software that detects tiny changes in color in any video— even from a phone camera—that can be used to detect heart rate. Skin gets ever-so-slightly redder when blood flows underneath it. With just a propped-up phone camera and this technology running behind it, you can monitor an infant or patient's health without plugging them into a heart rate monitor. Far more comfortable for them!

What's more, your camera is getting better at understanding what it's looking at. Google Lens is essentially a search box from your camera. Take a photo, and Google's years of visual machine learning come into play—it can tell you what you're looking at. A photo of a flower yields more information than just *it's a flower*; it might tell you the species, the conditions it needs to survive, and more. A photo of a restaurant might yield information about the restaurant's name, hours, menu, and address. And of course, this same visual analysis can translate any written sign the camera sees, so you're never lost when traveling.

And with all this machine vision progress, including even simple things like autofocus and image stabilization, assume that blurry photos are soon to be a thing of the past.

So the camera on your phone *today* is probably cooler than the one in your novel draft. Go update it!

THE OTHER SENSORS

Phones today have GPS, accelerometers, compasses, and more. Beyond just navigating you around (and figuring out the shortest routes, even within encased structures like football stadiums), this yields a lot of messy motion data. Zendrive combines all that data to figure out when the bearer of the phone is in a car crash (as distinct from, say, someone just dropping their phone), and the technology is used by other companies to automatically call a loved one, an ambulance, or a tow truck.

PUTTING THE SCIENCE IN FICTION

Other phone sensors let you count your steps instead of getting a fitness tracker (they know what the movement of a step "looks" like). They let you play augmented reality games, where the phone overlays content on top of what the camera sees, or virtual reality games, where you're immersed in the game—and for both of these, the other sensors let the phone know if it's up or tilted, if you're facing north or south, and so on, placing both you and it into the virtual play space. Your compass is actually a magnetometer, which means that metal detector apps are somewhat legit. Many phones have a barometer, which helps your fitness app know how many flights you've gone up.

Ambient light sensors automatically change your phone's display when it's light or dark out—particularly useful when you're driving in and out of tunnels in the daytime. And even the microphone has more uses than you'd think: Apps let you "play" wind instruments like a digital ocarina by blowing into the mic and covering the instrument "holes" on the screen with your fingers.

So if your science fiction phone can't do any of these things ... you need a darn good reason.

CONTEXTUAL ADAPTABILITY

Between phones knowing your location, motion, and a fair portion of your activity, they can already adapt to their situations. Motorola and Apple already have a phone setting that automatically reads texts and emails out loud when it detects that the person is in a moving car so people don't text and drive (yes, they let you opt out overall, or if you specify that you're not the driver). Google's Android will pull up different suggestions (weather, events it thinks you'll like, etc.) depending on where you are and what you've recently been searching for. Even Twitter will recommend different trending tweets depending where you and your phone are.

In addition, if your phone knows where you are in relation to other objects it can interact with, it can make them behave accordingly. There are already smart locks for your front door that unlock when your phone is in proximity, and lights and ambient music you can program to turn on when your phone is in a certain range or area. Your phone can be your TV remote, it can automatically start certain smart coffeemakers when the sun goes up, and so much more.

And, while Motorola and Proteus Digital Health have developed the "authentication vitamin" pill, which turns on when it hits your gastric juices and broadcasts out an authentication code for your phone or other device, it's easy to imagine this expanding to include turning on different things depending on the state of your stomach. (Alerts for gyms nearby, perhaps?)

YOUR SCIENCE FICTION PHONE NEEDS TO STEP IT UP

If all these things are happening *today*, your futuristic phone had better be much cooler. With the combination of the Internet of Things, where more items are connected, plus constant connectivity, phones almost act more like the terminals of yore than a stand-alone gadget. They can access any piece of information, from anywhere, and with any amount of processing needed. Plus, their sensors make them much smarter about what's going on around them for things that aren't already connected.

But more than just being a piece of technology in itself or being an extension of the technology in the world, the phone is now an extension of *you*. Your habits, your locations, your preferences … the more the phone knows about your context, the more it shifts into an extension of your wants and needs into the real world and acts upon them for you.

When writing your own phone/communicator/bracer/whatever you'd like to call it, remember all the things that the phone in your pocket can already do. Phones of the future should be at least this cool, if not far cooler. With that said, Go-Go-Gadget-Kickass-Future-Phone!

CHAPTER 34

CGI IS NOT MADE BY COMPUTERS

by Abby Goldsmith

Does your novel or story involve computer-generated imagery (CGI)? Does it take place in virtual worlds, like *The Matrix* films, or books such as Neal Stephenson's *Snow Crash* (Bantam Books, 2000) or Scott Meyer's *Off To Be the Wizard* (47North, 2015)? What about massive multiplayer video games like the one in Ernest Cline's *Ready Player One* (Crown, 2011)? Does your story include technological illusions, or digital manipulations of people's sensory input, like in TV series such as *Westworld, Dollhouse,* or *Lost*?

As a 3D animator, I shake my head with exasperation every time I see an author's wrong interpretation of how video games or virtual realities are created. Hyper-realistic graphics don't pop into existence by magic. Unprecedented visual effects cannot be created or maintained by one lone genius, or even by a tiny secret crew.

Yet this is the implication in novels such as *Ready Player One, The Three-Body Problem* by Liu Cixin (Tor, 2015), and *Daemon* by Daniel Suarez (Dutton Adult, 2009). These impressive, immersive virtual reality games were apparently created by a secret team that is so improbably small, they're able to remain untraceable. In the Otherland series by Tad Williams and the Wool series by Hugh Howey, the secret team is apparently small enough to vanish without anyone noticing. Oh, and the amazing graphics are apparently self-sustaining, now that the team is gone. The massive virtual reality doesn't need upgrades or maintenance at all. Ever.

I'm left to suppose that magical artificial intelligence fairies are adding creative graphics and artistic touch-ups, as needed.

THE MISCONCEPTION ABOUT CGI

In these fictional examples, and in many others, the book or TV show implies that a tiny team of artists—let's say no more than twenty—are able to populate an entire world with graphics so amazing they're indistinguishable from reality.

This conceit betrays the author's ignorance of how visual effects are made. Computer-generated imagery is a misnomer. The impressive visuals you see in films and games are not generated by computers, but by large teams of human artists who put in long hours of work. They always have been, and they always will be, unless our technology passes a singularity.

Sure, the artists use software tools, such as products by Autodesk and Adobe—software written by human programmers—but the artists using those tools have traditional training in painting, sculpture, or animation. They're often overworked and underpaid. Many have aspired all their lives for a career in the entertainment industry and have practiced their art skills from childhood through college.

Where are they, in the mega-corporations of fiction and TV shows? It's as if they don't exist.

During the Renaissance in Italy, artists such as Botticelli and Donatello pioneered realism techniques in their artwork, imbuing their paintings with dimensions of reality that had been lost to Europe during the Middle Ages. As Leonardo da Vinci and Michelangelo competed for projects of epic scope, they impressed the mass audiences of their day. A Renaissance-era visitor to the Sistine Chapel might have attributed the magnificent ceiling to divine intervention. Perhaps the artist's hands were guided by an immortal presence, or perhaps he drank special wine or used special paintbrushes.

I believe we're undergoing a similar renaissance in art today. Visually spectacular films such as *The Lord of the Rings* and video games such as *The Elder Scrolls V: Skyrim*, look too authentic to have been created by human hands. Backgrounds and creatures are more detailed than anything painted by the old masters. So mass audiences assume there must be a secret ingredient. Unaware of cutting-edge proprietary tools at the disposal of digital artists, and unaware of film-grade training programs such as the Gnomon Workshop, the average person attributes hyperrealistic otherworldly imagery to "computers." They credit the tool, as if the artist is just an unskilled, interchangeable automaton.

THE VITAL ROLE OF ARTISTS AND ANIMATORS

It's easy to ignore artists and animators. They're often stashed in overcrowded buildings in unremarkable industrial parks. The teams are so large that no single person can be wholly credited for a particular scene or a particular character. Burnout rates are high, and many artists are fresh out of college or immigrants from other countries. A lot of film work is outsourced. On top of that, showrunners, and actors such as Andy Serkis, take credit for creating CGI characters. They claim responsibility for bringing these characters and fantastic worlds to life without acknowledging the enormous teams of artists who do most of the work.

When you see Spider-Man swinging between skyscrapers or King Kong roaring in chains, you can bet that some 3D animators made those characters move in a realistically convincing way. Motion capture can help artists, but it's only a starting point. Human facial expressions and motions do not wholly translate to an ape, or to a cartoonish human, or anything else that isn't real. Motion-captured facial expressions and movements are tweaked by animators. Every frame of film footage is artistically altered or exaggerated in order to make the character look less fake and more alive.

The process of creating a CGI character starts with a screenplay and storyboards, or a game design document. In pre-production, concept artists are paid to sketch visual concepts of every character, environment, weapon, and whatever else will be involved in the final product. A director or a committee approves the final character designs, ensuring that each character will fit within the overall mood and world of the film, game, or franchise.

Whether they're creating superheroes, dinosaurs, or talking cars, the general process is the same. Someone models the character or creature using a 3D program, such as ZBrush, Maya, Blender, or Autodesk 3ds Max. Skin and clothing textures get mapped to the 3D wireframe mesh, sometimes by a different artist. A specialist rigs the character to give it an underlying skeleton for the ease of pose manipulation. Each skeleton has to be custom fitted to the 3D wireframe mesh or the character will deform in unnatural ways during motion.

Once the rig is finalized and tested, the 3D animators can begin their work. Animators spend a lot of time studying motion, timing, and the way quadrupeds and bipeds move. Cinematic animators practice their craft with an emphasis on acting. Many take acting classes. Game animators tend to specialize in smooth loops, or cycles, as well as exaggerated motions that read well at a tiny size on the screen.

A programming team will script code that enables fur, hair, or scales to look realistic. Another team handles physics, such as fire, or objects that flop about. Another team handles lighting, with the purpose of making scenes look natural given the simulated weather conditions or environmental conditions.

The hyper-realistic backdrops of SF/F films are painted with a blend of photography and digital enhancements, plus the traditional painting techniques taught for generations. Costumed actors and sets are then composited onto those backdrops. It's called *digital matte painting*. A similar process is used to create the environments in high-end video games.

I spent my twenties as a 3D animator, and fairly often I'd hear non-industry people try to guess what my job entailed: "So, you draw on a computer?" Rather than launch into a long explanation, I'd say, "Yep, pretty much." But although I love drawing and spent years honing my sketching craft, those skills are just a subset of what I actually do. CGI work has more in common with sculpture and stop-motion animation than with drawing. Animation is more about a sense of timing, and of weight and motion, than painstaking illustration. Animators tend to be sketch artists rather than detail-oriented illustrators. I'm not meticulous; I'm impatient! I want to make a character kick ass rather than gaze off into space with photorealistic beauty.

However you define CGI, it is creative work, and it requires artistry. Computer code lacks an imagination. Code can translate data into visual representations of terrain or geometry, but it cannot visualize spaceships or dragons. A skilled programmer can write a script to simulate aspects of visual elements, such as lighting and physics, but programmers do not create the visual environments or the visual characteristics of characters. Software cannot pull together all the data of human perceptions and create something imaginary from it. That's up to human artists with creative minds.

PRE-MADE VERSUS CUSTOM CGI

It's possible that a lone genius can avoid hiring a huge team of artists by buying prepackaged environmental elements and prepackaged CGI characters. Online marketplaces such as TurboSquid, CGTrader, and Renderosity offer loads of 3D assets for sale. However, keep in mind that other low-budget gamemakers and filmmakers purchase and use the same assets. They tend to look prepackaged. If your virtual world needs customized anything, this is not the way to get it.

For customized work, you need to hire someone. And much like hiring a writer, it's hard to find someone who is the perfect match for your needs. The 3D artists and animators who advertise their services are doing so because they want to build up their portfolio or demo reel. They're inexperienced. Professional high-end artists with an impressive track record tend to be employed full time, and they value career stability over freelance gigs. They're unlikely to want to juggle extra work hours, and they'll be suspicious of sketchy corporations or weird geniuses. There are plenty of those in the entertainment industry. You learn to be wary.

The budgets of major films and games sustain hundreds of skilled professionals who are working intensively, full time, for several years. If your story includes a project with visual effects or immersive entertainment, please remember the team that must have created it. Every element in your digital world was planned, sculpted, textured, rigged, animated, and implemented by a lot of artists.

It's not a magical process. Only the final render looks like magic.

CHAPTER 35

WHAT'S POSSIBLE WITH CYBORGS AND CYBERNETICS

By Benjamin C. Kinney

First things first: There are already cyborgs among us. Early twenty-first-century medical science has plenty of ways to surgically integrate a device into your body: cochlear implants, hip replacements, deep brain stimulation, pacemakers, and so forth. Right now, the first few human beings have chips implanted in their brains that allow them to control a robotic limb directly with their thoughts. For example, the BrainGate clinical trials allowed its first tetraplegic patient to control a computer cursor in 2006, gave another patient control over a robot arm in 2012, and used muscle-stimulation techniques to restore control of the patient's paralyzed limb in 2017.

From here on out, we'll focus on cybernetics suited for space-opera life: mechanical or other devices controlled directly by the human brain.

THE HARDEST PART IS NEURAL DECODING

If you want to control your cyber-arm just as smoothly and naturally as your real arm, the key technology is *neural decoding*. That means understanding the activity in your nervous system so well that you can convert neural signals into a machine-readable format: in other words, the neural-to-technological interface. (I say "machine" for simplicity, but this would hold true for any technology.)

Neural decoding requires a *lot* of information. The system doesn't just need to know your goal (e.g., "pick up coffee cup"), it also needs to know where you want to move your arm (*kinematics*, e.g., "reach to the left of my water bottle") and how you would accomplish that with a pattern of muscles and joints in motion over time (*dynamics*, generally below our conscious control).

Imagine how it would feel to have a system that didn't use your own kinematics: You'd tell it what to get done, but not how to do it. That kind of system would feel less like controlling a limb and more like pressing a "bring me coffee" button. A big step up for a paralyzed person, but it's a far cry from making the cybernetic arm a natural part of your life.

BRAIN FUNCTION IS DISTRIBUTED AND HARD TO MEASURE

Your brain doesn't have single cells that do specific things, outside of the most basic sensory perception. Information is shared across the activity and connections of hundreds or thousands of brain cells (mostly neurons, but also other cell types called *glia*). When your brain controls a movement, no single cell carries all the relevant information. To decode the neural signals for arm movement, you need to measure the neural activity in most of those hundreds or thousands of cells.

This is a big technological sticking point: how to record so much activity from the brain? Current brain-computer interface (BCI) methods involve implanting a chip onto the surface, with dozens of tiny microelectrodes sticking down into the brain tissue below.

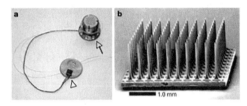

Figure 35.1: "BCI chip circa 2012. (A) Pedestal connector, grounding wires, and chip. Only the chip (B) makes contact with the brain. From Hochberg et al. 2006, Nature."

These electrodes don't penetrate neurons, but they get within a few hundred microns, which is close enough to measure electrical activity. Stick a hundred microelectrodes into the motor-control part of the brain, and you should be able to pick up activity in 50 to 150 random neurons.

It's like listening to a symphony orchestra by plucking out ten random musicians. You'll probably get the gist of the piece, but wouldn't it be better if you could choose which ten musicians? (On the upside, if you've randomly picked musicians, it doesn't matter if you lose track of a musician and replace it with a new one, which can happen as the electrodes move a little.)

Space-opera quality cybernetics will require one of three solutions: either a much bigger sample of neurons, a drastic improvement in our ability to extrapolate from a few neurons, or some way to identify exactly the right neurons to measure. Everyone's brain is unique, so if you want either of the biological solutions, they must be custom-tailored to each individual.

PERIPHERAL NERVES PROVIDE AN EASIER, BUT LIMITED, OPTION

You might be able to minimize the above two problems by recording from a peripheral nerve: For instance, to control your cyber-arm, we might try to decode signals in the nerves that would normally control your boring old human arm. Down there in your arm, you have far fewer neurons, and most of those carry the information you want: movement and sensation. But like all things in life, there's a tradeoff.

First, peripheral-nerve implants are no use at all for patients with spinal cord injuries or other nerve damage. You can't solve the problem at the arm level if the arm has lost its connection to the brain. Second, the arm nerve will only carry information about dynamics (joints and muscles) and maybe kinematics (movements), but not higher-level goals. Without also knowing the movement goal, your system has a lot more room for error compared with a brain-based system with access to all three kinds of information.

ACTION WITHOUT SENSATION IS POSSIBLE, WITH MAJOR LIMITATIONS

Can your fictional cyber-arm sense touch and motion like a human arm? If not, you'll encounter some problems, similar to a person with nerve damage. If you can't feel touch, you won't be able to grasp and manipulate objects. If you can't feel your body position (a sense called *proprioception*), you will lose track of your arm's location in space, and your limbs will start wandering all over the place as soon as you stop paying attention.

But there is a partial workaround, buried in that idea of "paying attention." There's another way to find out where your hands are and what they're doing, albeit one that takes work and vigilance to pull off. *If you can't feel your hands, you can learn to use them effectively as long as you're looking at them.*

THE LEARNING PROCESS IS REMARKABLY EASY

If you can record from the neurons in the motor-control areas of your brain, you'll have no problem learning the basic control of a prosthesis. Matt Nagle, the first human to receive a modern microelectrode array neural implant, was able to control a computer cursor immediately after a few seconds of software calibration because neural decoding interprets the brain's natural movement-control signals.

Hand transplant patients illustrate another trick: Most of the tendons that control hand movement (other than drawing the thumb toward or away from the hand) are controlled in the forearm, so a replacement hand could use intact nerves.

TRANSHUMAN PROSTHESES MIGHT BE IMPOSSIBLE

Can the human brain control truly inhuman things: an extra pair of arms, a pair of wings, a starship, Doctor Octopus? Goal-level control is certainly possible; Doc Ock thinks about his coffee cup and his robot arms will go get it. But it may be impossible to move your starship's steering flanges as naturally as you control your own arm. This is because the human brain is an evolved system that developed in parallel with our bodies, toward the goal of producing actions that improve our survival or reproduction.

Nearly everything in our brains is rooted in our motor and sensory capabilities, and vice versa. If you ask people to make yes/no answers by pressing a button, difficult questions (e.g., controversial moral judgments) lead to different movements: When you hesitate over a difficult call, even your arm hesitates to commit. Action is not like software uploaded into the brain; it *is* the brain. Radically different movement control would require a radically different brain.

THE BRAIN IS SHAPED BY THE BODY

Inhuman movement control would require an inhuman brain, but that's not nearly as impossible as it sounds. In the last section we saw what the brain has evolved to *do*, but we can also frame it as a brain evolved to *change*. We're born not with a detailed genetic program of our bodies encoded in the brain, but with the flexibility to mature and learn in the context of living in that body. This mutability is a phenomenon called *neuroplasticity*, which includes everyday learning, but also encompasses any persistent change in the brain. (Contrast "plasticity" with "elasticity," which would be a change that doesn't persist.)

Our brains' perfect fit to the human body is a consequence of life in that body, with countless moments of action, perception, and feedback. When scientists modify an animal's body right after birth, those changes to the body produce drastic changes in the brain. If the animal never uses its eyes, the visual part of its brain instead develops to control touch, hearing, or something else. However, these drastic changes require a young brain. Adult brains have less plasticity than young brains, and that difference runs deep in the motor system: Humans who lose a hand in accidents when they're adults have different patterns of movement and brain activity compared with people born without a hand. Maybe controlling a second pair of arms is more like learning a language: If you start young, the human brain can accomplish almost anything.

This is all conjecture, of course. A young human brain might be able to wire up appropriately for a nontraditional body, or it might fail. For example, the rest of the human brain might not function well without the patterns of movement and sensation that arise from its co-evolved body.

CHANGING THE BRAIN COULD HAVE CATASTROPHIC CONSEQUENCES

Here, at last, we may find a limit to human possibility. For the brain to control any kind of body, human or otherwise, it needs to start young. We can dream about rejuvenating the brain back to youthful levels of neuroplasticity, but that will always have a major, terrifying cost. After all, our brains stabilize for a reason. To destabilize the brain is to open all of it to change: our memories, personality, identity, and everything else. To return a brain to childhood is to wipe out its memories and personality.

We can't avoid this by targeting our rejuvenation at movement-control parts of the brain. As we learned earlier, our entire brains are rooted in motor and sensory capabilities, precisely the first areas we want to update for cybernetics. It might be technically possible to rejuvenate the human brain, with advanced drugs to reawaken the neuroplastic potential latent in every cell's genome. However, because that process would involve wiping away the brain's growth and experiences, few people would accept it voluntarily. This "treatment" is so harmful, it's the kind of thing a totalitarian space empire might force on conscripts and prisoners.

To add insult to injury, rejuvenating the brain could also cause brain damage. Animal research suggests that the brain's maturation mechanisms protect cells from long-term damage. If a brain spends an unnatural amount of time in a state of youthful plasticity, it would be at increased risk for psychiatric problems such as schizophrenia. Not something you want to cause, even in your space-empire soldiers.

We know a great deal about the possibilities for human cybernetics, but authors still have plenty of room to make choices. What will we achieve, and when? What are the as-yet-untested limits of the human brain? And most important of all, how far will our society go to find those limits?

———————•———————

CHAPTER 36

BELIEVABLE NANOTECHNOLOGY

By Dan Allen

Should nanotechnology be a "get out of jail free" card for fiction writers? Many undisciplined authors treat nanotechnology as a mystical, unexplainable method for accomplishing anything. This is the same as magic, and that sort of writing is more aptly called *science fantasy*. If you want to write fantasy, if Iron Man's Extremis formulation seemed believable to you, or if you want nanotechnology to be nothing short of divine omnipotence, read no further.

But if you want to understand the basics of nanotechnology, how it works, and how to write about it in a compelling way, you are on the right page. Just as Harry Potter can't do magic without a wand, a mistborn can't do magic without ingesting metals, and the tooth fairy won't take your tooth if it isn't under your pillow, there are basic rules to nanotechnology. To avoid mistakes that make your story read like a fourth grader's nonsensical ramblings rather than a piece of seriously awesome fiction, let's start with a short list of nanotechnology no-no's:

1. **BOGUS:** Nanobots take over everything or impart limitless energy to their hosts without *any* source of power.
2. **BOGUS:** Nanotechnology transforms living tissue into materials that aren't found in the body, like metal armor.
3. **BOGUS:** Nanotechnology is an electronic device you can spray from a can complete with batteries, radios, processors, and software.

Did you feel yourself starting to argue that last one? Shouldn't nanotechnology be able to do all those things? Isn't that what nanotechnology is all about: invisible engineering? Hold that thought. We'll come back to it.

Believable science fiction activates a reader's analytical mind, just as a note at the right frequency will cause a tuning fork to resonate. We want to find things that resonate with our readers, and we don't have to work too hard. Most of us understand the following basic principles from everyday life:

1. Conservation of matter (nanotechnology cannot make something from nothing)
2. Conservation of energy (making and breaking chemical bonds takes energy)

3. If it sounds ludicrous, it probably is—but not always!

Beyond the obvious conservation laws, there is one core concept to writing realistic nanotechnology fiction, which almost all writers miss: the idea is that the smaller something gets, the more specific, and limited, is its functionality. Nanobots, by their nature, have very limited—possibly just one—molecular function. They simply don't have enough atoms or ways to configure them to do more than one basic thing. Collections of them working together, like proteins in a body—that's a different story, but the blueprint for all that is millions of base pairs of DNA. Complexity requires organization. Organization requires specialization. Specialization requires variety, and variety requires exactly that: many things. But with nano-size, you only get one or two basic arrangements of the pieces. It's how those pieces come together that will form the basis of transformative nanotechnology.

Given that fundamental concept, how you wreak utter mayhem with nanotechnology, harness it, or stop it is the clarion challenge for both writers and engineers. The short introduction in the next section to the foundations of nanotechnology will give you numerous launching-off points for book research and idea discovery.

FOUNDATIONS OF NANOTECHNOLOGY

The concept of nanotechnology arguably began with a speech by one of mankind's greatest minds, Richard Feynman, at Caltech in 1959 called "There's Plenty of Room at the Bottom." At the dawn of the electronic age, the visionary physicist proposed radical ideas about the possibilities of controlling the world at the very small scale, from storing entire libraries on the head of pin (which we now do) to designer nanoscale machines and ingestible nanoscale medical diagnostics and robots (some of which are in FDA trials).

But how small is a nanometer (10^{-9} or 0.000000001 meters)?

Imagine a dog. It's about a meter long. How many fleas can you fit on the back of the dog? Several thousand, easily. A flea is about a millimeter, give or take—a thousandth of a meter. Now imagine a flea blown up to the size of a dog. How many bacteria can you fit on the back of a flea? A few thousand, comfortably. Bacteria are typically a few microns (millionths of a meter). Now image a bacterium blown up to the size of a dog. How many proteins can you fit on the back of a single bacterium? Thousands.

Now, at the size scale of a protein, we are finally measuring in nanometers. That's how small a nanometer is. And each nanoscale protein has how many atoms? Guess. That's right, thousands (give or take). This size scale can now be readily imaged with electron and atomic force microscopes, and scientists have begun to not only manipulate matter on the nanometer size scale but also create *functional* nanodevices that move, or break bonds, or light up when something is detected—like artificial proteins or lifeforms.

Let's dig a little deeper. By nature, nanotechnology is an interdisciplinary field with foundations in four different areas from which innovations begin and combine.

Nanobiology

Proteins are a few nanometers across, made up of groups of atoms (amino acids) linked together in a string that folds up into a functional nanomachine, nature's original "nanobots." Proteins make and break molecules, allowing us to metabolize energy and build new cells. Some proteins change configuration when they receive a chemical signal or are hit by light, like those used in our nervous system and eyesight. Others harvest electrons or aid in chemical reactions. For instance, a protein called glucose oxidase takes electrons from glucose by oxidizing them (like burning sugar). A diabetic's glucose test strip is loaded or "functionalized" with them—that's nanobiotechnology.

Proteins are the biological starting point of nanotechnology and provide a terrifying example of what happens when things go wrong. A misfolded protein, called a *prion*, if ingested will cause other proteins to misfold, resulting in a chain reaction that slowly turns your brain to mush: mad cow disease. If ever there was a rational basis for a doomsday nanotechnology disaster or zombie apocalypse, it is prions.

DNA is another nanostructure whose building blocks are called *nucleic acids*. Complex sugars (polysaccharides) are a third class: small, simple molecules joining together to form massive structures like redwood trees. And of course, there is the most dangerous form of nanobiology: the virus, a nanoscale object containing only DNA (or RNA) and proteins, capable of causing a cell to make copies of it until the cell bursts, releasing more viruses. All these kinds of biological replication by self-assembly are "bottom up" methods. But biological nanotechnology is only one corner of the four-sided interdisciplinary nanotechnology pyramid.

Nanochemistry

The second corner of the nanotechnology pyramid is chemistry. Chemists have made complex self-assembling nanostructures of all shapes and sizes using the basic buildings blocks from biology: proteins, DNA, and sugars, and added their own new categories: glowing nanocrystals able to detect cancer and nimble porphyrins that form complex 3D structures, not to mention soccer ball-shaped fullerenes ("buckyballs") that can be made into sensitive detectors as well as nanocages for delivering medicine to target cells.

Nanofabrication

The third foundation of nanotechnology derives from photolithography, nanoimprint, and other clean room "fab" technologies used in the manufacture of microchips. These top-down approaches are now defining transistors with minimum dimensions of only 16 nanometers, with 12 nanometers on the near horizon. We are literally making transistors the size of proteins. Commonplace nanotechnology (or microtechnology) includes transparent transistors (used in LCD screens) as well as printed flexible circuits, batteries and antennas, and complex microelectromechanical systems (MEMS). Notably, MEMS devices can harvest energy from vibrations and passing radio waves.

Nanomaterials

The last nanotechnology frontier is materials science, which has been working at the nanoscale since Roman times. Steel is a nanotechnology invention. Carbon dissolved in iron forms nanoscale defects when the iron is cooled. The defects are all tangled up in the iron crystal, like a nanoscale nappy hair rat extending all the way through the material. When the steel is stressed, the defects, all pulling on each other, can't migrate away from the stress point. So the steel doesn't deform. It is both hard and shatter-resistant, a property that pure crystals can't achieve.

Other nanotechnology materials innovations include superhydrophobic coatings—water literally balls up on a surface and rolls off—as well as growth of nanostructured crystal layers used in lasers and LEDs that engineer the quantum properties of electrons, and graphene and carbon nanotubes with astonishing world record properties like tensile strength and thermal and electrical conductivity.

WRITING ABOUT NANOTECH

Any of the four foundations can be the starting point for a nanotech adventure. Try this simple 3-step process:

1. **DO SOME EXPLORING.** Find out about something in nanoscience that gets your mind whirring or your heart racing. Call a professor or a graduate student in their laboratory—they'll talk your ear off. Reality is the conception point of great science in fiction.

2. **REASON TO EXTREMES.** Considering the technology you learned about, ask yourself a "what-if" question. This is the birthplace of sciece fiction—a dangerous curiosity of the unknown. At the end of this step, you should have both fanciful, mind-teasing possibilities as well as some serious and possibly unforeseen consequences for your technology run amok. For examples of reasoning to extremes, consider genetic engineering in *Gattaca* or cybernetics in the *Star Trek* Borg.

3. **CREATE NATURAL LIMITS.** Just like you need energy to grow, build muscle, or repair damage, so do all forms of nanotechnology. The likeliest energy source is unfortunately you, or perhaps sunlight. This brings up another useful limit: degradation. Small nanoparticles do not have thick layers of skin to protect them from solar UV light, heat, or reactive chemicals. Nanobots would tend to degrade quickly in sunlight or outside their designed environment such as the body. The body may also metabolize them, so perhaps you need a ready supply. Consider the economics of nanobots—people needing to constantly ingest or implant them to keep the benefits. Consider toxicity. Consider allergies or built-up immunity. Consider needing to take special vitamins or minerals to allow the nanobots to do their work.

With these basic concepts and tips, you are well equipped to write a compelling nanotechnology SF adventure. As for reality, will nanobots someday be implanted in our bodies to fight disease? Will they change our very nature and our society? In 1959 Feynman said yes, and he's been right on everything else so far!

CHAPTER 37

CRAFTING HOLOGRAMS

By Judy L. Mohr

Imagine driving through a parking garage looking for a perfect place to park. You find one just outside the main doors. You turn on your indicator and start to pull in.

STOP! A man in a wheelchair has appeared out of nowhere. You almost ran over him. Thinking that you could have killed this handicapped fellow, you step out of your car to apologize. As you walk around your car door and move closer to the man, you notice something odd. He's thin—as in 2D thin. He's not real. Yet his image is as clear as anything. Stunned, you stare at this image of a man in a wheelchair while he tells you that your perfect parking spot is actually a handicapped spot. A hologram wants you to park somewhere else.

Feeling guilty and sheepish, you get back into your car and look for another place to park.

It may sound like fiction, but it's not. Scientists in Russia have combined detection-and-recognition technologies with projection systems to solve a very real issue. If a handicap placard is not detected on your vehicle, an image of the man in the wheelchair is projected onto a curtain of mist directly in front of you. The image is very convincing, but is this really a hologram?

According to Merriam-Webster and the *Oxford English Dictionary*, a hologram is a 3D image formed from the interference patterns of a coherent light source. Put simply, a hologram is a virtual 3D image. It does not need a screen to be seen, nor does it need a source of monochromatic light. All that is needed is a light source of known, determinable characteristics and surfaces to bounce the light around. For something to truly be classified as a hologram, you should be able to look at the image from multiple directions, getting a feel for the 3D object hovering in empty space.

The Russian man in a wheelchair is actually just a 2D projection, but still a very convincing one—and one I would love to see in other countries around the world.

So, what about real holograms?

IT STARTED WITH *STAR WARS*

In 1977, R2-D2 projected an image of Princess Leia onto the big screen and the mainstream idea of using holograms for telecommunications was born. However,

George Lucas was not the first one to come up with the idea. What the public didn't know was that holograms already existed.

The first hologram was produced in 1947 by the British scientist Dennis Gabor while trying to improve the resolution of electron microscopes. With the advancement of lasers in the 1960s, holography developed into our current understanding of 3D-image transmission. In 1972, Lloyd Cross combined white-light transmission holography with conventional cinematography to produce moving 3D images from a sequence of recorded 2D images of a rotating object. So when George Lucas added holographic technologies to his futuristic story, it was by no means a stretch of the imagination.

However, I must admit that I'm still trying to figure out how R2-D2 was able to take an image of Leia's back when she was facing him during the recording, but we'll ignore that little detail.

Creating large-scale 3D images showing different views from all angles, similar to those portrayed in the *Star Wars* franchise, is not completely beyond the realm of our current technology. With clear, reflective plastic (or glass) and the right app, you can turn your smartphone or tablet into a holographic projector (Figure 37.1).

Figure 37.1: Using the plastic from CD cases, you can turn your smartphone or tablet into a holographic projector.

You can find many articles on the Internet detailing how to use the clear plastic from a CD case and your smartphone to create a moving holographic image of a jellyfish (or some other creature). There are even videos on YouTube that are designed specifically to use for the purpose. It's a fun activity to do with children that shows them how reflection works to form virtual images. (Actually, you don't need to have children to do this experiment—just an inquisitive mind.)

There are readily available units that use mirrors to magnify and project 3D virtual images of Matchbox cars and rubber frogs in free air. They come in a range of sizes, and every time I see one, the urge to pass my fingers through the image is uncontrollable. If you were to combine these simple holographic projectors with the current videophone technologies, the talking, interactive hologram used for communications in *Star Wars* instantly becomes a reality.

But what about the best holographic idea that science fiction has to offer: the holodeck from *Star Trek: The Next Generation*? I don't know about anyone else, but I remember sitting with my parents, gathered around the TV in awe as the first episode aired in 1987. Already big fans of *Star Trek*, my mother constantly begging to have a replicator, it was a collective "I want one" when we saw Riker open the doors to the holodeck and walk into the forest.

Unfortunately, unlike the holograms of *Star Wars*, the holodeck and its fully interactive environment are something we will never see. Projection systems may progress to the point that the 3D images are indistinguishable from reality; however, just the presence of a solid object would disrupt the image, creating shadows and distortions. This idea becomes further complicated with the fact that light cannot stop matter.

The scientific models for light can be incredibly confusing, with the ray and wave models used to describe reflection, refraction, and interference. Add the quantum model into the mix and even this scientist is lost. However, I can appreciate that current laser technology could potentially stop something with mass, but only by burning it to a crisp and blowing it up. Physical, tactile interactions with light are out of the question—at least the kind that won't injure us are out of the question. If you try to sit in a holographic chair, you will fall to the floor and potentially hurt your bum.

For the moment, I'll just ignore science fiction's suggestion that we might physically interact with holograms, enjoying a cup of tea with historic holographic characters. Regardless, projection and holographic-related systems have already had an impact on our everyday life—and it all starts with a pseudo-hologram telling you to park somewhere else.

●

CHAPTER 38

INFORMATION THEORY: DEEP THOUGHTS ON BUILDING HAL

By A.R. Lucas

Good science fiction starts with the question "what if?" It asks us to take what we know and stand at the crossroads of a myriad of possible futures. Technology is crucial to science fiction because it represents change. Sometimes it's a simple plot device, a way to get from A to B. Often it's a catalyst, something fundamental to the world we're about to explore, or even a character in its own right. And at technology's core is a fundamental but slippery concept: information.

Okay, don't leave yet. I know, it's not spaceships or killer mutant viruses, but it can be something far stranger. Don't believe me?

Take a number called Champernowne's constant. In Base 10, the number is a concatenated list of all numbers (12345678910111213…). It's what's called a *normal number*, which means its digits contain all numerical combinations equally, but that's not the cool part. The cool part is that Champernowne's constant, when translated into letters or bits or any other code, contains your next unwritten novel, the copy for this week's grocery flier, and Jorge Luis Borges's entire *Library of Babel*. You know, because of that whole all numerical combinations thing.[1]

Information theory is less than a century old, but it has changed our understanding of everything from physics to biology to computer science. It deals with the representation, communication, processing, and utilization of information.

DROWNING IN DATA AND CREATING CONTEXT

Information grows exponentially. This means that the current volume is always greater than the sum of everything before it. But too much information can overwhelm us, like the town of Ersilia in Italo Calvino's *Invisible Cities* (Harcourt Brace Jovanovich, 1974), which must be abandoned due to a lack of physical space.

The recent explosion of data has led many information experts to coin variations of the phrase "We are drowning in data, but starved for information." Data can multiply like the Tribbles on Captain Kirk's *U.S.S. Enterprise*, but without context, it's meaningless. Or worse, we can ascribe false meaning to it (google "spurious correlations" for a laugh), or make false assumptions.

1 von Baeyer, H. C. (2003). *Information: The New Language of Science*. Boston, MA, USA: Harvard University Press.

In the 1983 movie *WarGames*, the protagonist hacker, David Lightman, believes the computer system WOPR to be a simulation game instead of a military supercomputer. In fact, a military program and a computer game representing the same simulation may have the same programming, even though the consequences of engaging with one versus the other are very different.

The problem is Lightman interprets his interaction within the context he is expecting. He finds WOPR when asking for games and assumes that it is a game. False assumptions can enhance plot, and such problems may be unavoidable as information, like time, is relativistic.

DAMN YOU, HEISENBERG, THE ANSWER IS 42

Heisenberg's uncertainty principle states you can know either the exact speed or the exact position of an object, but not both. In fact, what you are trying to measure does not exist until you try to measure it. This means to get an answer, you must first ask the right question.

In Douglas Adams's *The Hitchhiker's Guide to the Galaxy* (Harmony Books, 1994), the supercomputer Deep Thought is built to solve the Answer to the Ultimate Question of Life, the Universe, and Everything. After 7.5 million years, the computer arrives at the answer: 42.

Deep Thought claims the answer seems meaningless because the programmers didn't know what the question was, and without the right question, quantum mechanics dictates that the answer is not just unknown, it is unknowable.

ENTROPY AS A MEASURE OF IGNORANCE

Probabilities are essential to information theory, but they often play tricks on us. Take the following example: I have two children, born two years apart, one of whom is a boy. What is the probability the other is also a boy?

Did you answer one-half to the question above? Unfortunately, that's incorrect. The answer is one-third. The possible combinations are BB, BG, GB (GG is not possible). Only one of these has a second B.[2]

Tricky, isn't it? Well, what if I tell you the taller of my two children is a boy? Height seems irrelevant, but it's not. It changes our probabilities. Now we only have two combinations: TB, SB and TB, SG. Probability is essential to information and information affects probability in surprising ways.

---

2 von Baeyer, H. C. (2003). *Information: The New Language of Science*. Boston, MA, USA: Harvard University Press.

Entropy is a measure of ignorance in information theory. An entropy of zero would represent complete knowledge, and an entropy of one complete ignorance or true randomness. (This should not be confused with probability itself, where both zero and one are less entropic states, and true randomness, the coin flip or 50/50, represents the state of highest entropy.) In thermodynamics, entropy can never be decreased, only held constant or increased.

Which unfortunately means the search for Deep Thought's right question may be impossible. If we knew everything, the information entropy would be zero and the universe itself might cease to exist. Yeah, it's a bit of a buzzkill. Blame Heisenberg.

TRANSMITTING A MESSAGE

Current science dictates that information transmission speeds cannot exceed the speed of light. This means your deep space communications could take a long time to reach home unless your faster-than-light (FTL) space travel technology extends to information, too. The Shannon-Hartley theorem tells you how much signal power you'd need and what the maximum amount of information you could send per unit of time without it becoming error-riddled noise.

Recently, there's been talk about using quantum entanglement to send FTL communications, but beware. The no-cloning theorem says you can't do this, and that even if correlation exists between two states it remains unknown until the states are verified against each other, which requires communication at the speed of light. For now, intergalactic snail mail is here to stay.

A COMMON LANGUAGE

A sender must represent information such that it conveys meaning to the receiver. Think of the prime numbers embedded in the alien message in the 1997 movie *Contact*. That string of numbers established the message as an intentional communication (not just noise) and mathematics as the common language. Communication imbues information with meaning and when technology is a character in its own right, developing systems of shared meaning can be a fundamental story challenge.

Returning to *WarGames*, WOPR is a doomsday machine. It relies on automatic fulfillment and cannot be unplugged or it will trigger nuclear war. This forces Dr. Stephen Falken and Lightman to find a basis for communication. The solution they arrive at is to have WOPR play tic-tac-toe against itself to teach it the concept of futility, as tic-tac-toe, when played without errors, always results in a draw (and in the case of nuclear war, the stalemate of mutually assured destruction). If you haven't heard of game theory, it's a useful tool to understanding how computers—and Vulcans—think.

EMPIRICAL TO ABSTRACT: IN OUR OWN IMAGE?

In the 1968 movie *2001: A Space Odyssey*, the computer HAL 9000 tries to destroy the ship's crew after overhearing that they plan to disconnect him following a series of malfunctions. Many viewers interpret the plot as a degradation of HAL's programming into human-like madness, but that assumes HAL is anthropomorphic. Instead, perhaps he is the opposite of mad, and his behaviors are pure logical self-preservation.

When developing artificial intelligence (AI) and other technologies, it is important to consider how they gather, process, and interpret information. The same image can mean disparate things to different people, and they share the common experience of being human. Push the boundaries when trying to devise logical frameworks for information processing and for communication between frameworks, and understand the limitations of your systems.

COMPLEXITY

Information theory tells us that the more complex a system is, the more entropy it has. If more entropy equals greater randomness, then the more complex our computing systems become, the less we can predict them. When they interact with a complex world, it is impossible to program responses for every potential scenario (too much data) or develop blanket rules that address every possible negative outcome.

Isaac Asimov's Three Laws of Robotics and his many writings about human/robot interactions and their unintended consequences demonstrate this. It is impossible to build complex systems of complete predictability. In recent literature, a hard takeoff (fast-learning) Artificial Superintelligence (ASI) and its potential unintended consequences are sometimes referred to as "the busy child." The unintended consequences may be malevolent or benign, but they must be there.[3] Entropy demands it.

---

3 Barrat, J. (2013). *Our Final Invention*. New York, NY, USA: Thomas Dunne Books

THE UNIVERSE SAYS, "HOLD MY BEER"

In *The Matrix*, the majority of humans go about their daily lives in a mundane, massive computer simulation while machines harvest the energy from their neural activity, sparking many late-night debates as to whether we are already living in the Matrix.

Turns out this may be true, on a far grander, though less nefarious, scale. Physicists are exploring the possibility that the fundamental building block of the universe may be not the quark or the lepton but the qubit, the base unit of quantum information. Space, time, and the universe as we know it may all emerge from the interaction of these qubits.

And remember, even though your next novel is lurking somewhere in Champernowne's constant, the pattern that makes it relevant doesn't exist until you write it.

CONCLUSIONS

Information theory is about interaction, and our interaction with information is changing our world every day, from artificial intelligence to quantum physics. However, if information theory is correct, as the complexity of our universe expands, so does its uncertainty, creating plenty of twists and turns for science fiction writers. The question is: Will any of them be stranger than the truth?

PART SIX

EARTH AND OTHER
PLANETS. YES, PLUTO
COUNTS!

CHAPTER 39

NEAR-FUTURE SCENARIOS FOR HUMANS AND PLANET EARTH

By Bianca Nogrady

For me, one of the greatest privileges of being a writer is being able to explore the "what-ifs."

These might be small what-ifs, like exploring what happens to fish larvae if marine noise pollution stops them finding their way back to their reef. They might be quirky what-ifs, like finding out how the waxing and waning of campfires influences our social development.

But sometimes—and this is happening more and more lately—my work as a writer forces me to confront the really big hairy scary what-ifs. Like, "what if the atmospheric concentration of carbon dioxide climbs above 550 parts per million?" or "what if we don't reduce our reliance on fossil fuels in time to adapt to renewable energy?" or "what if the world we are leaving our children is so harsh that many of them won't survive it?"

Over the last ten years of writing as a science journalist, a nonfiction author, and a fiction author, I have noticed some dramatic shifts in how I feel about the near-future prospects for our planet and our species.

Ten years ago, there was a lot of doom-and-gloom in the science media about our prospects, and dire warnings being thrown about that we were steering inexorably into an environmental hellhole. Many of the stories were about peak oil, peak phosphorous, peak everything-of-mineral-value; about the melting of polar ice caps and permafrost; about soaring carbon dioxide levels; and about how we needed to act.

Then I had the privilege of co-authoring a nonfiction book, *The Sixth Wave* (Random House Australia, 2010), with my friend Dr. James Bradfield Moody (who also happens to be an engineer, an innovation theorist, a World Economic Forum Young Global Leader, and a supremely clever fellow). This book put forward the idea that we are at the beginning of a huge wave of innovation that, like the Industrial Revolution, will transform our way of life and our economy, propelling us into a glorious new paradigm of sustainability.

THE OPTIMISTIC SCENARIO

We envisioned a world in which waste is an opportunity, in which nature is a source of inspiration for innovation, in which the digital and natural converge, in which information is global but stuff is local, and in which we shift toward service-based thinking rather than product-based consumption.

It was a wonderfully optimistic book. Despite the lack of initiative being displayed by governments around the world at successive climate summits (at the time and still now), it gave me hope that we may yet innovate to meet the challenges of climate change and peak resources.

While researching *The Sixth Wave*, I learned about some of the extraordinary innovations that are already a reality, like wave farms, plastic wood, landfill mining, the pricing of ecosystem services, green chemistry, car sharing, software-as-a-service, smart fridges, aquaponics, and green super-grids. These innovations are elegant, simple, and sustainable. So many of them caught my imagination not only as a journalist, but also as a fiction writer.

When I learned about kite power—which takes the principles of wind turbines but gets rid of all the unnecessary structural components—I immediately pictured a horizon dotted with the swirling waltz of high-altitude wind-power kites. I saw a design for large, gourd-shaped bamboo water collectors, which condense water out of the air, and knew I just had to find a place for those in my writing.

For a long time, I was actually excited about what the future would hold for humanity.

THE PESSIMISTIC SCENARIO

When I began researching my science fiction novel *Biohunter*, all of that changed. I wanted to explore what might happen if our greatest fears came true. What would our planet and our civilization be like if the worst of climate change came to pass, and if the resources that our world is founded on became too difficult and expensive to extract anymore? What if we didn't have oil or coal or liquefied petroleum gas, or iron or silver or rare earths? What if the polar ice caps largely melted and sea levels rose tens of metres? And what if temperature and rainfall patterns changed so much that large parts of the world became effectively uninhabitable?

I read a book called *The Long Descent* by John Michael Greer (New Society Publishers, 2008), which explores the theory that we are seeing the beginning of the end of our civilization. (Up your antidepressants before reading it, people. Trust me on this.) As has happened to so many other grand civilizations before ours—such as the Aztecs and the Romans—Greer argues that all we see around us will one day decline and rot. He predicts it won't be the apocalypse so many of us fear, but more a sad, gradual sequence of crashes and contractions as we descend back into the dark ages. Would the last person to leave New York please turn out the lights?

This depressing vision permeated my thoughts so much I began to have apocalyptic dreams of running, clutching my children, as a rising tide of oil pursued us across a barren landscape under a filthy sky. I found myself wondering how I and my family would survive in a world without oil, electricity, or even clean, fresh tap water. My little vegetable garden took on a whole new meaning as I began to imagine what life would be like if we relied entirely on it for our food.

PREDICTING THE HUMAN REACTION

With these scenarios in mind, I began building the world of *Biohunter*. I pictured a world where melting ice caps and glaciers had led to the flooding of most of the world's major metropolises, most of which had already been emptied by extreme weather events. Heat and drought had rendered large parts of the world's food-producing regions barren and uninhabitable. Governments had fallen as they became unable to provide their citizens with even the most basic infrastructure. The Internet and cloud had vanished like dust in the wind as grid-fail took down global electricity networks.

As populations migrated inland in search of reliable sources of fresh water and agricultural land, they formed their own self-governing, self-sustaining settlements, powered by renewable energy harvested from the sun and the wind, with not a fossil fuel in sight. Settlements grew and raised what they could to feed themselves and traded for the rest.

In the world of *Biohunter*, while there are now far fewer of us left alive thanks to the pressures of famine, disease, and war, there's still not enough to go around. Resource wars rage, but instead of wasting precious metal on bullets and bombs, conflicts are settled with bioweapons. They're easy to brew, don't take much material, and they're a guaranteed way to clear out a nice settlement and move in.

I thought this was all very depressing and apocalyptic until I had a conversation with a friend who commented that everything (apart from the biowarfare) actually seemed quite utopian. When I began to think about it, the world of *Biohunter* was also the world of *The Sixth Wave*, although it reaches that relative utopia only after having gone through the wringer of Greer's *The Long Descent*. I began to see that many of the innovations that James and I had envisaged when writing *The Sixth Wave* were manifesting in the world of *Biohunter*.

It's still a harsh, cruel world. Civil conflict rages between settlements over resources that we currently take for granted: clean water, arable land, salt, flour, or even human resources. And biowarfare is brutal and indiscriminate. It's no longer about soldier fighting soldier. It is an outright war of attrition where the victor takes all. The weapons are deadly and invisible, which makes them very difficult to protect against. The epidemic of Ebola in recent years provides a clear example of just how much damage something as minuscule as a virus can inflict on a population.

THE RISE OF SOLARPUNK

And then I discovered solarpunk. It was one of those serendipitous moments where my day job (journalism) and night job (aspiring novelist) came together.

The editor of an environment news service asked me to look into the nascent solarpunk movement for a feature. I discovered a young subgenre that is reaching for a more positive, sustainable, and realistic view of humanity's near future. While *Biohunter* shows a world rising from the ashes, solarpunk wills for us to achieve the same result without having to hit rock bottom first.

As solarpunk advocate and brand strategist Adam Flynn wrote, in a post on the Hieroglyph website, "We're solarpunks because the only other options are denial or despair." The solarpunk movement, which emerged largely as a hashtag on Tumblr and Twitter, takes some inspiration from an article written by author Neal Stephenson in the *World Policy Journal* in 2011, which called for science fiction to deliver some much-needed "techno-optimism" to the population and enthusiasm to scientists and engineers.

So, after all these ups and downs, I'm now allowing myself to feel a little bit of optimism that we may yet find our way to a positive future.

CHAPTER 40

THE FUTURE OF ENERGY

By K.E. Lanning

Energy is an essential part of our lives and, like the food we eat, it is entangled in our economy, politics, and our culture. The definition of energy is: *power derived from the utilization of physical or chemical resources, especially to provide light and heat or to work machines.*

PRIMARY SOURCES OF ENERGY

Currently, we have several primary sources of energy: fossil fuels, crop-based fuels, biofuels, nuclear fission and fusion, geothermal sources, hydropower, and solar and wind power. Let's go through each one of these briefly.

Fossil Fuels

Fossil fuels are organic sources that Mother Nature has cooked and processed for us to harvest: coal, oil, and natural gas. These fossil fuels are tapped by mining for coal or via drilling, either vertically or using the new technology of horizontal drilling for oil and gas. Fossil fuels have become environmentally and politically unpopular with concerns over pollution and climate change. The recent rise in popularity of wood heaters has exacerbated air pollution in cities, like London, that had previously moved away from coal stoves to reduce pollution.

Crop-Based Fuels

Crops grown for fuels, such as sugar cane or corn, must have energy expended on them to plant, harvest, and process them into an energy source. These crops also take precious land and water from food production and potentially create instability in our food prices, due to the gyrations of the energy market. Utilizing crops as fuel is more of an issue for various pollution concerns than drilling for fossil fuels.

Biofuels

Biofuels, which utilize waste turned into fuel, are excellent for "killing two birds with one stone" by burning cooking oils or other carbon waste products instead of dumping them into landfills. However, negatives of these carbon-based energy sources are potential pollution from spills or waste, and air pollution of many forms from burning these carbon-based fuels.

Nuclear Fission and Fusion

There are two types of nuclear energy: fission and fusion, which are opposite processes. Nuclear fission splits large uranium atoms, which releases energy in the form of heat. It's the form of nuclear energy source in current power plants, and it produces clean power. However, there are two huge caveats to this energy source: First, if an event occurs and the reaction can't be controlled, there is a real potential for runaway reactions with catastrophic results to life. Second, massive amounts of nuclear waste are produced as a byproduct and are being stored at nuclear plants with no long-term storage plans—this waste takes thousands of years to decay to safe levels of radiation.

Nuclear fusion uses the same process as our sun to produce energy, by fusing two hydrogen atoms to create a helium atom, which releases an enormous amount of power. Fusion energy is the ultimate solar power but is still in a development stage. The technological issue to nuclear fusion as an energy source has been the challenge of creating pressures and temperatures within a container that can maintain an environment for fusion to occur. The positive of this difficulty is that there aren't issues of runaway reactions because the reaction will die unless all systems are functioning. Only minor radioactive waste occurs from fusion and the time of decay to safe levels is fifty years.

Multiple countries and companies are racing to achieve the goal of a nuclear fusion power plant. Over the past decade, breakthroughs have been achieved via supercomputers, which allow scientists to model the complexities of fusion reactors. Fusion will be a Prometheus moment for humankind—solving our pollution issues with plenty of energy for our future needs.

Geothermal Sources

Geothermal energy emanates from the molten core of the Earth. It is clean and sustainable, but as a major energy source, it tends to be limited to areas near tectonic plate boundaries, where the geothermal gradient is most divergent, meaning you don't have to go very deep into the Earth to find a very different temperature from the surface level.

A heat pump uses underground pipes to tap into the differential temperature between the underground and the air, but it is a much smaller scale device simply for heating and cooling of buildings.

Hydropower

Hydropower is an ancient and nonpolluting power source that's limited to areas of major rivers. From the industrial age to now, hydroelectric dams provide a massive amount of electricity, but they alter fish migration and drainage, affecting the environment. "Run-of-the-river" hydroelectricity captures kinetic energy without the use of dams, but is a relatively small source of energy. Wave and tidal power are just in the initial stages of research at this point, and localized to shorelines.

Solar and Wind Power

Solar and wind are renewable sources of small magnitude energy, but they're not continuous.

These lesser magnitude energy sources are well matched to accomplish smaller needs: houses, buildings, and vehicles. A renewable energy company, RidgeBlade, has designed smaller scale turbines built into the ridgeline of a roof—a perfect match for powering a home. Economically, solar panels are competitive with traditional power sources, and the next generation of solar power is on its way. Every inch of a man-made object could absorb energy: windows, walls, and roofs. Perhaps one day you will drive down a sunny road and charge your electric car. However, with these intermittent low-magnitude energy sources, battery backup systems are a must for truly getting off a power grid.

Wind and solar as stand-alone power sources can, however, have negative impacts. Solar and wind farms impose themselves into the landscape and environment for minimal capture of power for large energy needs, so may not be an optimal use of land. Solar fields can negatively affect the surrounding plant, insect, and animal life. Wind turbines can augment main power sources, but are intermittent and can be an environmental issue. The large concrete foundations of wind turbines impact the land even after the turbine itself is taken away. In an environment such as a mountain ridgeline, this would forever alter the drainage—and scar the landscape.

THE FUTURE OF ENERGY

If we want clean air and water, we have to attack the energy problem on several fronts. For our large energy needs we must develop nuclear fusion or some source that has similar attributes. Every aspect of our lives must be analyzed for maximum capture of sustainable energy, coupled with efficient use of those varied sources. In addition, renewable sources would allow power availability during outages of a regional power grid. We must upgrade our power grid for maximum efficiency and possibly utilize underground routing to circumvent inadvertent damage to power lines. But as a part of the plan, we must wean ourselves away from burning carbon as a power source.

Recently, I visited an exquisite and wholly sustainable building at the Brock Environmental Center in Virginia Beach, Virginia. Paraphrasing from their website, "The Brock Center exists in concert with its natural surroundings, with minimal impact on the land, air, and waterways. It has a net zero impact on the environment and is a model for green building techniques, energy efficiency, water use, beauty, and inspiration."

Can we imagine a natural world of brilliant blue skies and clean water dotted with independent and sustainable buildings, solar-powered vehicles, and industries powered by clean nuclear fusion?

Humans now have the power of the ancient gods—the ability to create or destroy our world. We have to visualize a balance between humans and the natural world—then demand it.

CHAPTER 41

EARTHQUAKES: FACT VS. FICTION

By Amy Mills

If there's one type of natural disaster my home state of California is known for, it's earthquakes. In 2017 alone there were more than 500 2.5-plus magnitude earthquakes in California, and more than 20,000 2.5-plus magnitude earthquakes in the world. The title of the largest earthquake of 2017 is held by an 8.2 magnitude earthquake off the coast of Mexico. That's a lot of shaking.

Earthquakes were in the news for a few notable reasons recently: the movie *San Andreas*, an earthquake disaster movie released in 2015, an article in *The New Yorker* about the Cascadia Subduction Zone in the Pacific Northwest, and a devastating 7.3 magnitude Iran-Iraq earthquake that caused more than 500 casualties. Earthquakes are unpredictable, potentially deadly, and a great device in fiction to provide quick devastation and destruction.

THE MYTHS

To help you get earthquakes right, here are a few common misconceptions, and a couple tips, for writing earthquakes in fiction.

Myth #1: Earthquakes Can Be Predicted

Earthquakes are unpredictable. Natural disasters don't have a "season." They are a constant threat that can strike day or night, in the summer or winter. Despite extensive research on the subject, earthquakes cannot be predicted with sufficient precision to say what day an earthquake might hit, what month, or even what year. However, due to statistical analysis, scientists *can* provide long-term forecasts to give a likelihood of a large earthquake happening in the upcoming years. One of the most popular predictions of today is that a large earthquake, often cited as "The Big One," is due to hit California in the next couple decades.

There is *some* level of prediction, however small. Many countries, including Mexico and Japan, do have earthquake early warning systems in place. These early warning systems can't provide hours of warning, but they can provide precious seconds, enough time to get under something sturdy or get out of a building.

Myth #2: A Huge Earthquake on the San Andreas Fault Could Obliterate California

Not necessarily. While damage would be extensive and there would be loss of life when California's most famous fault line rumbles, we probably wouldn't be looking at a replication of the 1906 earthquake in San Francisco. California has some of the strictest building codes for earthquake safety in the United States. Though the state isn't earthquake proof, measures have been put in place to limit the damage and/or loss of life. While the San Andreas is scary, scientists believe anything larger than an 8.3 magnitude earthquake is unlikely, and it wouldn't be able to trigger a tsunami, either (tsunamis generally occur from earthquakes in subduction zones, which the San Andreas is not).

Myth #3: The Ground Will Split Apart

Sorry. Even if it does make a cool scene, the ground does not split open in an earthquake. Earthquakes are produced by faults slipping next to each other, not away from each other. No friction means no earthquake. Not to say there couldn't be ground failures (landslides, spreads, cracks in sidewalks and asphalt), but there would be no gaping chasm in the street for your character to plunge to his death. Don't worry! Soil liquefaction, which we'll talk about later, can provide some pretty nasty devastation instead.

Myth #4: A Magnitude 7 Earthquake Behaves the Same Way in Any Part of the World

Sadly, no. The survivability in the aftermath of an earthquake can be highly dependent on building codes and emergency preparedness. Retrofitting existing buildings to bring them up to code can be expensive and infeasible for poorer countries. In some ways, it's not about how strong the earthquake is but rather how safe the infrastructure is. This is why the damage and deaths from earthquakes can vary so greatly between countries even if they experience the same magnitude of earthquake. Not only that, but the timing of the earthquake could change everything. Consider the 1989 Loma Prieta earthquake in San Francisco. Despite the earthquake rattling San Francisco during rush hour, the casualties were relatively low. Why? Because the San Francisco Giants and the Oakland Athletics were in the World Series. Many residents were settling into watching the game—not driving on the roads.

WHAT CAN YOU EXPECT IN AN EARTHQUAKE?

Depends on magnitude. Earthquakes are measured by magnitude on the Richter scale, which ranges from 0 to 10-plus. Magnitude is not as straightforward of a concept as some would think. The scale is logarithmic, so every additional step in magnitude is 10 times bigger than its predecessor. The points below generalize a range in magnitude and what the expected damage would be.

- **0 – 2.9 MAGNITUDE:** This earthquake would not be felt.
- **3.0 – 3.9 MAGNITUDE:** "Was that an earthquake?" This earthquake may be felt by an individual if she's awake on an upper floor of a building, although she may not link the shaking with an earthquake. The rumbling would feel similar to a rumbling truck passing by.
- **4.0 – 4.9 MAGNITUDE:** "We're having an earthquake." This earthquake would be strong enough to wake up an individual from sleep. Picture frames may crash on the ground and windows could break, but the damage is relatively low.
- **5.0 – 5.9 MAGNITUDE:** "Duck and cover!" This earthquake would be strong enough to cause slight damage to well-built buildings and considerable damage to poorly designed structures. At this magnitude, the population would probably panic.
- **6.0 – 6.9 MAGNITUDE:** "Hold on!" At this magnitude, an earthquake would cause considerable damage to a city. Furniture would be overturned and buildings may be tipped off their foundations. Throughout a city, monuments and statues would be toppled, and roads would be damaged.
- **7.0 + MAGNITUDE:** "&#%!" Most masonry and wooden structures would be destroyed in this type of earthquake. Around a city, transportation would be severely disrupted as bridges could collapse, rails could be bent, and roads could be cracked. The city would be in chaos.

EARTHQUAKE SIDE EFFECTS

Earthquakes in and of themselves are dangerous enough, but they can also trigger other disasters to make an earthquake situation that much deadlier. Here are four side effects of earthquakes that you can write into your fiction.

Soil Liquefaction

Soil liquefaction is the phenomenon where water-saturated soil strength is diminished by rapid loading. In nonscientific terms, when soil with high water content gets shaken—like by an earthquake—the soil turns into a liquid. Soil liquefaction is especially common near rivers, lakes, and beaches and can cause buildings to tip, their foundations sinking into the earth.

PUTTING THE SCIENCE IN FICTION

Infrastructure Collapse

I think this is everyone's biggest fear in an earthquake—and with good reason. Buildings and bridges aren't earthquake proof, and the scariest earthquake damage pictures are the ones with crumbled buildings. Building codes are designed to prevent collapse as much as possible, but nothing can prevent cracked concrete or falling debris. This is why it's extremely important to duck and cover under something sturdy during an earthquake.

However, keep in mind if you're writing futuristic SF that earthquake technology will only get better and better. Even now, there are some pretty awesome earthquake safety measures being utilized in bridges and buildings. For instance, some structures have been built on base isolators (flexible bearings that separate the foundation of the structure from the ground). The idea is similar to the suspension system in your car. A very expensive suspension system. In California, a few structures are already built (or were retrofitted) with base isolators. These include the San Diego-Coronado Bridge, Los Angeles City Hall, and the San Francisco-Oakland Bay Bridge. Japan, however, is the reigning leader of earthquake safety in infrastructure. The country utilizes base isolators, pendulums, and even giant curtains to help dampen the blow of an earthquake.

Tsunamis

Tsunamis are giant ocean waves triggered by underwater land disturbances, such as landslides, volcanic activity, or earthquakes. Tsunamis—in relation to earthquakes—occur only from earthquakes in underwater subduction zones (like the Cascadia Subduction Zone off the coast of the Pacific Northwest). If you want a tsunami in your fiction, make sure the earthquake happens in the water.

Utility Failures

The higher the magnitude of earthquake, the more likely key utilities will fail. Power lines, sewer lines, water lines, storm drain systems, gas lines—all can fail. This could mean sinkholes, gushing water from water main breaks, leaking sewage, destroyed cell phone towers, inability to process debit or credit card transactions due to lack of electricity, and no water or electricity for days or weeks or months. Broken gas lines and downed electrical lines can spark fires, which caused much of the property damage in the 1906 San Francisco earthquake. In fiction, it's important to address these side effects of a massive earthquake, as they'll cause most of the problems post-earthquake.

There you go! A few misconceptions and facts about earthquakes. As a friendly PSA, make sure you have an emergency plan in case there is an earthquake in your area. And if the ground does start moving, remember to get under something sturdy, cover your head, and hold on.

●

CHAPTER 42

IMAGINING CLIMATE CHANGE

By K.E. Lanning

Science fiction was born asking the question, "What if?" Writers explore parallel universes, cruise subatomic particles, travel in space and time—just name it and science fiction readers are ready to hitch a ride. But climate fiction (cli-fi) is a relatively new subgenre of science fiction, springing out of the growing concern over climate change. After reading a 2006 article from the Intergovernmental Panel on Climate Change, activist Dan Bloom penned the term *cli-fi* to describe a subgenre of speculative fiction that emphasizes the effects of climate change.

The Earth's climate is not a static beast—the geologic history of the world is rife with sea level changes due to natural cycles of warming and cooling. Dinosaurs roamed near inland seas until a cooling trend caused a series of ice ages, lowering sea levels. Subsequently, humans moved onto the Americas across newly exposed land bridges. Since the end of the last ice age, we have been in a period of melting ice and rising seas.

GLOBAL WARMING IS AN OLD IDEA

Global warming is not a new concept—scientists have studied the greenhouse effect since the 1820s. But in 1896, Svante Arrhenius, a Swedish chemist, concluded that human activity was contributing to this warming trend. In 1938, G.S. Callendar presented evidence that humanity's use of fossil fuel might cause climate change. Over the span of modern history, a chart juxtaposing the rise of carbon dioxide to human population growth tracks ominously. Scientists warn that intense warming could shift the ocean currents into a different orientation—no one knows what havoc this could bring to the equilibrium of our world.

However, burning fossil fuels is only a part of our influence on the planet. Humans have created a complex puzzle of shifts in the environment to the water, air, and land, some as surprising as methane bubbling up from the rotting vegetation submerged under dammed-up reservoirs. A large mirror indeed is needed to view our impact on the globe.

IMAGINE DRASTIC CLIMATE CHANGES

The current climate of the Earth provides an excellent petri dish for human propagation, but what if the climate shifted back to that of the Cretaceous or Jurassic—would we adapt to the jungle or be eaten by a burgeoning population of, dare I say, a new generation of dinosaurs? Or if the climate shifted to a brutal ice age, would massive crop failures cause famine around the world and decimate the human population?

Eco-fiction has certainly been around—Frank Herbert's *Dune* (Chilton Books, 1965) beautifully builds a world of sand and tenuous human existence. But in the 1970s, the recognition of human influence on climate change initiated a call for action. Ursula K. Le Guin's *The Lathe of Heaven* (Charles Scribner's Sons, 1971), a beautifully surreal novel, illuminates the effect of human population intersecting the delicate balance of the world. *The Lorax*, written by the venerable Dr. Seuss (Random House, 1972), though not a specific global warming book, spoke to the children of the 1970s of the plight of the environment and our direct impact on the Earth. The legendary environmentalist Edward Abbey wrote *The Monkey Wrench Gang* (Lippincott, Williams & Wilkins, 1975), a controversial novel of extreme activism and his most famous work of fiction.

With human populations exploding and industrial capacity fleeing to countries with no environmental controls, the resulting pollution is overwhelming our fragile ecosystem. The climate talks in Paris illustrate the difficulties, but also the urgencies of curtailing pollutants which alter our world. We now have a new globalization of *fear*.

CLI-FI AS INSPIRATION

That tickle of fear has sparked a new world for science fiction writers to delve into—the cli-fi novel. In this new millennium, Earth's rising temperatures brought a wave of cli-fi novels to the bookshelves. Renowned author Margaret Atwood wrote the gut-wrenching trilogy MaddAddam [*Oryx and Crake* (Nan A. Talese, 2003), *The Year of the Flood* (Nan A. Talese, 2009), and *MaddAddam* (Bloomsbury Publishing, 2013)], set in a dystopian future when a geneticist decides that the human population needs a bit of culling to save the Earth from the human beast. A major writer in the cli-fi genre is Kim Stanley Robinson, notably his *Forty Signs of Rain* (Spectra, 2004). British author Jeanette Winterson wrote *The Stone Gods* (Houghton Mifflin Harcourt, 2008), set on a degenerating planet similar to Earth. Paolo

Bacigalupi published his critically acclaimed novel, *The Windup Girl* (Night Shade Books) in 2009, a near-future novel exploring a post-petroleum world.

The key to effective cli-fi is creating an engaging protagonist lost in a dystopian or post-apocalyptic story without beating the readers over the head with overt political agendas. The writer's characters take us on the journey, with a human voice carrying the message of devastation, but also the hope of redemption. Climate fiction can fill us with fear or possibly even excitement of a new and altered world to explore.

What if the polar caps melt and sea level rose hundreds of feet? Cities and entire countries might disappear like the fabled Atlantis. Social and political chaos would reign as populations migrate to dry land—humans on the move with strife and despair in their pockets.

Bookshelves drowned in thoughts of ocean's rising? Or perhaps frozen in an impending ice age? *What if?*

—————•—————

CHAPTER 43

HOW THE OCEAN WILL KILL YOU

by Danna Staaf

The ocean covers 71 percent of our planet and probably leaks into at least that much of our collective psyche. You can't dip your toe in a tidepool without getting bitten by symbolism. The depths of the sea represent humanity's unconscious; maritime weather stands for fickle fate; fish denote Jesus; and the white whale—well, we all know about him.

The ocean has shaped high fantasy like Ursula K. Le Guin's Earthsea series and hard science fiction like David Brin's Uplift books, adventures like Jules Verne's *20,000 Leagues Under the Sea* and thrillers like Peter Benchley's *Jaws* (Doubleday, 1974).

The immense popularity of these last two titles, however, has contributed to one of the most common misconceptions about the ocean among readers and writers alike.

THE OCEAN CAN KILL YOU, BUT PROBABLY NOT IN THE WAY YOU THINK

When they hear that the ocean is dangerous, most people think of great white sharks, giant squid, maybe even sea serpents. But the most dangerous thing in the ocean is actually . . . water. Because you can't breathe it.

In the United States, about thirty-five hundred people die every year by drowning. About half of these deaths occur in swimming pools and bathtubs, while the other half occur in what the Centers for Disease Control and Prevention calls "natural water" settings: the ocean, lakes, and rivers. So compare 1,750 annual deaths by natural water to less than one by shark (some years there are no fatal shark attacks) and zero by squid (there's never been a confirmed fatal squid attack).

In addition to suffocation, water can play another unpleasant-and-sometimes-fatal trick: hypothermia. You may have noticed that sitting for an hour in a 70-degree pool chills your body like sitting in 70-degree air never would. That's because water is an excellent conductor of heat, whisking the warmth away from your skin far faster than air. Many a shipwreck survivor, saved from drowning by a life vest, has died of hypothermia before help could arrive.

Real people who work or play in the ocean, like divers and sailors and surfers, focus most of their safety precautions on these water-related risks. Fictional characters can do the same. Life jackets don't just languish under benches in case of emergencies—boaters, canoers, and kayakers are often required or at least strongly recommended to wear them at all times. Depending on your story, this may be an unnecessary detail or a great opportunity to inject characterization. ("Excuse me, I have to run home and change into my tangerine pants to match this vest.")

And if you do want to hurt or kill a character in the ocean, it's tragically easy to find inspiration in real headlines. Operating a boat under the influence. Night swimming alone. Ignoring the dive computer's warnings. Such risky but all-too-common behaviors can easily cause hypothermia, drowning, or both.

MOST ANIMALS IN THE OCEAN ARE NOT SHARKS OR WHALES

But I know, I know. Sometimes you just have to threaten your characters with a deadly animal. In that case, may I suggest a cone snail or a blue-ringed octopus?

Marine biologists have a name for the large, but not terribly abundant, creatures that receive a disproportionate amount of attention from the popular media: *charismatic megafauna*. Big animals like dolphins and great whites sure don't lack for star power—but their entire existence depends on an uncounted number of smaller species, from algae and coral to sardines and snails.

In fact, the ocean is Earth's premier showcase for the diversity of animal life. It's got dancing flatworms, sea cucumbers that breathe through their anuses, sailing jellyfish, octopuses that dress up like shrimp, shrimp that can break your thumb . . . I could go on and on.

Most of these creatures are invertebrates, animals without a backbone. And some are truly bizarre. In college, my invertebrate zoology professor said that if he had to pick a group of animals that came from outer space, it would be the echinoderms—the group that includes starfish, sea urchins, and sea cucumbers.

Instead of having a left and right side like we're used to, they have five-pointed symmetry. Instead of a proper circulatory system, they pump raw seawater through their bodies, using the pressure of the water to move their feet. They can regenerate their arms and even their guts. Aliens among us, indeed.

In fact, many writers have drawn inspiration from the marine realm for creating alien and fantasy life forms. Invertebrates offer an almost endless diversity of shapes, forms, and behaviors to stir the imagination (see chapter 26, "Writing Outside the Human Box," and chapter 31, "Tentacles: From Octopus to Alien").

If you're writing horror, try looking up marine invertebrate parasites. There's a barnacle that grows entirely inside the body of a female crab and compels her to tend the barnacle's eggs as though they were her own. There are blood-sucking isopods (relatives of the garden-variety pill bug) that feed exclusively on fish tongues. In the most disturbing case, one particular species of isopod actually replaces the fish's tongue with its own body.

THE OCEAN WE'RE USED TO IS UNNATURALLY EMPTY

But if you're not inventing a new species or traumatizing your readers, if you're just writing a few boat scenes or a romantic walk on the beach, do you really need to know about all this biodiversity? Plenty of people who live in coastal towns never see much more than seagulls and seals. However, it's worth remembering that today's ocean is the product of centuries of overfishing.

It's hard to pinpoint exactly how long humans have been extracting life from the sea at a greater rate than it could be replaced. Steller's sea cow, a cousin of the manatee, was hunted to extinction by 1768. The development of industrial fishing techniques and an increased global desire for protein went on ramping up the harvest, leaving drastically depleted oceans that seem "normal" today.

Are you writing historical fiction or creating a fantasy/alternate world? Try filling the oceans with turtles and fish twice the size of a person. Pack in the whales like sardines. Consider reading accounts of historical abundance, like this passage from Richard Henry Dana Jr.'s memoir *Two Years Before the Mast*, set in the year 1834:

> "We were surrounded far and near by shoals of sluggish whales and grampuses [orcas], which the fog prevented our seeing, rising slowly to the surface, or perhaps lying out at length, heaving out those lazy, deep, and long-drawn breathings which give such an impression of supineness and strength. . . . I stood leaning over the bulwarks, listening to the slow breathings of the mighty creatures—now one breaking the water just alongside, whose black body I almost fancied I could see through the fog; and again another, which I could just hear in the distance— until the low and regular swell seemed like the heaving of the ocean's mighty bosom to the sound of its own heavy and long-drawn respirations."

On the other hand, is your writing set in the future? Consider that whales may become wholly extinct, as in the charmingly cheesy 1986 movie *Star Trek IV: The Voyage Home.* And charismatic megafauna aren't the only ones who will be affected. It's also reasonable to speculate on the demise of coral reefs and mangrove forests, each habitat a haven for innumerable small fish and invertebrates.

We often think of the ocean as powerful and dangerous. It is. But at the same time, many marine animals and ecosystems are fragile and endangered. To incorporate both aspects in our writing is to give to the sea what we try to give to all of our characters—depth.

CHAPTER 44

●

HABITABLE ATMOSPHERES

by Lynn Forrest

Within a few episodes of the revived *Doctor Who* series, I found myself sucked into the Doctor's universe. When he didn't travel to some place or time on Earth—particularly a version of London—he was on a different world. A world that, in general, was warm or cool enough with the right kind of atmosphere to wander around without special gear.

As much as I enjoy the show, I can't suspend belief enough in those episodes to think, "Sure, humans and Time Lords can breathe there just fine." (I could write a full chapter on what's wrong with the ATMOS burn-the-atmosphere-to-cleanse-it story line.) Unfortunately for the factual science fiction writer, multiple factors have to come together to let humans or human-like people live on the surface of a planet, and those things can't coincide on a whim.

Let's break down the key ingredients for a habitable (Earth-like) atmosphere on a given world:

1. sufficient planetary mass to provide the gravity that keeps the atmosphere in place,
2. a magnetic field,
3. a reasonable distance from its parent star (not too close, not too far), and
4. oxygen in the atmosphere itself.

THE IMPORTANCE OF GRAVITY

Your characters probably don't want to float away from the planet they're on, and neither should your atmosphere. Every object in the universe attracts other objects with a force proportional to its mass and its distance from those objects. This applies to the molecules within the atmosphere, too. On Earth, the acceleration due to gravity—the gravitational force between objects on Earth and the Earth itself—is about 9.8 meters per second squared, often referred to as 1 *g*.

By comparison, Venus's surface gravity is about 91 percent that of Earth, Mars about 38 percent, and Earth's moon about 16 percent. Which of these celestial bodies has an atmosphere? The ones with higher gravity. The moon lacks an atmosphere altogether, and the average atmospheric pressure at the Martian surface is about 0.6 percent of Earth's (the complex topography of Mars strongly affects the pressure at any given location). On the other hand, Venus boasts a surface pressure ninety-two times *greater* than Earth's.

Clearly, gravity isn't the only reason these planets have or don't have an atmosphere. Venus provides a shining example of the runaway greenhouse effect: Any oceans it may have had boiled away millions of years ago, creating an oppressive wasteland that destroyed a NASA lander less than an hour after it reached the surface. Mars lacks a magnetic field, a topic covered in more depth in the next section. But a planet must have some gravity to pin its atmosphere in place.

MAGNETIC FIELDS: A PLANET'S SHIELD

Thankfully, the Earth has a magnetic field that's produced by a complicated process involving Earth's solid core—solid due to high pressures, not low temperatures—surrounded by molten rock. Since the Earth rotates quickly on its axis, the spinning core creates what some call a *geodynamo*. (That's as far as I'm comfortable explaining it. Find a friendly geologist for the full scientific details.)

This magnetic field is important because it acts as a shield, protecting Earth's atmosphere—and us—from the Sun's solar wind. The highly charged particles that make up the solar wind get deflected by the magnetic field. Without it, the solar wind would strip away part of our atmosphere, including the ozone layer protecting us from ultraviolet radiation. Some theorize that Mars, which has a very weak magnetic field, lost much of its atmosphere due to the solar wind even though it's farther from the Sun than Earth is. Imagine how much less atmosphere we'd have without our magnetic field!

Conversely, Venus doesn't generate a magnetic field at all. As a result, the solar wind has stripped molecules from Venus's atmosphere for millions of years, taking away its hydrogen and thus removing its ability to create water. Why hydrogen? It's the lightest element and can more readily escape Venus's gravity.

THE INGREDIENTS FOR BREATHABLE AIR

When the air is dry, Earth's atmosphere is about 78 percent nitrogen, 21 percent oxygen, 1 percent argon, and 0.04 percent carbon dioxide (and, sadly, rising). It has trace gases as well, such as methane—yes, the stuff cows produce—and water vapor when the relative humidity is above 0 percent, which is almost always. For us to breathe without assistance, the air should be at least 19.5 percent oxygen. (Note that levels above 22 percent are considered "oxygen enriched." Since fire consumes oxygen, I shouldn't need to explain why a largely or entirely oxygen atmosphere would be Armageddon levels of bad.)

Where does the oxygen come from? Thank the nearest plants for breathable air. Some oxygen was present when the solar system formed, but photosynthesizing organisms generate far more of this molecule necessary for life as we know it. Basically, photosynthesis uses energy from the Sun to pull carbon from carbon dioxide and releases oxygen as a by-product. (The air is the biggest source of carbon for plants!) On Earth, cyanobacteria produced the initial influx of oxygen into our atmosphere. Volcanoes contribute some oxygen as well, but not enough to bring us to our current 21 percent concentration.

I'd argue a habitable atmosphere is a breathable one, but we could get away with living on Mars if we lived inside pressurized domes and carried oxygen tanks with us when we walked outside. If you'd like to learn more, Robert Zubrin's excellent book *The Case for Mars* (Free Press, 1996) delves into the science and logistics behind a feasible Martian colony. Unfortunately, the average Martian surface temperature is a frigid -58° F (-50° C). Which brings me to the next point....

THE GOLDILOCKS ZONE

Yes, there is such a thing as the Goldilocks zone. It has more respectable titles such as "habitable zone" or "life zone," but the Goldilocks term will always stick in my head. True to its title, this is the region in which a planet is neither too hot nor too cold for liquid water.

Liquid water is key for life. Water freezes once the temperature reaches 32° F (0° C) and evaporates at 212° F (100° C). If you want your Earth-like planet to be comfortable for your human or humanoid characters, you want it to be "just right" for vast amounts of liquid water.

Mars could be that way if we added greenhouse gases to its atmosphere. Robert Zubrin proposed the use of fluorocarbons to kick-start the process. Thawing the surface of Mars would release more carbon dioxide, which would add more greenhouse gases to the atmosphere, which would continue warming the atmosphere—a positive feedback. (Great for Mars, but Venus shows why it wouldn't be great on Earth.) Eventually the Martian surface would become warm enough to maintain liquid water, that water would release oxygen from the soil, and then we could start bringing plants to Mars. Imagine how cool it would be to farm on Mars. "Interplanetary Gardener" has a neat ring to it. (I'm sure Mark Watney from the 2015 movie *The Martian* would have appreciated a more hospitable climate for his potatoes.)

PUTTING THE SCIENCE IN FICTION

If the right ingredients are in place, terraforming a world to make it more Earth-like is possible and could make a great story. However, Zubrin's method is time-consuming and thus couldn't happen overnight, despite what was implied by the 2000 animated movie *Titan A.E.*

A RECIPE FOR A HABITABLE ATMOSPHERE

First of all, start with a decent-sized rocky planet. You need a solid surface for characters to stand on and enough mass to produce sufficient gravity. Then pick a star: it can be like Earth's or it can be a hotter or cooler star. The key is to slide your planet into an orbit that's within the Goldilocks zone for liquid water. Give it a sprinkle of photosynthesizing organisms, a generous helping of water, a few billion years, and voilà! Human-friendly planet.

Just keep your characters from showing up early.

This is a highly adaptable recipe. You can always put your characters on a more hostile world where they need protective gear or on a planet where only a small region is human-friendly, such as the poles or along the equator. Planets can have seasons and complex topography, too!

●

CHAPTER 45

AGING PROPERTIES

By Gwen C. Katz

So there's an episode of *Star Trek* where Data travels three hundred years back in time and his head gets cut off and later they find his head and reattach it to his modern body and get him working again. (*Star Trek* plots sound weird when you summarize them.) But wait. His head is three hundred years old. Are we supposed to believe that three-hundred-year-old electronics will still function perfectly? Okay, maybe Data's positronic brain is made of advanced future materials that don't degrade.

How about the *Doctor Who* episode where Rory is replaced by a plastic Roman centurion and spends two thousand years guarding the Pandorica? (*Doctor Who* plots sound *really* weird when you summarize them.) We're explicitly told that Rory is made of regular plastic, and if you have any hand-me-down toys from your parents, you know that most plastic gets yellow and brittle within a few decades. But two-thousand-year-old Rory is still fully functional.

One of the most common scientific errors in epic science fiction and fantasy is failure to consider the effects of aging. These genres have time scales covering hundreds or thousands of years, and often important artifacts are passed down through that time. Inevitably, these artifacts are intact, shiny, and ready to use. In real life, however, very few objects survive for thousands of years, and those that do are usually rusty, crumbling, or otherwise in poor condition.

HOW AGING WORKS

The main chemical reaction that causes materials to age is oxidation, and the main culprits are oxygen, water, and light. Let's have a look at some common materials and how these factors affect them.

Metal is well known for its tendency to oxidize (rust) when wet. But individual metals oxidize in different ways. When iron and its alloys oxidize, the rust flakes off, revealing a new surface that can continue to oxidize, allowing the object to eventually rust away completely unless the surface is protected by paint or another finish. There's not much hope for the fragments of Isildur's sword after three thousand years.

When copper and bronze oxidize, however, the oxidation sticks to the surface, forming an attractive patina that protects the object from further damage. Objects like the Statue of Liberty can therefore last for centuries in good condition. Bronze statues age so well that most of them were lost not through aging, but through deliberate destruction when they were melted down to make cannonballs or new statues. Surviving artifacts can, however, be distinguished from new objects by the patina.

Gold does not oxidize under normal circumstances. An ancient gold artifact can indeed remain in shiny, like-new condition, although if it's been handled, the soft metal will show a lot of wear.

Paper is subject to many kinds of environmental damage, including fire, mold, and insects, and everyone is familiar with the yellowed, brittle texture of old paper. But truly old paper might not age as poorly as you expect. The yellowing is caused by lignin, a chemical present in wood pulp that can turn acidic in the presence of light, and wood pulp only became a ubiquitous papermaking material in the late nineteenth century. Before that, most paper was made of recycled cloth fibers, which did not contain lignin. Depending on the papermaking process, ancient books could last a very long time if given the right care.

Plastics are the least stable common material. This may surprise you if you've heard the old factoid about a plastic bag taking five hundred years to break down in a landfill. While it's true that plastic takes an incredibly long time to completely decompose, it doesn't take very long at all for it to stop being good plastic. Different types of plastic have different chemical compositions, but they're all made of polymers, which are vulnerable to various kinds of degradation. Sunlight can create free radicals that age polymers much like they age your skin. Long polymer chains can break into shorter molecules or become linked to each other, making the plastic brittle. Poor Rory would probably break at his age.

One of the most dramatic examples of aging plastic is cellulose acetate, the material film is made of. Cellulose acetate quickly degrades, releasing acetic acid, which gives the film a strong vinegar smell and causes the degradation to accelerate. As it degrades, the film shrinks, buckles, and becomes fragile enough to shatter when handled. This process can begin within a decade, and it's irreversible.

DELAYING AGING

To protect an object from aging, the first step is selecting the right materials and preparing them correctly. Acid-free paper circumvents the problem of yellowing. Painted or varnished metal is sealed away from oxygen and will not corrode.

Glass and ceramics, while fragile, are made of stable minerals that generally don't degrade over time.

Favorable conditions can also do a great deal to prevent aging damage. Egyptian tombs preserve artifacts incredibly well because they are shielded from light, water, and (if the tomb is fully sealed) oxygen. Bogs provide a dark, oxygen-free environment that preserves organic materials well. A spaceship traveling through a vacuum with no exposure to air or water would be protected from most aging effects, at least on the outside.

But beyond damage caused by external factors, there's another principle called *inherent vice*, which refers to materials that, by their very nature, are unstable and don't last. For instance, magnetic storage like cassettes and VHS tapes will gradually lose their charge and be erased over time, even if they're stored perfectly—and playing a tape causes it to be erased faster. Sorry, Star-Lord, there's not much chance that you're still listening to that cassette from 1988.

Once aging damage occurs, it's usually difficult to do much about it, but an entire field, art conservation, is dedicated to preserving objects and restoring them if they've been damaged. Sometimes striking results are possible.

The ubiquitous lead white paint used before the twentieth century was not only toxic but unstable. Its white pigment, lead carbonate, decomposes into black lead sulfide in the presence of hydrogen sulfide—a gas released by Victorian gas lamps. Illuminated manuscripts from Victorian libraries ended up with a garish "photo negative" look because the brightest white areas had turned black. However, treatment with ordinary hydrogen peroxide oxidizes the lead sulfide to lead sulfate, which is white and stable. Badly degraded paintings have been beautifully restored to their original appearance by this method.

If your space opera or fantasy epic spans hundreds of years, think about the condition everything is in. Are things worn out or broken? Do important artifacts need to be carefully stored and handled? Have things been destroyed intentionally or through neglect?

Just don't expect me to believe that a steel sword without a speck of rust on it is three thousand years old.

PUTTING THE SCIENCE IN FICTION

CHAPTER 46

GRAVITY BASICS

By Dan Allen

Get a big trampoline or one of those coin-eating toys for donations at the mall that looks like a trumpet shape where you put a coin in the top and it spirals around and around faster and faster until it drops through the middle. If you have a trampoline, put a heavy person in the middle and roll tennis balls or soccer balls across the trampoline and watch what happens. If you play enough, you will figure out the laws of orbital mechanics and you won't need to do any math.

These toys have surfaces the same shape as a gravitational field with a massive object in the middle. The trampoline is like Earth, with an object in the center. The penny eater is a black hole—that's why you don't get your money back. After some good play time on the trampoline (or a lot of lost coins), you should understand a few following key principles.

ANGULAR MOMENTUM—WHEN YOU JUST CAN'T STOP

You can't just fall into the Sun or back to Earth, a planet, moon, or even into a black hole, unless you are really far away and accidently aim straight for it, like NASA did with their failed Mars lander. To approach any gravitational object that you are moving past, you have to slow down somehow. You might try air-braking in an atmosphere or firing retro rockets. Similarly, to go from launching off the surface of an object, such as an asteroid, to orbiting the object you need to transition that upward speed into angular speed moving lateral to it. More angular velocity will give you a bigger orbit. Trajectories that trade off speed for distance from the Sun are called *elliptical orbits*. Trajectories with constant speed follow circular orbits.

ORBITAL CHANGES

Given what we already know, if you are in a circular orbit, such as Earth's, and you change speed, you just went into an elliptical orbit. The difference in velocity you need to change orbits is called *delta-v* (or Δv, meaning change in velocity; pronounced "delta-vee"). All you need is an impulse of energy in a particular direction to change the shape of an orbit from circular to elliptical and then another burst to change back to circular and match orbits with a new planet such as Mars. (You can try that on the trampoline, too.) The real trick to changing orbits is timing it so you end up in the new orbit at the same place as your destination planet. If the timing doesn't work out given the amount of delta-v you can get with your fuel, you are "outside the launch window."

To orbit closer to a sun, you need to lose angular velocity. To orbit farther a way, you obviously need more. Similarly, to change from one orbit to another on a minimal effort basis, you will take a mostly tangential (around the sun) path. A more direct path heading radially (toward or away from the sun) will cost you more fuel. Just remember the key concept: To leave a circular orbit, or enter one, you have to change velocity—you need delta-v. Use that word in your writing and you will definitely start to sound authentic.

GRAVITY CALCULATIONS

When you just need enough reality to make your story plausible, don't look up formulas on Wikipedia and do calculations from scratch. Just scale everything from Earth's gravity. It's easier and you'll be less likely to make a mistake. It is as easy as multiplying or dividing with your calculator app.

Tip #1: Escape Velocity Is 1.4 Times Orbital Velocity

Once you are in orbit, you are more than two-thirds of the way to escape velocity. This is the speed at which you can get away from the "gravity well" and not get pulled back by gravity, ever. By way of example, escape velocity on earth is 11.2 km/s, so minimum orbital speed is 11.2/1.4 = 8 km/s. That's eight kilometers every second! You really gotta move. Since Earth's diameter is 40,000 km, at that speed it takes 40,000/8/3600 sec/hr = 1.4 hours to get around Earth in low orbit or about eighty-five minutes (ninety minutes if you are out of the atmosphere).

Tip #2: Orbital Time Near the Surface Doesn't Depend on the Size of the Object

This is a really weird, but true, result. If two planets or moons, or even asteroids, have density similar to Earth, it will take about ninety minutes to get around in low orbit. Size doesn't matter! (Only density and distance from the surface.)

Tip #3: Gravity Drops Linearly Inside a Planet

In fact, gravity is zero at the center. Anything dropping through a cored planet or asteroid will bounce up and down the shaft just like a yo-yo, until it fries, slows down from air resistance and gets stuck in the middle, gets crushed by pressure, or hits the walls and dies a gruesome but exhilarating death.

Tip #4: The Force of Gravity Scales Linearly With a Planet's Diameter

Halve the diameter of a planet and you get half the gravitational force at the surface. Earth has a diameter of about eight thousand miles, so an eight-mile-wide asteroid has 1/1000 earth's gravity. But even if you weigh in at a slim 0.35 pounds, you should probably go easy on the tribble jerky because when you get back to Earth, it all comes back.

Here is where this idea comes from. A planet's mass grows as the cube of its radius, but the force at the surface drops the square of the distance to the center of gravity (center of planet). So there is only one factor of radius left over: Double the radius, double the gravity.

Tip #5: Orbital and Escape Velocities Also Scale With Diameter

Since I already told you that the orbital times are the same for objects of similar density, you immediately know that orbital speed scales with diameter, too. Earth's escape velocity is 11.2 kilometer/sec. So to get off an asteroid with 1/1000th the radius you need to be moving at 11.2 meters/sec or about 25 miles per hour.

MAKING THE JUMP TO LIGHT SPEED

Now prepare to go where no accountant has gone before: general relativity.

Virtual reality theme park rides take advantage of our body's inability to distinguish acceleration from gravity to make it feel like we are accelerating when really we are just tipping. With visual miscues, you can't tell if you are accelerating in a car or leaning back. Einstein's general relativity principle goes one step further. It says that not even *light* can tell the difference between gravity and acceleration. So the experiment you just did on the trampoline with soccer balls or coins at the mall also works with light. Yes, gravity bends light, or more accurately, gravity bends space and light travels straight through bent space. So just like the trampoline mat stretching, space stretches in the presence of gravity.

It is hard to imagine in 3D, but think of the lines on a ruler getting farther apart the closer you get to a gravitational object. Closer to the star, distances seem longer. The equivalent way to look at it is that time depends on the curvature of space (gravity). The more gravity, the slower time runs. This idea is explored in the 2015 film *Interstellar*.

Astronomers even use large gravitational objects like galaxies as "gravity lenses" to collect and bend light toward us from even more distant objects beyond.

Imagine a gravitational field as a sand trap or a bog. If you want to get from one side to the other you can either walk through it (slow) or go around (faster). Light always takes the shortest, quickest path from one place to the next. So light passing a star will bend. It takes a direct path through a curved space time, traveling the quickest possible route from one place to another. Gravity refracts light, just like water or glass.

The closer you get to a black hole the more the light bends, until you can see your own backside around the black hole. But it wouldn't be pretty because the gravitational gradient would have stretched you out like a piece of taffy.

Like the coin trap's slope, the curvature of space becomes infinite at the event horizon of a black hole. So time literally stops, just like a space traveler approaching the speed of light. The closer you get, the slower time moves. So actually you can't reach the event horizon. The closer you get, the faster the universe behind you moves. Stars are born and die in a tick of the clock, galaxies form and collide, galactic superclusters orbit super-superclusters and before the whole universe can die the black hole glows itself out of existence (thanks to Hawking radiation). So as long as you don't mind having your subatomic particles ripped apart in the extreme gravitation field, you can just happily wait it out on the event horizon scoping your backside as your quarks run amok.

In fiction, gravity matters, and in space, matter gravitates.

PART SEVEN
SOMETIMES, IT REALLY IS ROCKET SCIENCE

CHAPTER 47

REALISTIC ASTRONOMY

By Tom Benedict

Despite the close link between astronomy and science fiction, few science fiction stories include the basic tool of astronomy: the telescope. Those stories that do tend to stand out, either because they got the details right or because they got them so very wrong. In the interest of having more stories that get the details right, here are some common misconceptions about the business of optical astronomy, a look at how optical astronomy is done today, and speculations about astronomy's future.

TELESCOPES IN *DEEP IMPACT*

A good place to start is the 1998 movie *Deep Impact*. The first telescope scene, in which a high school astronomy club is watching the sky and one of the students, Leo Biederman, spots a strange object, is actually pretty accurate. Amateur telescopes outnumber professional observatories by a huge margin, so many transient events—supernovae, comets, or Earth-killing asteroids and comets—are reported first by amateur astronomers.

Where the movie's portrayal of astronomy began to break down was in the second telescope scene, in which Dr. Wolf confirms Biederman's object at the Adrian Peak Observatory. After aiming the telescope with a hand paddle, Dr. Wolf sits down at a bank of monitors next to the telescope to munch pizza and see what Biederman saw.

Unfortunately, the light from a computer monitor or desk lamp is enough to blind a detector that's sensitive enough to image the night sky. Like the reader of a good mystery novel, telescopes have to be kept in the dark. Modern observatories are controlled from rooms located somewhere else in the building or from a remote site far from the observatory.

Increasingly, astronomers aren't even the ones making the observations. It's more efficient and cost effective for observatories to hire professional observers and telescope operators to collect data, process it, and hand it over to the astronomers so they can use it for science. An accurate portrayal of that second scene would've had Dr. Wolf eating pizza in his office, requesting target-of-opportunity time for Biederman's object to be observed by an observer (who might have had pizza of their own).

All of this means that the classic science fiction setup—the lone astronomer witnessing that magic moment when they, and they alone, see the doomsday asteroid, and the fate of the world rests upon their shoulders—really doesn't happen. That moment is more likely to be experienced by an amateur like Leo Biederman, or by an astronomer in an office thousands of miles from the telescope.

MODERN OBSERVATORIES

Observatories are in the business of taking on-sky data and handing it over to astronomers for analysis. The modern observatory resembles, in many ways, a cross between a university research laboratory and a medium-sized factory. Depending on the size, the staff of a modern observatory ranges from a handful of employees up to several hundred and includes every role you'd find in a typical office—accounting, HR, purchasing, IT, etc.—as well as the software developers, engineers, and technicians required to keep the place running, the observers and telescope operators who take data at night, and the staff astronomers.

Astronomers themselves typically make up only a small percentage of the staff at a modern observatory, and some telescopes don't employ staff scientists at all. Most astronomers work at universities rather than observatories.

The data is collected by electronic detectors, almost all of which are cryogenically cooled to reduce heat-induced signal noise. Astronomical detectors are almost all black-and-white devices. Color images are built up by taking several exposures with different filters in front of the detector. As backward as this may sound, it provides the most flexibility for gathering scientific data. Rather than only gathering red, green, and blue pixel data like a color detector, this allows an astronomer to request data through other filters that can pick out a single emission line or image wavelengths the human eye can't see.

It also allows astronomers to make new filters to fit a particular science case without having to replace the detectors in an instrument. What this also means, though, is that the pretty color pictures we see on posters and in calendars have to be made, after the fact, by combining black-and-white images.

In addition to the telescope itself, the kinds of machinery you find in a modern observatory include all of the machinery typical of a large building such as elevators and air conditioners, as well as the kind of machinery found in a factory, such as cranes, forklifts, scissor lifts, air compressors, and hydraulic plants. Some observatories have their own machine shops and welding shops as well. Larger observatories have their own clean rooms for working on detectors and lab space for working with optics and electronics.

OBSERVATORY DRESS CODE

Contrary to popular belief, practically no one at an observatory wears a lab coat or a pocket protector. On the rare occasions when lab coats are worn, it's almost always by technical staff working around optics. When instruments are disassembled for servicing, that lab coat is traded out for clean room garb identical to that worn at factories that make computer chips. If there were an observatory dress code, it would be jeans and a shirt.

Figure 47.1: Time to wear the lab coat

Along with the myth of the lab coat goes the myth of technobabble. Although every technical and scientific field has its own form of jargon, for the most part people use everyday language to describe what they're doing. For example, someone at an observatory is less likely to say, "Affix that support mechanism to the unstable apparatus" than they are to say, "Brace that thing. It's wobbly."

The only time technical jargon comes into use is when it specifically applies. A lens really is a lens, and will be called a lens by layman and engineer alike. But when talking about optical aberrations, the optical engineer will speak in terms of Zernike coefficients because that really is the right term to use. If a part of your story hinges on a technical point, be sure to look up the proper terms. Otherwise, plain language works just fine.

PERSONALITIES IN ASTRONOMY

There is no single overarching personality type that defines the people who work at observatories. As with any other professional field, they run the full gamut.

I've worked with introverts, extroverts, focused people whose entire lives revolve around their professions, and people who have any number of outside interests. Those interests have included music, photography, art, dance, cooking, sports, woodworking, and even pursuit of their own field in some other direction like home shop machining, DIY electronics, and robotics. When writing characters to inhabit an observatory, be sure to develop them the same way you would develop any other character.

THE FUTURE OF ASTRONOMY

None of these details are likely to change in the foreseeable future, even into future science fiction settings. But the larger scale picture changes constantly and has a couple of clear directions.

New telescopes only get built if they fill a niche that isn't already filled. At the moment the three big drivers are mirror size, image quality, and access to new wavelengths. Desire for larger mirrors that will let us see farther out into space has led us to build a slew of new telescopes including the Giant Magellan Telescope, the European Extremely Large Telescope, and the Thirty Meter Telescope. Desire for better image quality leads us to build these new telescopes in remote parts of the world at high altitudes with stable air. Desire for new wavelengths drives development of new detectors, and to put telescopes in places where certain wavelengths aren't blocked by atmospheric absorption, such as the South Pole or out into space.

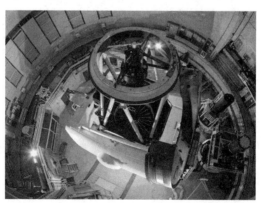

Figure 47.2: The Canada-France-Hawaii Telescope

Another key driver for future development is time. There are only 365 nights a year, or about 3,000 hours available for observing. Weather and technical failures eat into that, so the actual figure is considerably less. This is true regardless of the size of the telescope or the instrument suite available to it. Some science programs require large blocks of uninterrupted time that may run into tens of thousands of hours of sky time. This has led to the development of dedicated survey telescopes that host only a single instrument, such as the Large Synoptic Survey Telescope, the Hobby-Eberly Telescope Dark Energy Experiment, and Pan-STARRS—a telescope dedicated entirely to early detection of Earth-crossing asteroids and comets. (Sorry, Mr. Biederman.)

If you are writing a story that includes a telescope that doesn't already exist somewhere in the world, make sure it fills a niche that addresses at least one of these points or a new point that might become a consideration in the future, such as having telescopes on the far side of the moon or orbiting some distant star. And be sure to give it an appropriate name. If the previous paragraph didn't convince you that astronomers don't always come up with great names, this might: The OWL Telescope was a conceptual design by the European Southern Observatory. OWL stands for "Overwhelmingly Large."

Be sure to use your imagination.

———————•———————

CHAPTER 48

IMAGING OVER LONG DISTANCES

By Judy L. Mohr

The satellite whizzes overhead, its alignment reconfigured by the technician in some bunker in a secret location. After moments of clicking at the keyboard, a series of images flicker across the screen. Details of the landscape come into focus, but that detail is not enough. The technician taps the keyboard again, clicks the mouse, and the cameras on the satellite overhead zoom in. They've found him. They can see exactly what he's wearing and the backpack slung across his shoulder. Oh no … The hero is now in danger. Run, sly spy! Run!

While Hollywood would in reality take those zooming-in shots using a hover drone, believe it or not, the concept that the moviemakers are trying to portray is very real. As much as you might try and hide, you can't: The spy satellite will see you.

It's not a simple matter of just taking a picture like you would on your cell phone or digital camera. In reality, there would be a series of images captured, in conjunction with behind-the-scenes algorithms and corrective optics to compensate for atmospheric effects in real time and during post-processing.

MIRAGES AND RIPPLED GLASS

Most people have firsthand experience with the effects that the atmosphere has on light. Think about driving down a long, straight road on a sunny day. In the distance, you see shimmering above the road, and what some might believe is a wet patch. However, the closer you get to the origins of the mirage, the effects diminish and practically disappear. Instead, the wet patch has moved to a location farther into the distance. This mirage effect is caused by heat rising off the ground, but the effects that air movement has on light need distance to propagate before our eyes can detect it. The farther into the distance you look, the greater the scintillation. It's because of this effect that the stars twinkle at night.

Within the field of optics, one can think of the atmosphere as a thick pane of glass, but not just any glass. I'm talking about that rippled glass commonly used in bathrooms. If you were to shine a light through that glass, you would get a rippled pattern on the wall behind it where some parts are brighter than others. Now imagine that the rippled pattern in the glass was constantly moving. The bright sections of light would be flickering—they would be twinkling.

Imagine trying to take a picture of something that is constantly moving in an erratic way. For short-exposure images, the resulting speckle pattern can make it difficult to identify the shape of the original object (see Figure 48.1). For long-exposure images, you get a blurry mess. It might turn out to be quite an artistic image, but for someone on the ground trying to take pictures of the stars, or a satellite trying to take surveillance images of the ground ... Not a good thing.

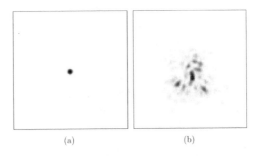

(a)   (b)

Figure 48.1: The effect of the Earth's atmosphere on stellar light. (a) A simulated stellar image taken from space (no distortions introduced by the atmosphere). (b) The real situation where a speckle pattern is seen in the short-exposure image due to the aberrations induced by the atmosphere. [Source: Mohr (2009). "Atmospheric Turbulence Characterisations Using Scintillation Detection and Ranging." Ph.D. Thesis, University of Canterbury.]

In reality, the atmosphere is not a single sheet of glass with a moving rippled pattern. It's actually multiple sheets of glass, each with different characteristics. In some cases, that layered sheet of glass is incredibly thick. However, if you were able to determine exactly how the layered sheets in the atmosphere were rippled and how they were changing with time, you could compensate for the resulting twinkling effects.

SURVEILLANCE IMAGING IN THE DESERT

Advancements in digital imaging are progressing every day. The latest smartphones now use 16 megapixel cameras and digital zoom to narrow in on that long-distance detail.

However, those spy films often show the hero in the desert of the Middle East taking images of the target from miles away. Over those distances, the scintillation would make a standard image so fuzzy that detail would be hard to distinguish. Some people might argue that if you use a camera with a telescopic lens, you'll easily take the detailed image you require—but it's not that simple.

PUTTING THE SCIENCE IN FICTION

Even if you had the best camera in the world with the most expensive optics mounted on front, unless you employed some level of post processing the resulting image would still be fuzzy. However, like in the stellar situation (Figure 48.1), if you could model the effects that the atmosphere has on the light, you can compensate for it. The equations for the horizontal problem are significantly more complicated, but it is doable.

In fact, in 2002, researchers from ADFA (Australian Defence Force Academy) in Canberra, Australia presented to the world single-frame images obtained of a house located ten kilometers away from their imaging system (over six miles). If there had been a person standing at the window at the time the photos were taken, you would have seen them in those photos (see Figure 48.2).

Figure 48.2: Single-frame image from a telescope sequence obtained over a horizontal distance of ten kilometers (over six miles). [Source: Jahromi, et al. (2002). "Image Restoration of Images Obtained by Near-Horizontal Imaging through the Atmosphere." DICTA2002: Digital Image Computing Techniques and Applications, 21–22 January 2002, Melbourne, Australia.]

If you combine the technology developed for imaging over long-distances from 2002 with the digital camera technology of today … Let's just say that I have no problems in imagining that surveillance photos could easily be taken of me, and I would never know it.

LONG-DISTANCE IMAGING AVAILABLE TO ALL

Imaging over long distances has been an area of research for many years. Granted, large portions of the research have been initiated by military and spy-related activities, but other sectors also benefit from the technology: astronomy (which is how I came to be in this field myself), telecommunications, civil aviation, and users of Google Earth, just to name a few.

You read that correctly, folks: Google Earth has taken advantage of satellite imagery for years. In 2007, Google Earth undertook a massive campaign to image my home city, Christchurch, New Zealand. The initial images blew everyone away, using a combination of satellite imagery, aerial photography, and geographic information systems. Since then, Christchurch has suffered massive earthquakes, leveling whole areas of the city, including the central business district. All of those initial Google Earth images are now not accurate enough to use. New images have been taken, but most of the residential areas are now cheap, minimal-rendering, satellite images. Even so, the detail in the images is impressive.

Take the image of my own house and surrounding neighborhood (see Figure 48.3). Due to copyright issues, this particular image was not acquired from Google Earth, but rather a company in the United States that specializes in satellite images for commercial use. While the level of detail visible in this image is better than the cheap, minimal-rendering images currently used on Google Earth, the image itself is similar in quality to the original images from 2007, but with post-quake details.

Figure 48.3: Satellite image of my house and surrounding neighborhood.

You can clearly see my big red roof (the only rectangular house), complete with the chimney flu and the white vented port by the back door. My SUV is in the driveway, and the garbage wheelie bins are by the fence. There are all the trees on my property, and the neighbor's patio with the umbrella covering her picnic table.

This image was taken using a satellite that is *years* old. Just imagine what information can be gleaned if you actually took the time to focus and acquire a series of images using the latest imaging technology.

Given the public-domain research available in this field, most of which is *years* old, it's no stretch of the imagination to believe that a satellite could take a photo of you and determine whether you were holding a tennis ball or a basketball. However, that spy agency is going to need ground-based surveillance footage if they want to see you peel that orange.

PUTTING THE SCIENCE IN FICTION

CHAPTER 49

RELATIVITY AND SPACE-TIME

By Dan Allen

In the 1800s, life was good. Steam engine-riding folks in Europe were all in on the new electromagnetics of James Clerk Maxwell, and soon Guglielmo Marconi would send sound over wireless waves in the ether.

But there were two dirty little secrets that threatened to destroy that idyllic steam-powered world of the late nineteenth century. Queen Victoria herself, if she knew them, would have kicked the bucket—or at least fallen off the fantastic flushing toilet of Thomas Crapper.

These two great puzzles, when solved, opened to us the power of the atom and gave birth to the nuclear age, effectively obliterating the steam era—much to the chagrin of all the steampunk fans who still fantasize about it.

One of these dirty little secrets was the "ultraviolet catastrophe." The solution to this conundrum came from combining a bit of math from Niels Bohr and Albert Einstein's idea of the photon, giving birth to the funky modern science of quantum mechanics.

The other dirty little secret was the electromagnetics of moving objects. (Eek, it didn't work!) And it was all because of this little (huge) problem called the speed of light.

THE STEAMPUNK WORLD

To figure out what this special relativity business is all about, let's put on our riding goggles and take a brisk ride in a bouncing buggy back in time to the late 1800s.

To a scientist of this era, things were simple. Wiggling charges created electromagnetic waves in the ether. Everyone's properly calibrated pocket watches and ivory cane measuring sticks agreed, even if they were moving past each other fast enough to kick up dust from the cobblestones (all while wearing dapper waistcoats and top hats, of course).

The fundamental premise of the pre-Einstein world was that events that happen at the same time for me, happen at the same time for everyone—a world good enough for Galileo Galilei and Isaac Newton.

There is one teensy little problem. With those rules, when you happen to move past electrical charges that are being accelerated (like by an antenna), the charges generate electromagnetic waves before they are even moved—wait, what?! That is because by riding on a train you can get your flashlight to shine at the speed of light plus forty-five leagues per hour, so causality breaks down.

I will spare you the math. It's bad, and when you're done with three pages of it, you get equations that are nonsense. So … if you like a world where none of the rules make sense, consider yourself a steampunk scientist! Smoke your pipe with no thought of lung cancer, ride a steamboat across the Channel, and use some burning magnesium for your photograph flash. The speed of light—poppycock!

HOW EINSTEIN SAW THE WORLD

It all began when Albert A. Michelson and Edward W. Morley flabbergasted, flummoxed, and discombobulated themselves and the whole scientific world by accidentally proving there is no unseen "ether" in which everything in the universe is suspended, like some kind of cosmic Jell-O fruit salad. Shortly after, Einstein decided that a few ideas had to change.

The first postulate or premise of Einstein's ether-less universe was that everybody experiences the same laws of physics regardless of their frame of reference. It is a reasonable assumption, given that there is no "stationary" ether that we move through. Einstein simply abandoned the idea that there is some magical "north pole" or other fixed object in the universe that we can say is "not moving." At the time, this was quite a cheeky thing to do and the height of impropriety.

What this means is that if I shine a flashlight, the beam shoots out from my flashlight at the speed of light, as expected. If a planet or star or galaxy whizzes past at close to the speed of light, it doesn't matter. Or, by the same token, if I whiz past a planet at close to the speed of light, my flashlight still sends out light at the speed of light. The big idea is it doesn't matter if you are sitting still or moving. In fact, according to relativity you can't even know whether I'm moving past you, or vice versa!

It is very fair. Everything about Einstein's work has that pragmatic feel to it. That never-failing "simple, easy, works for everyone" math expunged all the great quirkiness of science of the steam era.

But wait, there's more!

Postulate number two (and this is the kicker) is that everybody measures the same speed of light, regardless of whether they are in a box with a fox, or on a boat or in a train.

SPECIAL RELATIVITY

That last point had some interesting implications. It meant Einstein had no choice but to relate the experiences of people moving past each other using a kind of transformation worked on by brainiacs with names that started with L: Hendrik Lorentz, and Joseph Larmor (and some people's names that don't start with L, such as Woldemar Voigt and Henri Poincaré). This "Lorentz transformation" is the basis of special relativity and is one of the great hammers that struck down our romantic and mysterious world of the 1800s and took us into the nuclear age of mutually assured destruction and TV advertisements.

The first conclusion is that the universe is like a picture with a width axis and a length axis. All the dimensions of space are like one axis. And the second axis is another kind of distance: time. All events take place somewhere in this "picture" called *space-time*. The distance between two events is measured along both time and distance, like the distance between two pixels in a photograph being a combination of horizontal and vertical distances. Now, you can stretch one axis on a picture and distort it without changing the details of the picture. This is what happens when we convert happenings in one reference frame to another. Length and time get stretched in each picture to make the total space-time distances the same.

Is the speed of light mysterious and mystical? No, it is just the scale factor our universe uses to relate time and distance. Time has units of seconds, so we scale it by the speed of light in units of meters per second or miles per hour to change it into a distance. It is not mysterious at all. Even worse (steampunk fans flee while there is still magic in the world), the speed of light is the same for everybody. You see, unfortunately for philosopher friends, relativity is *not* about things being relative, like my morals vs. yours. It is about *absolutes*. There is one speed of light for everybody, all day, all the time, ever. Not very romantic at all.

So, what does it all mean?

THE IMPLICATIONS OF SPACE-TIME

Distances in space-time are constant for observers having a picnic in the countryside as well as those riding first class on steam trains. Unfortunately, that has some consequences for pocket watches and ivory-handled measuring sticks and canes. If we didn't allow these space-time "pictures" to be distorted, when we shine a light from a lantern on a steam train, that light moves at the speed of light plus some—which Einstein made illegal. Instead, to move from my reference frame watching the train go by to the reference frame of the brakeman holding the lantern, I have to distort my measurements of distance and time in just the right way so we agree.

Now, the distance between two points in two warped pictures may be the same, but that doesn't mean the X and Y axis values are the same. For example, up two and over one is the same distance as up one and over two. One observer may see events as having more X (spatial distance), while the other observes events as having more Y (time). But only this space-time distance, the combination of distance and time, is conserved. That means if we watch a horse race and start and stop our pocket watches to time the race, and you are on a train and I am not, our measurements simply don't match up. And that is okay. The Lorentz transformation will settle whose pocket watch is running fast—no gentlemen's duel necessary.

Our space-time pictures in our respective "reference frames"—the one on the ground and the one moving along at a heady clip down the track—work just fine for each of us. But when we examine each other's space-time picture, we find it distorted relative to our own, liked a warped woodcut of an idyllic Victorian family with perfectly behaved children and a mother soon to die from tuberculosis.

Events are no longer simultaneous for everyone. You say the revolver shots in the duel happened at the same time, but when I move past at close to the speed of light, I see them happen at different times. My clock runs slower than yours, and strangely things aren't so far away as they used to be when I looked at them before I caught the express trolley.

Of course you've all heard this before, and most of us think it sounds mystical: *time dilation*, the effect of slower time when you get close to the speed of light; and *length contraction*, the idea that distances to objects ahead of you appear shorter when you head toward them at speeds close to the speed of light.

But it gets worse. Moving electrical charges or currents generate magnetic fields, right? So if I move past some charges, it's the same as a current moving past me. There has to be a magnetic field. Thankfully relativity changes your electric fields into my magnetic fields and vice versa in a wonderfully symmetric way that makes the whole math simple enough to express all four of Maxwell's equations of electromagnetics in a single (matrix) equation.

WHAT HAPPENS AT THE SPEED OF LIGHT

Without going into the math, which starts out not too bad then gets a little woolly, like food left out of the icebox, the idea is this: There is a parameter called γ (gamma), which starts out a 1 (things act like steam era objects), then as you get close to the speed of light, γ gets bigger and bigger and goes to infinity as you approach the speed of light. This gamma factor is what we plug into the Lorentz transformation, like a sort of cosmic currency exchange for measurements. That parameter tells me how to stretch your universe picture (space-time) to make it agree with mine on the timing of events and the measuring of distances. It is that simple.

But it's also really cool. When moving at the speed of light, time stops relative to other reference frames because you've stretched space-time infinitely, so the distance between any two times is immeasurable. Now, stretching space-time that much would require an infinite amount of energy, which is why you can't reach the speed of light if you have any mass at all.

We can see this concept of stretched or "dilated" time with subatomic particles that are generated by cosmic rays in the outer atmosphere. We know their lifetimes because we can make them on Earth, too. They should decay and disappear before they reach the surface of Earth, even travelling at close to the speed of light. But they actually make it to Earth's surface to mess with our electronics just fine. How is that possible?

When those particles are generated moving at close to the speed of light, they look down at Earth and say, "Not so far, I'm gonna make it." Now, if we on Earth could see into their internal clockwork mechanisms as they flew by, we would notice that their system is running slow. So we say, "Well, of course they made it. They were decaying slowly." One worldview has a tall picture, and the other a short and wide one. In both pictures the particles make it to Earth.

That is how Ender Wiggin in the Ender's Game novel series by Orson Scott Card managed to outlive everyone from his era, by traveling at close to the speed of light most of the time. His internal clock ran slower, along with all his electronics, to avoid violating the speed of light. His picture was "stretched," spreading out the distance between points in time for him. He moved from one point to the next and then the picture was squished again when he returned and stopped. He traveled a greater distance across space and a shorter distance across time—fair enough? (Incidentally, you can move across the picture and back in space, but only in the forward direction in time. Otherwise, the math hits the fan and you are back where we started with steampunk non-causality and things happening before they are caused.)

So, the next time your dinner party discussion about Franco-Prussian relations is interrupted by an Orwellian machine that abducts you and heads out into space, you'll find that the distance to the star you are headed for is much shorter than it appeared from Earth. But when you get back to Earth after only a few months journeying among the stars, you will find that everything has changed, Rip Van Winkle. You are suddenly in the digital age. Thankfully, your tightly wound pocket watch still works.

————————●————————

CHAPTER 50

MISCONCEPTIONS ABOUT SPACE

By Jamie Krakover

It's fun to think about "what-ifs." And there are a lot of really cool possibilities when it comes to space travel. Unfortunately, a lot of the awesome things we see in science fiction movies and even books are less than realistic. That's not to say you can't stretch the truth and explore options, but if you want your writing to be believable there are some concepts about space travel that will help build a foundational understanding.

How do we as writers decipher reality from Hollywood? How do we create fiction that could be realistic and that is an extension of our world without making it overdramatized and fake? We research. In an effort to put my rocket science to good use and help my fellow writers, here are nine common misconceptions about space travel.

MYTH #1: PEOPLE AND OBJECTS IN SPACE EXPERIENCE ZERO GRAVITY

In space we call it *zero gravity*, but gravity isn't really zero. Gravity is the pull one object has on another. It's why things fall to the ground when you drop them, because the Earth has a gravitational pull. But when you're in space, you are actually in free fall. This is why it gives the appearance of weightless, or "zero," gravity. In space you are outside the gravitational pull of another body. Because of this you will keep free falling because there is nothing to pull you toward it. In other words, you are falling in an infinite hole because there is no bottom to hit. So while zero gravity is slang for what space travelers experience, they really are just free falling continuously with no end.

MYTH #2: THERE ARE FORMAL DIRECTIONS IN SPACE

In space, up, down, left, right, etc., are all relative to your current position or the position of another object. It's easy to get disoriented because there is no north or south, forward or backward—it's just a vast expanse. Without other objects to orient against, it would be hard for someone in space to figure out which way is up.

Literally. Because "up" as we know it doesn't really exist. The minute a person in space flips over or reorients, "up" is a completely different direction.

This is one reason why the quote "The enemy's gate is down" from Orson Scott Card's *Ender's Game* is so famous. Because in space, "down" is relative to what direction you are facing. Orienting in space isn't easy. There's no floor or ceiling, and that's a difficult thing for the brain to wrap itself around. But Ender identifying the enemy's gate as down, helped him orient within the battle room where they were in a near weightless environment with no frame of reference. Therefore, directions in space are usually given in reference to other objects to help the human mind wrap itself around which way is designated as up.

MYTH #3: FLYING IN SPACE IS LIKE FLYING ON EARTH

Unfortunately, it's not even close. It's not like cruising around underwater, either. Sure astronauts train in the water, but that is mainly to help simulate the feeling of "weightlessness." Astronauts often build and maneuver heavy objects in space, so training in water helps simulate a lighter load. That said, maneuvering in space is extremely difficult. There's no friction.

When Isaac Newton said an object in motion stays in motion until an external force is applied, he meant when you push on something it will keep going forever until something else stops it. On Earth, a lot of times that something is friction (or a car or a wall or another person). In space, there are very few things to stop objects in motion. If you move something it will presumably go in the direction pushed, forever, unless it hits something else or enters into the gravitational pull of another object (see Myth #1). In which case, the object will then take on a new direction and continue on in that direction until affected by something else.

Even worse, you can't just wave your arms in space like you can in water and move around. Space is a vacuum. There's no air around you to displace and therefore move yourself. Without some kind of jet pack to propel you, you would be stuck floating in the middle of nowhere. (Or speeding through space in whatever direction you happened to be going.)

Where it gets tricky is when you add in the fact that things can go (for lack of better words) up and down, left and right, and front and back. But you can also spin around those directions in what's called yaw, pitch, and roll.

When you combine those directions in different combinations, there are a lot of different ways an object can move (as described by the six degrees of freedom). It can pitch and go down, it can roll and go forward, it could do everything at once, etc.

If you have an object spinning toward a planet through space, it's pretty hard to get it to stop. If it hits something else, it's likely to be sent spinning off in a completely different direction forever, or until it encounters another object or gravitational pull.

Search for *gyroscopically stabilized CD player in microgravity* on YouTube to see a great video that shows how difficult it is to stabilize a spinning object in space.

MYTH #4: STUFF "BLOWS UP" IN SPACE

Science fiction space battles are the best. Watching spaceships blow up is really cool. Unfortunately it's extremely unrealistic. Again, space is a vacuum. There's no air, which means there's no oxygen in space. Without oxygen, you can't have fire. And without fire there can be no explosions. Sad, but true.

The corollary to this is, if you have an oxygen-rich environment like a spacecraft, you can have fire inside portions of the craft or in the engines if it has an oxidizer (liquid oxygen).

MYTH #5: HOW PEOPLE DIE IN SPACE

The last thing a person would want to do in space without a pressurized suit is hold his breath. You'd actually want to exhale air so the vacuum of space didn't pull the oxygen out and cause your lungs to rupture. The remaining oxygen in the human body would cause it to bloat. After bloating, a person would likely lose consciousness. From that point, the person would probably die from hypoxia or an embolism because the body is strong enough to keep the bloating contained.

People also can't freeze in space. Although space is extremely cold, in a vacuum, heat transfer works very differently. Your body would maintain its heat and keep heating itself. In fact, you'd probably overheat before you froze. That said, your blood will not boil in space. While space is cold enough for liquids to boil, and lower pressure means a lower boiling point, your blood has no direct exposure to space. Therefore your blood won't boil. It's protected by your skin and the rest of your body.

Lastly, people don't run out of oxygen in space. Well they do, but that's not what kills them. If a person was in a room with no oxygen source, she would die from the excess of carbon dioxide exhaled. Since blood rich in carbon dioxide is poisonous to humans, that is what would kill someone, not the lack of oxygen.

MYTH #6: THERE'S SOUND IN SPACE

Sound needs something to compress or vibrate against in order to create waves, which is what we hear. In space there's no air; it's a vacuum. Therefore, there's nothing for the vibrations to compress against. Which means space is a sad and quiet place. And if you could have awesome space explosions (which you can't: see Myth #4), you wouldn't be able to hear them.

MYTH #7: CREATING A GRAVITY ENVIRONMENT IN SPACE IS EASY

They don't call it rocket science for nothing. There isn't a magic button you can push on a spaceship that will suddenly conjure gravity. The way to create gravity in space is to create a force that will push objects in a certain direction. On Earth, that direction is toward the floor or the ground. On a spaceship, that's a little harder to simulate. You have to do it using rotation.

If you spin a bucket of water in a circle upside down at the right speed, the water will be pressed against the bucket and won't spill regardless of whether the bucket is right side up or upside down. Using this same theory, you can spin a spacecraft at the right speed such that the people and the objects inside are pressed against the outer walls of the craft. This creates a gravitational environment.

Where things get tricky is how you actually go about doing this. There are many arguments as to whether a giant spinning ring or a spinning tethered craft would work better. Both have pros and cons. Regardless of which option you choose, it's an expensive endeavor to simulate gravity. Making something that large spin is difficult. There are a lot of logistics that go into how you get something to spin at the right speed. Too slow and you don't get enough gravity. Too fast and you make people sick.

Once you get a craft spinning, it should sustain itself (see Myth #3). But if for some reason you have to stop the spin or you want to do more than orbit (i.e., travel to other planets), things get tricky. It's hard to make a ship go the direction you want it to when it's spinning. (Go watch the video mentioned in Myth #3 again.)

MYTH #8: THE SUN IS ON FIRE

It's not really on fire, but it is really warm, blazing hot in fact! In addition, the Sun can also be quite dangerous in space. Radiation is a very real concern. On Earth, the atmosphere helps protect people from the Sun's radiation to some extent. However, in space there is no atmosphere, so space travelers are at a much higher risk of receiving higher doses of radiation. Protecting against radiation, especially large galactic cosmic radiation events, requires quite a bit of shielding. Radiation shielding can be one of the heavier parts of a spacecraft. If a spacecraft doesn't have enough shielding, a solar flare or event could wipe out an entire crew.

MYTH #9: A LIGHT YEAR IS A MEASUREMENT OF TIME

Sure it has the word *year* in it, but a light year is actually a measurement of distance used by astronomers to try and reduce the use of large numbers in their calculations. One light year is about 5.9×10^{12} ft, which is a 59 followed by eleven zeroes. A HUGE number. The Sun is 92,960,000 miles from the Earth, or 0.0000158 light years. Unfortunately, that's a rather ugly number as well. But when you start talking about other star systems that are tens of hundreds or even thousands of light years away, things look a little cleaner when you can say something is one hundred light years away.

And that wraps up nine misconceptions about space. This is by no means an exhaustive list of things people don't quite get right about space travel, but hopefully it helps put a few things in this vast universe in perspective. After all, they wouldn't call it rocket science if it was easy.

CHAPTER 51

REALISTIC SPACE FLIGHT

By Sylvia Spruck Wrigley

Science fictional space flight involves three steps forward and two steps back. Swooping through the sky in a one- or two-man cockpit, surrounded by windows for a clear view of the starry-filled sky, a meaty joystick for the controls. The pilots are obviously the epitome of cool (this is of course standard for any pilot!), and piloting a spaceship looks suspiciously similar to a video game. The pilot isn't focused on computers and instruments but reliant on fast hand-eye coordination and quick thinking. Space flight is all about the maneuverability, as our trusty pilot stares out the windows to see what's coming.

If there's a fleet, they are all oriented the same way up and neatly lined up. They apparently do this by instinctively knowing the level plane on which they are flying, as if all of the ships were skimming a great invisible lake.

It's true that, if you get your private pilot's license, you will be taught to fly visually: that is, to keep your bearings by staring out the window. Once you progress from there, however, it's all about the glass cockpit and the instruments. Tell fighter-jet pilots that they need to maneuver by looking out the window and they'll laugh you out of the room. That just isn't fast enough.

In our universe, the reason an aircraft banks as it turns is to change the lift force: As the aircraft inclines toward the side of the turn, the lift force gains a horizontal component that forces the aircraft to turn. However, in space, you are flying in a vacuum and there is no lift force.

ILLUSIONS AND DISORIENTATION IN SPACE

The most common cause of death for the solo pilot at high altitudes isn't crashing in a high-speed obstacle course. The real risk is falling prey to illusions. The problem with flying is that, if you aren't able to see the ground and a horizon, your brain gets confused and lies to you.

This is why the basic private pilot's license is bound by visual flight rules, which only allows for flight within sight of the land and with clear visibility. The next stage of training is the instrument rating, which, as the name implies, trains the pilot to rely on the instruments in the cockpit rather than believing his eyes.

If you aren't instrument-rated and you fly into a cloud, losing sight of the ground, you are in trouble. Statistics from the National Transportation Safety Board show that you are unlikely to survive. Your life expectancy drops from decades to *178 seconds.*

So here's the thing: Flying in space is a lot like flying in cloud. You have no point of reference for up and down and whether you are flying straight on or in a turn. And once you lose these references, you succumb to disorientation. Technically, once you fly away from your colonized planet, if you are still staring outside instead of relying on your flight computer, you are likely to get tangled into an illusion and turn your spacecraft upside down in less than three minutes.

You cannot stop the illusion; the best you can do is train yourself to ignore it. This means disregarding everything your brain and body are telling you and believing the instruments. You need to be looking in, not out.

It's not just humans who have this issue, by the way. Radar studies have shown that, although European starlings can maintain straight and level flight when flying in overcast conditions, birds flying within the clouds fly erratically, suggesting that they are equally disoriented in the absence of visual cues.

Once you lose that visual frame of reference, your brain lies. Luckily, it lies consistently enough that we've learned to catch it out.

The graveyard spiral is probably the most well-known example of dangerous spatial disorientation. Common in poor weather conditions and night flights, the pilot loses the ability to judge the orientation of the plane.

What happens is that, without visual reference, you enter a banking turn. You initially can "feel" the turn, let's say to the left. However, if the turn continues for twenty seconds or more, you'll end up feeling that the aircraft is no longer turning. It feels absolutely as if you were flying straight with the wings level.

If you try to continue the turn, you'll go into a much steeper left turn. More likely, you'll want to be sure you have straightened out, but the straight-and-level aircraft will feel to you as if the aircraft is turning and banking to the right, even though you are now wings level. The compelling belief that you are now turning right will lead you to go back into the left turn. And the plane very slowly and gently flies in circles, a downward spiral that tightens as the aircraft descends. Your speed will increase until eventually you will escape the clouds and/or impact the ground.

Here's what's happening in the body to cause this disorientation according to Medical Facts for Pilots from the Federal Aviation Administration (www.faa.gov/pilots/safety/pilotsafetybrochures/media/SpatialD.pdf):

In this kind of turn, the fluid inside the canal starts moving initially, then friction causes it to catch up with the walls of the rotating canal. When this happens, the hairs inside the canal will return to their straight up position, sending an erroneous signal to the brain that the turn has stopped—when, in fact, the turn continues.

If you then start rolling out of the turn to go back to level flight, the fluid inside the canal will continue to move (because of its inertia), and the hairs will now move in the opposite direction, sending an erroneous signal to the brain indicating that you are turning in the opposite direction, when in fact, you are actually slowing down from the original turn.

The problem with a graveyard spiral in space is that its very existence means you're generating mild gravity as you tighten the spin. But honestly, if we start thinking hard about gravity within our dog-fighting spacecraft, and if we pay too much attention to the science, they'll all implode into a black hole of improbability anyway.

More pertinent for our science fiction stories, then, are the visual illusions that aren't reliant on problematic laws of physics.

Autokinetic effect gives the pilot the impression that a stationary object is moving. Specifically, a stationary small point of light in a dark or featureless environment, like a star-filled sky in space. This illusion is caused by very small movements of the eyes, which the brain misinterprets as movement of the stationary object. It means that we would find it incredibly difficult to tell the difference between a star and an approaching spaceship.

In *Generation Kill* (Putnam Adult, 2004), Evan Wright tells how, during the second Gulf War, the U.S. Marines reacted to town lights about forty kilometers away. The autokinetic effect led them to believe that a large combat force was moving out to attack. An airstrike was called in for fifteen kilometers away, the estimated position of the lights. There was nothing there.

MOTION-INDUCED BLINDNESS IN FLIGHT

The opposite of the autokinetic effect is motion-induced blindness, which causes objects to disappear from sight. A retired military aviator describes the phenomenon in an e-mail to *RoadRUNNER* magazine:

> This is a great illustration of what we were taught about scanning outside the cockpit when I went through training.
>
> We were told to scan the horizon for a short distance, stop momentarily, and repeat the process. I can remember being told why this was the most effec-

tive technique to locate other aircraft. It was emphasized repeatedly to not fix your gaze for more than a couple of seconds on any single object. The instructors, some of whom were veterans with years of experience, instructed us to continually "keep our eyes moving and our head on a swivel" because this was the best way to survive, not only in combat, but from peacetime hazards (like a midair collision) as well.

We basically had to take the advice on faith (until we could experience for ourselves) because the technology to demonstrate it didn't exist at that time.

It's easy to see this effect yourself by looking at one of the demonstrations online, which usually consist of a spinning grid with a single dot in the middle for focus and three yellow dots near the edges. There's an example at www.michaelbach.de/ot/mot-mib.

If you move your eyes around as described by the pilot above, the yellow dots remain clearly in sight. But if you focus on the dot in the middle, you'll discover that the dots disappear from view. Michael Bach has a configurable version of this test (found at the URL above), in which you can slow the movement right down and increase the size of the dots. They still disappear.

These two illusions alone mean that your fighter pilot flying through the stars has two problems. The autokinetic effect makes her think that the distant lights are incoming spacecraft coming to shoot her down. Meanwhile, motion-induced blindness makes the actual incoming space craft invisible to her.

Now that would be an interesting space battle!

PUTTING THE SCIENCE IN FICTION

●

CHAPTER 52

WASTE MANAGEMENT

By Gareth D. Jones

A lot of people don't give much thought to their waste (or rubbish or garbage, depending on where you live). They just throw it out and somebody else takes it away. People are generally more aware of recycling, resource efficiency, and sustainability than they used to be, but still have little idea how that works in practical terms.

Most writers who set their stories in space (or elsewhere for that matter) probably give the topic of waste management little thought, too, unless your story happens to be about the mutating power of toxic waste, but as with many other aspects of everyday life it can be something that appears in the background of your story and add an important detail to the society or ambiance you're going for.

If you're writing a story in a postapocalyptic, dystopian, or steampunk setting or in a ruthless dictatorship where slave labor is used for menial jobs, feel free to write anything you like. If you're writing a story that is contemporary or set in the future, though, it would be nice to see something based on current technology or an extrapolation thereof rather than something hopelessly outdated that makes me want to send you an email and offer to take over the Total Waste Management contract for your galactic empire and bring it into the twenty-first century.

SPACE JUNK VS. RENEWABLE RESOURCES

We all love the scene in *Star Wars* with the garbage compactor, and the time the Millennium Falcon hides among the garbage being jettisoned from the super star destroyer. But, we have to ask, could a closed system like a space station or starship, or a society in general, afford to throw away that amount of material into space?

When the U.S.S. Enterprise in the 2013 movie *Star Trek Into Darkness* turned out also to have a garbage chute to jettison huge quantities of material into space, I watched on in disbelief; not at Kirk and Spock's highly dangerous flight, but at the ridiculous waste. That material should be recycled onboard or stored up to be returned to a planetary base to be recycled. The cost involved in getting anything into orbit makes it far too valuable to throw away when it could be easily sent back to Earth on a returning shuttle.

The 2008 movie *WALL-E* was even more preposterous. How could they be throwing that amount of waste into space if the ship was mankind's only home for centuries? The volume of material being thrown out would probably have amounted to the entire mass of the ship after a few decades. Materials are not infinite. Give some thought to where they came from and where they go when people are finished with them. Please don't throw your waste out an airlock or have a laser waste bin vaporize it.

HEALTH AND SAFETY

In an episode of *Dark Matter* I half-watched recently, the team were imprisoned on a space station and some of them were sent down to the waste department to work. Here they were sorting the waste for recycling (hoorah!) and sending the rest for incineration. The waste was on a conveyor belt being handpicked. That's getting rather old-fashioned even now.

Optical and magnetic sorting mean many waste streams can be sorted mechanically, and this would surely improve in the future. Admittedly, this was a punishment detail so it was perhaps deliberately labor intensive. Next, they had to wheel the residual waste on trolleys into a large incinerator room. That was ridiculously inefficient. Of course, somebody then shut the door, locking them in, and turned on the incinerator. Who designed that system? Did nobody carry out a hazard and operability study when they were designing it? What madman would design a system that allows a good chance of death for the operators?

I've managed hazardous waste incinerators in the past. Every system has an alarm, a backup, an alarm for the backup, and a backup for the alarm. There are safety interlocks and emergency stops and there is nothing designed to allow the operator to be incinerated. On a related note, boilers and high-pressure steam systems are often a source of peril when somebody jams a valve and the system overpressurizes and explodes dramatically. Boilers have pressure relief valves that will open to vent steam safely, and if that doesn't work they have bursting discs that give way under pressure and vent steam in a controlled manner. When you're designing your Imperial Galactic incinerator, or any other technology, don't just throw in a convenient way to put your hero in mortal peril. Imagine you're the system's designer (which you are) and design it properly. Then come up with a more convincing way to threaten your protagonist.

LANDFILL

In an episode of *CSI: Crime Scene Investigation*, a murderer admits to having dumped a body in an old quarry. When the CSI team arrive, the quarry has been tuned into a landfill. The operators never found the body because they drained the water and just started throwing waste in. Landfills are not just a hole in the ground. They're specially engineered with impervious lining, venting systems for gas, and pumping systems for leachate. They would have found the body while constructing the landfill. In some countries, old landfills are now being mined for the valuable materials that were dumped in them for decades: plastics, glass, and metal, including trace amounts of many precious metals that are often present in greater quantities than they are in virgin ore and are much more easily extractable. In fact, precious metals are also being extracted from road sweepings, which contain trace amounts from exhaust catalysts and, bizarrely, from sewage sludge incinerator ash.

Developing countries where huge urban waste dumps are still common will often be crawling with poor, barefoot workers looking for materials to sell for recycling. The efficiency with which this health-and-safety-nightmare of a system works even now is impressive and goes to show that with a little thought, waste can become a resource instead of a liability. Particularly if you're setting up a colony on a new planet, this kind of resource efficiency and environmental technology would likely be built-in from the start.

HAZARDOUS WASTE

I've been working with hazardous waste for eighteen years and so far it's failed to mutate me into any kind of superhero. Which is a shame. Mutagenic and teratogenic waste can cause mutations in cells or in embryos, but the other hazards associated with them mean that even if you bathed in the stuff you would likely die from toxins before you were to mutate into a sentient samurai tortoise.

Sadly, radioactive waste doesn't glow. If somebody has been exposed to radiation and developed radiation sickness, this does not automatically make them radioactive. The kind of radioactive waste I've dealt with is Very Low Level waste from research laboratories rather than nuclear power plant waste, but Low Level Waste is much more likely to crop up in real life. X-ray machines and various bits of medical diagnostic equipment contain radioactive sealed sources, which are rather small and potentially deadly.

The important thing to remember about protecting yourself from radioactivity is time, distance, and shielding. Minimize the time you spend in contact, maximize the distance, and get some shielding. I won't go into all the complexities of half-lives, radionuclides, and the effects of alpha, beta, and gamma radiation, but if you're going to use radioactivity it's worth getting an idea of what's involved.

BIOHAZARDOUS WASTE

Biohazardous waste could be a number of things: bodily fluids and body parts, genetically modified organisms, cell samples, agar plates and the like infected with a disease of some kind, gloves and wipes contaminated with biological agents, or needles and other sharps infected with the same. They don't all automatically require full-body suits to protect you from them, and they won't all kill you on contact. A lot of research labs and hospitals put their biohazardous waste through an autoclave to kill off anything dangerous, so piles of waste waiting to be collected may already be harmless.

CHEMICAL WASTE

Chemicals come with a fabulous variety of hazards: corrosive, flammable, toxic, irritant, harmful, spontaneously combustible, oxidising, explosive. Mixing them together can cause dramatic reactions, so generally all of the different hazards are stored separately, even while awaiting disposal. Unless you're a chemist (which I'm not), it's very difficult to know which chemical will react in what way, but there are such a huge number of possibilities that it's worth thinking of some dastardly and original way to feature chemical waste in your plot.

Remember, in the future not everything will be made of plastic, not everything will be disposable, and most things still won't mutate you into a supervillain. Give some thought to the resources your society consumes and what they do with the waste. And unlike in real life, have fun playing with toxic waste!

———————•———————

CHAPTER 53

ENCLOSED ECOSYSTEMS AND LIFE-SUPPORT SYSTEMS

By Philip A. Kramer

Closed ecological system (CES) is a broad term that encompasses any self-sustaining and closed system in which matter does not leave or enter. These artificial habitats can be built in space, underground, or underwater, but no matter where they are, chances are they are closed for a reason. Whether it is an underground bunker in a postapocalyptic setting, a distant planet in the early stages of colonization, or a spacecraft carrying the last remnants of humanity, the environment outside is not hospitable. To ensure long-term survival, the occupants must maintain a well-balanced air and water system, a continuous food supply, and a reliable source of energy.

So far, no artificial enclosed ecosystem has successfully supported human life for long periods of time. Even the astronauts on the International Space Station get regular supply runs and have to exchange personnel. The largest CES was Biosphere 2, which sustained eight crew members for two years; however, they had to resort to some extreme measures to keep oxygen and carbon dioxide levels in normal ranges, and many of the plant, animal, and insect populations died off.

Creating and maintaining a CES is difficult, as many fluctuations or imbalances can cascade into environmental collapse without continuous monitoring and support. Here I will discuss a few of the misconceptions about enclosed ecosystems and life-support systems and suggest ways to get them right in your story.

MYTH #1: WASTE IS USELESS AND SHOULD BE DISPOSED OF

You see this in many stories set in space; the airlock door opens and a stream of garbage is ejected into the vacuum. This might be acceptable for short-term missions, where all the supplies needed are carried along, but for an ecosystem intended to last for a long time, being wasteful is not an option. It is a matter of *mass balance*. In most situations, it won't be possible to obtain resources from outside the enclosed system, so if your characters are ejecting waste of any kind out the airlock, soon there won't be anything left. By the same principle, if some waste product cannot be recycled, it will build up and eventually consume all of the precursor materials.

Getting It Right

When creating a life-support system for a fictional crew, they must adhere to a strict recycling policy. Most solids, such as plastics and metals or glass, can be melted and recast into any number of shapes. Of greater importance is the conversion of gaseous, liquid, and solid wastes into breathable air, drinkable water, and edible food. Solid organic waste, such as material from dead plants, animals, or their excrement, contains large amounts of nitrates, phosphates, and other inorganic compounds that serve as fertilizer for plants.

Having a "living soil" or cultured hydroponic system is also necessary, as bacteria, like those found in the human gut, are great at breaking down complex organic molecules and making them accessible to the roots of plants. So far, there is no easy way to convert waste, carbon dioxide, and water into an edible food source, outside of a biological system such as a plant. Such plants can be consumed as food, and the cycle is repeated.

MYTH #2: WATER EVAPORATES AND CONDENSES, BUT THE TOTAL AMOUNT DOESN'T CHANGE

You hear this often in terms of a large environment like the Earth, where water rises from the oceans and falls again as rain, and it is true for the most part. Only a few processes create or break down water, but in a small, highly balanced environment, they can make a huge difference. Water is made and destroyed in biological systems during condensation reactions and hydrolysis reactions, respectively.

The most significant of these reactions occurs in the mitochondria, the energy-producing organelle in nearly every cell. In the mitochondria, oxygen receives four electrons from the electron transport chain and is reduced to water. Yes, nearly all of the oxygen you absorb through your lungs is converted into water. The reverse happens in plants, where water is hydrolyzed into oxygen during the construction of carbohydrates during photosynthesis.

Getting It Right

The balance between animal and plant life on the ship should ensure a stable supply of water, but water can be made and eliminated artificially if there is ever an imbalance. Electrolysis, breaking water into hydrogen and oxygen, can be accomplished with a little electricity. That process can be reversed by burning hydrogen in the presence of oxygen. Storage of oxygen and hydrogen or water should be in place to deal with small fluctuations. Humidity and condensation can cause severe damage to electrical systems, especially in zero gravity, where air currents can become stagnant. This also increases the risk of mold. Cold surfaces or specialized air filters can trap the water vapor and return it to storage.

MYTH #3: PLANTS CONVERT CARBON DIOXIDE INTO OXYGEN, WHILE ANIMALS DO THE OPPOSITE

Unfortunately, the biochemistry isn't so simple. Oxygen is not converted into carbon dioxide in animals. As I already mentioned, nearly all of the oxygen you absorb is converted into water. Carbon dioxide is released from the breakdown of metabolites like sugar, proteins, and fats. This takes place in the mitochondria. In plants, oxygen is made when both carbon dioxide and water are converted into carbohydrates like glucose during photosynthesis. This occurs in the chloroplast in plants.

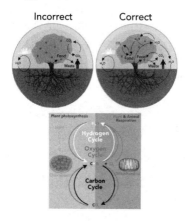

Figure 53.1: Food, water, and air cycles

Another misconception is that producing oxygen is all plants do. In reality, plants have mitochondria too, and they consume oxygen and carbohydrates and produce carbon dioxide and water. When the lights are on, plants tend to produce more oxygen than they consume, but without light, they will suck up the oxygen as hungrily as we do.

Getting It Right

Even as little as 1 percent concentrations of carbon dioxide can cause acute health effects such as fatigue and dizziness, but even higher concentrations (7 to 10 percent) can lead to unconsciousness, suffocation, and death within hours. To control fluctuations in carbon dioxide, scrubbers can be used. However, carbon dioxide is an intermediate step in oxygen and carbon cycles, so this artificial means to lower carbon dioxide may cause downstream effects on plant growth and lower oxygen concentration. This occurred accidentally in Biosphere 2 when carbon dioxide was converted into calcium carbonate in exposed concrete.

Materials like metal oxides and activated carbon can be used in carbon dioxide scrubbers and the carbon dioxide can be released at a later time. Large variations from the normal 21 percent oxygen are more easily tolerated than variations in carbon dioxide, but long-term exposure to greater or lower concentrations can lead to many acute and chronic health effects. Adjusting the amount of artificial or natural light available for photosynthesis is an effective means of controlling oxygen concentrations.

MYTH #4: ENERGY MUST BE PRODUCED WITHIN THE ECOSYSTEM

No closed ecological system is completely enclosed. If it were, it would soon succumb to the laws of entropy, making it a very cold and dark place. Something has to enter the system, and that thing is energy. The energy driving the weather, the currents, and the very life on this planet is coming from the Sun.

Getting It Right
Most common energy sources:

- Solar
- Wind
- Water
- Geothermal
- Gas
- Fusion/fission

The first four examples are the only types applicable in a completely closed ecological system, since energy can be moved into the system without any exchange of matter. A major drawback, however, is that the habitat can't leave the source of the energy. A spaceship powered by the Sun will have a hard time operating in interstellar space.

Any technology that requires the use of combustible fuels or fissionable (uranium 235 or plutonium 239) or fusible (hydrogen 2 and 3, deuterium and tritium, and helium) materials will have to be resupplied on a regular basis, so they are not suited for long-term ecosystems. By nature of their by-products, they cannot be reused for more energy, but they have the benefit of being disposable and can be used as a form of thrust in spaceships without upsetting the mass balance.

OTHER CONSIDERATIONS FOR ENVIRONMENTAL CONTROL AND LIFE SUPPORT

Size

Closed ecological systems can come in all shapes and sizes, but the larger the better. Larger ecosystems, like the Earth, can sustain much more life and complexity and take longer to collapse if poorly maintained.

Nutrition

The nutritional demands of a human are more than getting the right amount of calories. There are many essential trace elements, minerals, amino acids (nine of them), and fatty acids (omega 3 and omega 6), and nearly everything that is classified as a vitamin, which cannot be synthesized by the human body. Until these things can be synthesized by machines, a complex ecosystem of many different plant and animal life forms would be required to maintain optimum human health.

Temperature Regulation

Heat will build up rapidly in most enclosed systems, even in the cold of space, especially when you have heat-generating electronics around. Heat needs to be dumped back into space as thermal radiation, usually a high surface area radiator that circulates a fluid capable of picking up heat in the interior and dispensing with it outside. The opposite may be true in the deep ocean or underground, where heat may be drawn out of the enclosed system, and insulation will be necessary.

Air Circulation

This is particularly important in zero gravity space, where hot and cold air will no longer rise and fall, respectively. To prevent air stagnation, humidity fluctuation, and condensation, air needs to be well circulated. Filters are also necessary to remove any particulate matter such as skin cells or microbes.

The Human Element

Most enclosed ecosystems designed to support human life have not lasted nearly as long as they were intended to. Why? Because they failed to factor the human element into the equation. People get lonely and fall in love, personalities clash, and people fight. Close quarters and a limited food supply can cause even the most patient and respectful of people to lose their temper. In Biosphere 2, the eight crew members were barely on speaking terms by the time they exited, and two of them got married soon after.

PART EIGHT

STAR WARS AND THE
FAR FUTURE

CHAPTER 54

FASTER-THAN-LIGHT TRAVEL

By Jim Gotaas

The universe is a *big* place.

The fastest spacecraft currently planned is NASA's Parker Solar Probe, designed to launch in 2018 and approach the sun, with a maximum speed of two hundred kilometers per second. At that speed, we could go from the Earth to the Moon in about half an hour. Pretty fast, huh?

Even if our crewed spaceship could reach that speed, it would still take 6,400 years to reach the *nearest* star, Proxima Centauri. There has been much speculation about different forms of slower-than-light (STL) travel that could cut that time substantially. But if we accept Einstein's special theory of relativity, it would take us just over four years of travel to reach Proxima Centauri. Without faster-than-light (FTL) travel, four years to our nearest neighbor is probably too long for most stories. That said, there are a lot of interesting classic stories that are based on various types of STL, where current physics is obeyed, but advanced engineering work is needed.

THE BASICS OF FTL

There "ain't no such thing." Sorry.

Specifically, most scientists and engineers believe current physics says that FTL is impossible. Einstein's special theory of relativity states it would take infinite energy for a material object (like a spaceship) to travel at the speed of light. That *infinite* doesn't mean just lots and lots of energy, but literally more energy than exists in our universe. So the speed of light is the absolute speed limit in our reality.

Special relativity also predicts that actual FTL would lead to the breakdown of cause-and-effect. This is too complicated to really go into here, but basically, special relativity says that every person (technically, the theory refers to every "frame of reference") moving with a different speed sees the universe differently. In particular, if FTL occurs, even the order in which things take place can change. There will be some people who "see" the ship arrive before it's left!

So as far as current real science is concerned, we're stuck without FTL. But there are *possibly* some loopholes, which we'll explore.

From the earliest days, science fiction has wanted to play out on the big stages. All but the most hard-core SF purist is willing to bend the rules a bit for the sake of a good story involving galactic empires. So science fiction has come up with a number of imagined methods for FTL, some with more scientific plausibility than others. If you want your story to *sound* scientific, you'll need to face up to the problem of real interstellar distances, but be prepared to wave your hands a bit and mutter the accepted "magic words" to play the game properly.

There are dozens of different names and ideas used for FTL technology in science fiction, but we'll take a brief look at four main types.

WARP DRIVE

Most *Star Trek* fans are familiar with its warp drive through the use of "dilithium crystals." Depending on which generation you belong to the special effects vary, but the basic idea is the same. You start your warp drive and break through the light barrier, allowing you to have adventures all over the galaxy. There's usually no scientific justification for this, but at least you're facing up to the whole light-speed limit issue. This is an accepted trope in science fiction, and you're allowed to switch it on yourself in your stories, although calling it *warp drive* may evoke images of *Star Trek*. If you want to spend a little more time waving your hands about and sounding more expert, you can name your own version of FTL drive, or simply mention the Alcubierre drive. (This is an actual scientific idea, first developed in 1994, but more recently revived to the point where NASA scientists are actually looking at a variant—but still only in theory!) For more detail, see chapter 11 in Michio Kaku's book *Physics of the Impossible* (Doubleday, 2008).

HYPERSPACE

Hyperspace is an old idea in science fiction, encouraged by the fact that it's a real mathematical concept. Although it sounds interesting, in mathematics *hyperspace* simply refers to a set of dimensions beyond the normal three spatial directions (left-right, forward-backward, up-down), so we can talk about a hypersphere or a hypercube in four (or more) dimensions.

The key to FTL through hyperspace is the idea that different hyperspaces may have different intrinsic length scales. So while in our normal universe Proxima Centauri is just over four light years away, we can imagine a more compact hyperspace in which the distance is much shorter—let's be absurd and say four kilometers. In *that* hyperspace, traveling to Proxima Centauri at the speed of a normal car would only take a few minutes. So if we shift our ship into hyperspace, we can get there very quickly. Depending on the needs of your story, you can make the hyperspace journey shorter or longer by changing the size of your dimensions. There are examples in modern science fiction of having a range of hyperspaces with different scales so you can change your speed by moving up the hyperspace ladder.

In older science fiction, this alternate space was sometimes called *subspace*, implying that it somehow lay beneath our normal 3D world.

There are two main versions of hyperspace in current science fiction:

The first type has hyperspace accessed through gates that are fixed at certain locations in the galaxy, often making their location an important political and strategic consideration. On television, *Babylon 5* jumpgates were of this sort, created by unknown advanced aliens sometime in the past.

Another version allows individual large ships to enter and exit hyperspace directly with their own engines at any point in space. Again in *Babylon 5*, larger ships can have jump engines that allow for direct access to hyperspace, although it saves them energy if they can use a jumpgate instead.

WORMHOLES

Wormholes are usually described in terms of shortcuts across space by *folding* it.

The key is that if you take two points that are separated by, let's say, five feet on a single very large sheet of paper, you can bring them closer together by folding or bending the sheet of paper until the two points are almost touching. So if a fast snail (racing at three feet per hour) needs to travel from point A to point B, it will take her about an hour and forty minutes crawling along the paper. But if you helpfully fold the paper so that A is on the top and B is on the bottom as the paper touches itself, the snail can simply hop across, bypassing all that real space and taking only a minute or two.

Of course, this requires the existence of an actual higher physical dimension in which our ordinary space can be "folded," as well as a technique for bending our space in the first place. There are two main versions of these wormholes.

In many cases, the wormholes are imagined to be naturally occurring, a result of some sort of natural folding of our universe. This is the sort used, for example, in David Weber's Honorverse series.

Another version has the wormholes being engineered and fixed in space (a bit like the jumpgates in *Babylon 5*); this fits in with the artificial gates of the 1994 movie *Stargate*, or 2015's *Interstellar*.

Wormholes have a bit of scientific plausibility in that they are mathematically allowed by Einstein's general theory of relativity. One classic version in physics is known as the Einstein-Rosen bridge. Unfortunately, we don't know how to actually create them yet.

(For more detail, see chapter 11 in *Physics of the Impossible* and chapter IV in *The Science of Interstellar* by Kip Thorne [W.W. Norton & Company, 2014].)

HYPER JUMPS

Another version of FTL is called the *jump* or *hyper jump*. Here you simply fire up your jump engine and are transferred instantaneously to somewhere else. This often includes ideas about the energy required for your jump drive going up as the mass of your ship and the distance jumped increases.

This form of FTL is used in the "reimagined" latest version of *Battlestar Galactica*. If you want to add some plausibility, you could describe a possible mechanism behind this such as the creation of a very short wormhole that connects the two points in space for an instant.

FTL IN YOUR STORIES

So you want to make use of the big stage of the universe outside our own solar system? Well, if you just use one of the four standard ways discussed in this chapter (warp drive, hyperspace, wormholes, or hyper jumps), you can usually get by with just mentioning it in passing. However, science fiction readers enjoy new and exotic ideas, so if you can build a world in which you invent some wildly different and strange way to create FTL travel, you just may have a winner!

CHAPTER 55

CRYOPRESERVATION

By Terry Newman

The first thing to remember about cryopreservation is that it's a very tricky business. The second thing to remember is that frostbite is very painful. Plus, also remember that you have to be very careful about extrapolating from one example—say the freezing of bull semen (no sniggering, please)—to a rather more complicated situation such as people freezing. Some people, when asked what their idea of cryopreservation is, mutter, "That's all about freezing Walt Disney's head, isn't it?" No, it isn't.

Cryopreservation, as performed by biologists, is actually carried out for two different ends. The first objective is to maintain the structure of biological tissue as close as possible to the functional biological state for subsequent analysis. If you can do this, you might be able to image the biological tissue in as natural state as possible, at a particular time—even capturing cellular events, such as secretion, as they occur and potentially capturing the biochemical constituents of cells and tissues in their appropriate compartments.

The second objective is to permit freezing, and eventual recovery to a fully functional state, of the biological material. This potentially allows for long-term storage, usually at low temperature, with suspended animation. It doesn't matter if the material, while it is being stored, is in a natural state. A seed, after all, is biological tissue in a form of suspended animation, and it can do remarkably well without going anywhere near a fridge.

These two different approaches to cryopreservation do not go hand in hand. For microscopic and other analytical studies, the cryopreserved biological material should be frozen as quickly as possible, otherwise the fine structure of the cells and tissues will be disrupted by the physical and chemical effects of ice crystal growth. These are not good; in fact, they kill cells. Cryopreserving for future viability is all about controlling the freezing of cellular water to prevent damage and that does not require very fast freezing but controlled freezing.

THE TRUTH ABOUT LIQUID NITROGEN

Let's clear up one thing straight away, despite what many novels and *Terminator 2: Judgment Day* would have you believe: Liquid nitrogen is not a great freezing agent. Yes, it is quite cold (–195.79° C), what we scientists call a bit nippy, but it has quite a small range between its melting and boiling points. This means that if you put something warm into your liquid nitrogen (sitting happily in a vacuum flask), the heat will initially cause the liquid nitrogen to boil. This will form an insulating layer of nitrogen vapor around the object you are trying to cool, which prevents further rapid heat loss.

This is why you can actually very briefly dip your hand in liquid nitrogen (DO NOT TRY THIS AT HOME—OR ANYWHERE!). This is called the Leidenfrost effect. You can see the same thing happen when you put drops of water into a very hot pan.

However, you can get very nasty burns if your clothes are cooled by the liquid nitrogen and then come into contact with your skin. No insulating gas layer is possible then. If you ever have to visit the doctor to get a skin lesion frozen off, the doctor will use quite a high-pressure jet of liquid nitrogen on you. Here the jet effectively strips away the insulating layer of gas to expose the skin to more very cold liquid. Alternatively, you can cool a metal rod in nitrogen and press that against the skin. One way to get around this limiting effect is to make liquid nitrogen slush—a mixture of solid and liquid nitrogen. The heat then removed from the specimen turns the solid into a liquid, rather then the liquid to a gas. This is achieved by putting a small quantity of liquid nitrogen, in an insulated container, into a chamber that can be cooled by a vacuum pump. The resulting liquid nitrogen "Slush Puppie" is a good way of freezing a small amount of biological material and suspensions.

Figure 55.1: An electrically stimulated locust neuromuscular junction frozen milliseconds later using ultra-rapid freezing with a liquid helium-cooled copper block. The sample was then prepared for electron microscopy by freeze-fracture replication, which produces a platinum-shadowed replica of the fractured tissue surface, with white shadows. Membranes can fracture down the center of the bilayer producing an external (E) face and a protoplasmic (P) face. Each of the small particles represents a single

PUTTING THE SCIENCE IN FICTION

membrane protein and is approximately 10nm in size. The large proteins of the pre-synaptic bar (PSB) are thought to be calcium channels. The arrows indicate the position of synaptic vesicles, fused by the freezing process.

EN—External face of the nerve membrane. PM—Protoplasmic face of the muscle membrane. Micrograph prepared by the author.

One of the fastest ways of freezing biological material for ultrastructural analysis is to "slam" it against a liquid helium-cooled ultra-pure copper block. This produces ultrarapid freezing. I used to do this a lot; it's really cool. (Sorry, I just had to get that pun out of the way.) The electron micrograph shown is of a neuromuscular junction of a locust that was frozen milliseconds after being electrically stimulated. Small membrane-bound vesicles have been captured as they fuse with the nerve membrane. Each of the small particles on the smooth areas is a membrane protein some 14 nanometers in size. A nanometer is 10^9 meter, or one billionth of a meter. If that doesn't boggle you, just consider *a nanometer is to a tennis ball what the tennis ball is to the Earth*. That's small.

THE NEED FOR ULTRARAPID FREEZING

The objective when freezing for ultrastructural studies is to freeze the tissues so very fast that large ice crystals cannot form to disrupt this delicate nanostructure. The cell water is said to become vitrified—glasslike—and you effectively get a snapshot of the tissue and can capture transient events, like the membrane fusion shown. However, even with the very fast freezing rates that are produced by slamming, you only get this glasslike appearance in a very superficial layer below the contact area (less than 10 micron). This is all because of physics. You simply can't get the heat out of biological material any faster. And this is the problem with freezing tissue for viability: There is nowhere for the ice crystals to grow where they can't do damage.

The results of the largely disappointing freezing rates available to us are that you get large ice crystals forming in tissue and they disrupt the structure, bursting membranes and organelles and that will eventually kill cells and tissues—catastrophic for organs! You don't come back easily from that state when you are put onto defrost. There is another very important effect as well: As water freezes to form pure ice crystals, salts within the cells become concentrated, causing damage thanks to chemical and osmotic effects. If the ice crystals form outside the cells, in the extracellular space, water being drawn out of the cells will cause chemical and osmotic damage within the cells themselves. Slower freezing rates can cause water to freeze outside cells, with the cells themselves dehydrated and damaged by the growing internal salt concentration.

Cryopreservation is therefore a different matter when you are considering freezing for subsequent recovery. That's all about controlling the freezing rate and the amount and state of the water in the cell.

CRYOPROTECTION OF BIOLOGICAL TISSUE

Time for a reminder of some basic biology. The cell is the basic structural and functional unit of any living thing. A tissue is an ensemble of similar cells, usually from the same origin that work together to carry out a specific function. Multiple tissues, working together, form organs. A lot of the work done on cryopreservation for viability has been carried out on isolated cells, like the aforementioned semen and blood components such as red blood cells. Cells are small, and therefore heat can be extracted from them relatively speedily. It is also relatively easy to extract water from, and infiltrate other substances, into a cell. Essentially, this means that isolated cells are ideal for the application of cryoprotectants. These substances are used to protect biological tissue from freezing damage; any discussion about suspended animation is a discussion about the efficacy of cryoprotectants.

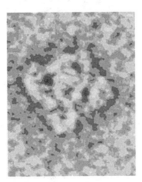

Figure 55.2: An isolated mammalian ryanodine receptor molecule, a type of calcium channel found in the many muscles. The preparation was ultrarapidly frozen in liquid/solid nitrogen slush and viewed under the electron microscope while still frozen. Freezing with cryoprotectants is ideal for this type of investigation. The four clamps at the molecule's corners and the central rim can be clearly seen. The whole molecule is 270 Å in width. An angstrom is a unit of length equal to 10^{-10} m. Micrograph prepared by the author.

Cryoprotectants come in two main classes, penetrating and nonpenetrating. Penetrating cryoprotectants are small molecules that dissolve in water and can easily cross cell membranes and affect the melting point of water. These cryoprotectants must not in themselves be toxic, of course, but you need to remember that their actions and toxicity at room temperature will be different than that as they approach freezing. They should also not precipitate or adversely affect the distribution of cell constituents. By entering the cell they will help prevent excessive dehydration of cells; some actually function by forming hydrogen bonds with biological molecules. Sugars such as trehalose and glucose can act as penetrating cryoprotectants.

Nonpenetrating cryoprotectants are large molecules that do not enter the cell—they still need to penetrate a tissue to surround the cells. Not everything is known about how they function, but they seem to have an effect similar to that of the proteins within the cells. Polyethylene glycol and polyvinylpyrrolidone are nonpenetrating cryoprotectants.

Another class of helpful compounds is sometimes referred to as *ice blockers*, and they can complement, by additions in small amounts, the cryoprotective actions of conventional cryoprotectives.

EXISTING CRYOPROTECTANTS

Some cryoprotectants occur naturally. Antarctic fish have evolved cryoprotectant glycoproteins, insects use sugars or plyols, and arctic frogs use glucose, but arctic salamanders can produce glycerol in their livers. Microscopic multicellular water bears (*Tardigrada*), can survive freezing by replacing most of their internal water with the sugar trehalose.

Cocktails of cryoprotectants have been developed to assist in freezing biological materials, and it's estimated that we are now on a sixth generation with regard to their success and ability to produce a form of vitrification. Vascular tissue, heart valves, corneas, and cartilage have all been successfully frozen. Progress has also been made on ovary and kidney tissue.

However, when red blood cells are infiltrated with trehalose, maximal survival rates are only in the 90 percent range, with functionality reduced to 60 percent. You can get increased functionality but with a reduction of survival. And remember, 90 percent is in pretty perfect conditions, cells in solutions, not where you need to perfuse a cryoprotectant through a dead body. Whole-body perfusions can be tricky at the best of times—like when the patient is actually alive with a beating heart.

I, for one, would not want to lose approximately ten billion neurons from my brain. Call me old-fashioned, but I don't really fancy coming back in two hundred years' time as something akin, at best, to a zombie.

CHAPTER 56

THE WEAPONS OF *STAR WARS*

By Judy L. Mohr

Franchise movies like *Star Trek* and *Star Wars* often spark imagination regarding the weapons of the future. The debates about how certain technologies could come about are steeped with speculation, sometimes loosely backed up by science. Although, some people question how much of science fiction is science fact.

The weapons depicted on the screen within *Star Trek* and *Star Wars* are all weapons of light. You have phasers of varying designs with their beams of light striking the enemy down. There are pulse cannons, sending a pulse of light to blow up the ships orbiting the planet. There are photon torpedoes on *Star Trek*, torpedoes with a light-based warhead. However, we can't forget the most coveted of all light weapons: the lightsaber.

Before I get too carried away in debunking certain fandoms about their weapons, let's turn our attention to the most important question in this argument: Is it possible to create weapons of light? The answer is yes and no.

THE DESTRUCTIVE FORCE OF LIGHT

For a moment, let's pretend that we're outside playing with a magnifying glass in the sun, torturing ants. It takes some careful maneuvering, but the sunlight can be focused into a fine point, and the ants … poof! And let's not forget about the number of fires that have been started by focusing that light beam on a patch of dry leaves. Ah, the joys of childhood science.

The concept of turning light into a destructive force is something that many of us have played with at some point. With the introduction of laser technology, it was only a question of when lasers would become powerful enough to be weaponized.

If your objective is to slice through an opponent using only a beam of light, you will be pleased to hear that the laser technology already exists and is commercially available. Lasers have been used to cut high-density materials, such as diamonds and metal, since the 1960s. In the 1970s, laser-cutting technology was used to cut titanium for aerospace applications. However, the power requirements for laser cutting are enormous. Just cutting 6.4mm (0.25in) thickness of plywood requires a laser of 650 watts. Laser surgery, commonly used in eye surgery, uses a 1,000-watt laser, minimum.

For a laser beam capable of slicing off the nose of an X-wing starfighter, the power generation unit would need to be the size of a tank, based on current technology, but this is rapidly changing.

LASER CANNONS ALREADY EXIST

With our growing demands for smaller, more powerful batteries for cell phones and laptops, power generation technology is growing by leaps and bounds. So much so that weapons such as laser cannons and laser rifles, the ones like the stormtroopers in *Star Wars* used, are now within the reach of our current level of technology.

In 2014, the U.S. Navy experimented with a ship-mounted laser weapon system (LaWS) to target small boats and unmanned aerial vehicles (UAVs) with promising results. (We'll blame the U.S. military for this incredibly exciting system name and acronym.) The system was installed on the *U.S.S. Ponce*, and videos of the tests can be found on YouTube. Personally, I feel sorry for that dummy on the dingy—to have its hand blown off by a beam of light. However, the accuracy of the system to take down a UAV … I'm impressed.

Today, similar systems have been mounted on several other naval vessels and land-based units, and have been deployed into the field. The current systems do take time to charge the laser unit between consecutive shots. It's not the near-instantaneous shots that you see in *Star Trek* with the phaser cannons, but if I remember rightly, there a few episodes in the TV series *Star Trek: Enterprise*, where they spoke about charging the laser cannons. There was definitely this conversation in *The Empire Strikes Back*.

Now, I can hear a few readers shouting at me, saying that *Star Wars* used pulse cannons, not laser cannons. The difference between these two systems is the amount of energy sent out at a time. A laser cannon, like LaWS, employs a constant beam of light—creating its destructive abilities in the same way you did with that magnifying glass and sunlight. The pulse cannon sends a short burst of high-intensity light, giving the system the chance to build up its deadly charge in between shots.

LASER RIFLES

Laser pointers are now so common that many people use them to tease their cats. Novelty designs exist in the shapes of guns and rifles, some sold as toys. However, true laser-based handheld military weapons also exist and are currently being tested by military and gun enthusiasts.

In 2013, gun enthusiast Rob Pincus released a video on YouTube comparing the performance of laser rifles with projectile rifles. At the time, the laser rifle was lethal to a stationary balloon. A moving target, on the other hand ... I shall hang my head in shame. A laser-based weapon like the one Pincus tested took far too long to charge. On the battlefield, a unit like that would be completely useless.

However, our level of understanding of power cells and fast-charging systems has dramatically improved since then, thanks to smartphones and tablets. It wouldn't surprise me if, in the near future, weapons like the laser pistol Han Solo sported on his thigh become a reality.

THE LIGHT-BASED GRENADE IS STANDARD ISSUE FOR MILITARY

In *Stargate*, the Goa'uld had a grenade-type device that would emit a strong pulse of light and a high-pitched sound that rendered the enemy unconscious. Variants of the stun grenade have been around since the 1970s, and are now standard issue for Special Forces soldiers.

The stun grenade goes by many different names: flash grenade, flashbang, and thunder flash, to name a few. These devices produce a blinding flash of light and an intensely loud sound of greater than 170 decibels, overloading the senses of the assailants and disorienting them. In some cases, assailants are rendered unconscious. The stun grenades are normally nonlethal.

LIGHTSABERS

What about the one weapon that so many covet: the lightsaber?

If you look on YouTube, you will find countless numbers of videos where people are demonstrating their homemade lightsabers. Some are just flashlights and LED rods fashioned to look like lightsabers. A few give the zooming-out beam that really does look like a lightsaber and can cause significant damage. However, if you take a close look at the latter category of videos, you'll discover that what was created was actually a glorified blowtorch, complete with the long, narrow, blue flame. Yes, they are extremely impressive—from a cosplay perspective—but are they lightsabers?

To put it frankly, no. The lightsabers portrayed in the *Star Wars* films are swords constructed from a laser beam of some description—it's made of light, hence its name. Now comes the next question: Like the laser cannons and guns, will we ever see a lightsaber in reality?

Well, I will gladly admit that the fight scene in *Star Wars: Episode I—The Phantom Menace* between Darth Maul, Obi-Wan Kenobi, and Qui-Gon Jinn was a serious bow-down-to-the-Sith moment. It was spectacular on so many levels. Never mind that the science behind their weapons was seriously flawed.

Power generation is one thing, and as I've mentioned already, it won't be long before we have a lethal laser unit that would fit in the palm of the hand. However, turning a laser beam into a functional sword is something that is pure science fiction.

Cutting down the enemy is only one requirement for a sword. A sword must also block the strike of another swordsman. No matter how hard you try, a light beam would never be able to stop another light beam. Dare I say it, even the glorified blowtorches that people have fashioned to look like lightsabers would have no hope of stopping the beam from another lightsaber. Stopping something of mass is possible, but at this stage, only by burning it to a crisp and blowing it up.

Let's for a moment assume that the lightsaber's blocking capabilities come from the force that flows through all things. The lightsabers portrayed in the movies have a visible beam that is approximately one to two meters long (one to two yards), depending on the design employed. Beyond this range, the lightsaber appears to be harmless; either that, or the Jedi would frequently be cutting holes in the decks of the ships they're on. There are two things wrong with this picture.

First, light travels faster than the human eye can process. As such, to see the beams from lasers, one of two things has to happen: either the photons from the laser interact with particles in their path, for example dust or ionizing atoms; or a long-exposure image is taken using an exposure time beyond the capabilities of the human eye.

Second, any photon emitted from a laser will continue along its path until stopped by some energy-absorbing material. You cannot generate a laser beam with a finite length stopped only by clear air. Those photons need to interact with the surrounding air particles in some fashion, often resulting in a flash of light concentrated at the point of interaction. To render a high-powered laser beam harmless after a short distance, traveling through only air, one would need to employ another science fiction method to either teleport the light photon to the start again, or bend the beam back upon itself with a micro-singularity.

Science fiction is often the birth of modern technology, and many of the ideas come from *Star Trek* and *Star Wars*. Because of the inspiration fueled by these franchises, we now have laser cannons, and phaser pistols are just around the corner. The lightsaber? Let's just leave that one for those who are strong with the Force.

●

CHAPTER 57

HOW TO DESIGN A
PRACTICAL SPACESHIP

By Eric Primm

Science fiction loves a beautiful starship. From the Minbari Sharlin to the Empire's Star Destroyers to the Borg Cube to the Heart of Gold, aesthetics rule. From a practical standpoint, most starships in science fiction are poorly designed. They're made to elicit awe, but a ship designed from the viewpoint of economics and efficiency would be visually boring. Even in post-scarcity societies, engineers would still strive for efficient designs, which drive out wasteful extravagances.

Poor designs are costly in terms of downtime, maintenance, and resources. Most important, a bad design puts lives at risk. In the vacuum of space, even small design flaws will quickly escalate into life-threatening problems. While contemporary spaceships are often based on aircraft, the operating environment is drastically different, but safety would be the primary limitation. Engineering is the discipline of balancing functionality with risk to make the possible practical. To make functional spacecraft, engineers would study the failures of past and contemporary designs. Here we'll focus on shape, windows, and manned fighters.

SHIP SHAPE

To support life within, a starship must contain atmosphere. Since outside of the ship is vacuum, the structure must be sealed tight. Another way to think about them is to consider spacecraft big balloons. Inside the ship, the atmosphere must operate at a pressure that supports life. Because of the differential pressure outside and inside, the atmosphere tries to equalize by pushing on the ship's skin. Logically, the skin is pressing back on the atmosphere to contain it. This means that even when not moving, the ship's structure has a force applied to it. In engineering terms, the structure is pressurized.

Airplanes and submarines are vehicles that undergo pressurization, and in general, these craft have a rounded shape because the best shape for pressurization is a sphere due to the pressure pushing equally in all directions. Practical starships would be either spherical or cylindrical.

Add in maneuvers, environmental changes, gravitational fluctuations, weight modifications, pressurization cycles, etc., and it's easy to see that spaceships undergo a lot of force. The varying levels of force have an effect on structure, known as *fatigue*. Yes, structures get tired. Instead of getting irritable and needing a nap, structures tend to crack. The aerospace industry found this out with the de Havilland Comet, a commercial airplane that crashed due to catastrophic cracks. Cracks at square window cutouts grew large enough to cause problems. As the study of fracture progressed, engineers learned that sharp corners create stress concentrations, which is as bad as it sounds. The sharper the corner, the higher the stress concentration, the more likely the crack initiation.

Therefore, designs that have gentle curves have less cracks. Windows on aircraft minimize stress concentrations. Doors on submarines are rounded at the corner for this same reason. A civilization advanced enough to build spacecraft will understand fatigue and fracture, and while their technology would be much more advanced than the current understanding, they would implement these basic design touches to ensure the safest vehicle possible.

Rounded designs, like commercial aircraft and submarines, are good examples of efficient structure. The best science fiction example is the space station Babylon 5. It's cylindrical, which is close enough to a sphere for a good engineering tradeoff. The worst science fiction example is the city ship from the TV series *Firefly*. It's creative while being an engineering nightmare.

WINDOWS

Space is huge with not much to see. Regardless, science fiction spacecraft tend to have windows, and even worse, they have windows so that the pilot can ... erm, pilot. Sylvia Spruck Wrigley already talked about the dangers of visual piloting in chapter 51, "Realistic Space Flight." Since she is correct that spacecraft would be piloted by instrument, the pilots don't need windows, which are basically holes in the structure with something transparent filling them. In other words, windows are failure points.

Putting important functions of the ship near weak points is not a good design. Despite the mission, chances are good the ship will encounter debris in space. Whether environmental factors like micrometeoroids, debris from battle, or trash left behind by inconsiderate people who also probably talk during movies, the ship will take damage. Therefore, navigation and the rest of the command center would be located away from the outer surface and buried deep in the ship. As it takes damage, the critical functions can still operate.

In fighter craft, windows are especially useless. Science fiction is correct in that missiles would be guided by tracking software instead of by hand. In most science fiction stories, fighter pilots use their sight to target enemies with guns. But in space, combat between fighters would not be like aerial dogfights. Smart militaries would keep their attack craft black to match the background of space, making it difficult to find. When fighting in the depths of space, black ships would be difficult to spot visually. Even in a planetary system with a star, the counter tactics for visual targeting would be to position the ship against a background of black space.

Targeting software would be needed for all weapons. With screens being relatively cheap technology, it makes more sense to have a solid structure outside with a screen and targeting computers inside.

Since visual cues aren't needed for daily operation, command and control can be located anywhere on the ship. Starships, especially battle craft, would bury their decision centers in the heart of the ship, where damage is unlikely. *Battlestar Galactica* does this well. Instead of operating like an aircraft, the Galactica bridge is reminiscent of a submarine.

Unfortunately, every ship in the *Star Wars* universe fails this one. The Millennium Falcon is cool but hangs the pilots out there to be targeted. Despite the prevalence of droids and artificial intelligence, the vehicles in *Star Wars* rely on visual ship-to-ship combat. While this is more exciting, it's incredibly reckless. I should turn in my nerd card now. As much as I love the iconic *Star Wars* designs, those ships reflect that instead of science fiction, *Star Wars* is science fantasy.

MANNED FIGHTERS

When the X-wing starfighters first appeared on screen during *Rogue One: A Star Wars Story*, an actual cheer went up in the theater where I saw the movie. The silhouette of that spacecraft evokes the feeling of the entire franchise. It represents hope. The X-wing starfighter is also an unnecessary risk of life. At the time of the franchise's creation, drones were not war machines. *Star Wars* extrapolates its space battles from air combat. But as modern armies are finding out, the weakest part of a fighter is the human inside it.

This is a truth that will carry into the future, and a spacefaring civilization would advance drone technology to be its main fighter force. Instead of a carrier ship loaded with fighters, the practical starship would control unmanned craft. The pilots can be located safely within the depths of the command ship, each controlling a single craft or squadron of drones. Warfare already includes significant signal jamming efforts, known as electronic warfare. Modern militaries excel at this, and it is an easy assumption that advanced civilizations would understand and

PUTTING THE SCIENCE IN FICTION

conduct electronic warfare much better. *Battlestar Galactica* demonstrates this as static in the communication between the colonial Vipers and the main ship's crew.

As has already been established, visual flying and warfare are unnecessary, so why put a being in a craft separate from the big ship? If saving a life for the sake of life itself isn't enough, think about the time and money needed to train a pilot. The skills necessary for flight take a long time to develop, and by putting a pilot in a fighter, a significant investment is risked. Advanced civilizations would not accept these risks, and unmanned attack craft would be easily in reach of a society with artificial intelligence.

By removing the pilot, drones lose unnecessary weight, such as life support equipment, and become more maneuverable. The structure can be designed for flight that would harm a pilot. As stated earlier, structure undergoes significant forces, including anything inside it. Biological bodies are weak, and despite mitigating factors such as crash couches, exercises, and drugs, the physical body limits the forces that can be placed on the structure. By removing the body, the fighter can be smaller, more maneuverable, and more effective.

Unmanned craft are the future. The Cylon Raider in *Battlestar Galactica* is a great example, but those craft were autonomous cyborgs instead of drones. In the recent show, they also contain biological circuits. This is a potential limiting but not fatal flaw. For a counter example, the fighters from *Babylon 5* are beautiful but limited fighters.

CHAPTER 58

EXOPLANETS AND HABITABILITY

By Jim Gotaas

Why do writers want to know about exoplanets?

Perhaps you want to write *hard science fiction*, in the spirit of Hal Clement, Poul Anderson, Gregory Benford, or Stephen Baxter, stories that fit in the magazine *Analog Science Fiction and Fact*. The discovery of exoplanets provides new worlds unlike any in our own solar system. If you're more interested in space opera, these new planets give the chance to build stories with modern, exotic backgrounds. They may even trigger ideas for different types of stories.

ON TO GOLDILOCKS EXOPLANETS!

The Goldilocks zone (more scientifically the habitability zone) is the range of distances from any star that allows liquid water to exist on an "ordinary" planet, similar to Earth. This concept centers around the idea that life as we know it requires liquid water at some point.

In our solar system, given the Sun as it is now, the Goldilocks zone stretches from inside the orbit of Venus to outside the orbit of Mars. This tells us that things *aren't* always equal, since neither Venus nor Mars currently has liquid water. This is probably due to factors such as a runaway greenhouse effect for Venus and the smaller mass and lack of a magnetic field for Mars. (This is covered in more detail by Lynn Forrest in chapter 44, "Habitable Atmospheres.")

Outside the Goldilocks zone, we're fairly certain liquid water exists under the icy surface of Europa, one of Jupiter's Galilean moons. Here, tidal heating provides the energy to support liquid water. We don't know whether life can arise under these circumstances because we don't know exactly how our sort of life arose, or precisely what conditions it needs.

THE EXOPLANET MENAGERIE

We're getting a glimpse of the kinds of planets orbiting other stars. As of November 2017, we've identified more than thirty-five hundred definite exoplanets, with almost five thousand more still to be confirmed, with varying sizes and orbits around other stars. It turns out our old familiar solar system, with rocky planets close to the sun (Mercury, Venus, Earth, and Mars) and gas giants (Jupiter and Saturn) and ice giants (Uranus and Neptune) further out, isn't at all typical.

Instead, we have hot Jupiters, hot Saturns (also known as *puffy* planets, because their density is so low that they would float in water—if you had a big enough bathtub!), hot Neptunes, Super Earths, water worlds, and even Chthonian planets (*Chthonian* describing inhabitants of the mythological Greek underworld, their version of Hell). The latest models of solar systems require radical movements of planets during the evolution of such systems.

With existing techniques, we're more likely to find massive exoplanets that are close to their star, so the current catalog is biased toward these types. If you're interested in detection methods, check out the webpage Exoplanet Detection Methods Visualized at the Planetary Habitability Laboratory (PHL).

Some newly discovered exoplanets are *not* new to science fiction, such as Super Earths (rocky planets that are larger and more massive than Earth) and water worlds (planets that are completely covered by oceans). These are still exciting because there's now a scientific basis for stories about these worlds. But for our purposes, we're going to concentrate on the exoplanets that are really new and different from our own solar system and traditional science fiction.

What are these new worlds like? Planets are usually characterized in terms of their *mass* (often expressed as multiples of the Earth's mass), their *radius*, and their *elemental composition*. Beyond that, their physical state depends on the radius of their orbits (often expressed using *astronomical units* (AU), the average radius of the Earth's orbit about the Sun), and the type of star they orbit. The last two basically determine the star's habitability zone. Whether or not a planet in that zone can be considered Earth-like depends on the first three.

Astronomers have discovered a huge range of exoplanets. We're going to look more closely at just a few of them that are most unusual and unexpected.

Hot Jupiters

Like Papa Bear's porridge, these are just too hot. Roughly the size of Jupiter, their orbital radius ranges from 0.015 to 0.15 AU. For comparison, Mercury orbits at 0.39 AU. This means they're very hot, which affects their atmospheric composition, but if they're massive enough, they remain gas giants. (If they're *not* that massive, they can become *Chthonian* worlds.) Orbiting so close to the star, they are *tidally locked*, meaning that they always show the same face to the star (just as our Moon is tidally locked to Earth, always showing us the same face).

An early discovery in 2005 was the extrasolar planet HD189733b, about sixty-three light years away. With a mass about 13 percent larger than Jupiter's, this blue planet orbits the star every 2.2 days at an orbital radius of about 0.03 AU. Its dayside temperature is 1,700° F (927° C), with a nightside temperature of 1,200° F (649° C).

Current theories about the origin of planetary systems require that gas giants must form out where hydrogen can easily condense into a planet (such as Jupiter or Saturn). At some point, they migrate into a close orbit about the star and heat up dramatically. During this migration, smaller planets such as Earth would be flung wildly around the system.

Hot Neptunes

More Papa Bear exoplanets! Hot Neptunes are similar in mass to Neptune or Uranus, but their orbital radius is normally less than 1 AU (compared with 30 AU for Neptune). One example orbits the star Gliese 436 every 2.64 days, trailing a sort of comet tail as it moves, the result of atmospheric hydrogen boiling off into space. If a hot Neptune loses all its atmosphere, it can end up being a rocky planet similar in size to Earth.

Chthonian Planets

Yet more Papa Bears: Chthonian planets are to some extent hypothetical. They are basically supermassive rocky or metallic worlds, although we think they have evolved from hot Jupiters whose atmospheres have been boiled off by radiation from the star, leaving behind a solid remnant core. One suspected example is CoRoT-7b, located 480 light years away, which orbits at about 0.02 AU, is 70 percent larger than Earth and almost five times as massive. With a dayside surface temperature of about 3,600° F (2,000° C), if it has any atmosphere at all, it will be a tenuous one of vaporized rock.

POTENTIALLY HABITABLE EXOPLANETS

Welcome to Baby Bear's bowl of planetary porridge: These worlds are potentially "just right," lying in the Goldilocks zone. The key word here is *potentially*, since our current detection methods can't provide much detail about the masses or atmospheres of these worlds. You can find a graphic of some likely candidates at the PHL website, giving their astronomical designations and distances from Earth.

We don't actually have direct images of any of these exoplanets. They're all larger than Earth, but we have no estimates of their masses and we're not certain about their composition and habitability. We think they're roughly the right size and in the Goldilocks zone for their stars, but are subject to change as new interpretations or astronomical observations are made.

It's difficult to detect atmospheres of exoplanets, as you have to see the effects against the backdrop of the star's intense light. So far, all such examples are hot Jupiters or hot Neptunes. A variety of gases has been detected, including hydrogen, helium, carbon, oxygen, sodium, water vapor, carbon monoxide, and methane.

WHAT ABOUT MAMA BEAR?

Current techniques for finding exoplanets aren't accurate enough to give detailed descriptions of planets lying outside the habitability zone, which would make them too cold. Several hundred have been found, and astronomers have directly imaged four massive planets orbiting HR 8799, a young system (only 30 million years old, compared with the Sun's age of 4.5 billion years) located 129 light years from Earth. These planets have estimated masses about five to seven times that of Jupiter, at distances ranging from 14.5 to 68 AU.

WATCH THESE SPACES!

The list of confirmed exoplanets will certainly grow, and new telescopes will provide more information about their physical characteristics, including their atmospheres. In a few years' time, we may be able to describe many more of these planets much more completely. For exoplanet science fiction, these are exciting times!

FURTHER READING

- For up-to-date information about exoplanets, visit the NASA Exoplanet Archive at https://exoplanetarchive.ipac.caltech.edu.
- If you're interested in detection methods, check out the webpage Exoplanet Detection Methods Visualized at the PHL http://phl.upr.edu/library/media /exoplanetdetectionmethodsvisualized
- For the latest information about the habitable exoplanets that have been discovered, visit http://phl.upr.edu/projects/habitable-exoplanets-catalog
- A more leisurely explanation of most of these ideas can be found in *The Planet Factory: Exoplanets and the Search for a Second Earth* by Elizabeth Tasker (Bloomsbury Sigma, 2017)

CHAPTER 59

PRINTING THE FAR FUTURE

By Jamie Krakover

When looking at far future technology, one of the most popular pieces from science fiction is the replicator from the *Star Trek* franchise. The idea of printing anything from a meal to a needed item on demand, in a matter of seconds, is incredibly appealing. While 3D printing is exploding in popularity across numerous industries, how realistic is this technology application?

HOW 3D PRINTERS WORK

To answer that question, we first need to look at how a 3D printer works. Most 3D printers use some kind of material for a base, either a plastic, wax, or metal in the form of powder, wire, resin, or filament. Then a heat source such as a laser or electron beam is used to melt the material in a pattern designated by a design file typically from a computer-aided design (CAD) program. The material is laid out or fed along a pattern. The heat source then melts the material to the part being built. It sounds relatively simple in theory, but in reality there are a lot of concerns that go along with 3D printing.

As material is added to a build structure, there are a variety of ways things can go wrong. Everything from warping to gaps in the structure can occur. This makes for messy and damaged parts. When heating the material on the part build, stress can build unevenly, which causes cracking or other deformation in the part. Depending on the material and method of 3D printing, there are ways to prevent this from happening, but it involves careful planning and monitoring throughout the setup, printing, and even post-processing of the parts.

Another concern with 3D printing is the ability to repeatedly and reliably print parts. The smaller printers that in-home users purchase are not highly calibrated like the larger industrial printers used for more mainstream applications. Even with the same print program on a finely tuned printer, the end result can vary from print to print or even across different printers much like two Xerox printers at FedEx Office. Similar to how colors can slightly vary, or paper might jam more in one printer over another, no two 3D printers are exactly alike. And guaranteeing the same result from the same printer, let alone two different ones, can prove difficult. Depending on how finely calibrated the printer is, the user may get more variation in the part than desired.

If you can get past the possibility of deformations and part variability, the next concern is the surface roughness. For some applications a jagged surface isn't a problem, but you aren't going to get a smooth and/or shiny surface from a 3D printer. Parts coming out of a printer frequently have the consistency and roughness of sandpaper. Just as sandpaper has different levels of grit, 3D printed parts vary in surface roughness. Plastics tend to be smoother than metals, but printed parts usually have to be post-processed with some form of machining to reduce the roughness.

The part construction aside, there are additional issues with 3D printing. In *Star Trek*, a user requests an item from a replicator and within a few moments it appears. In real life, 3D printing isn't nearly that fast. It can take hours or even days depending on the size of the part and the speed of the machine. It can take up to an hour to print one small plastic trinket a few inches tall. The larger and more complex the part, the longer it takes to produce it. In addition, parts are constrained by the size of the 3D printing chamber. Small in-home printers can be purchased for as little as a few hundred dollars. But parts are limited to about a square foot in size. The bigger the chambers, the more expensive the printers. And while multiple parts can be printed at once if the chamber size allows for it, the speed and size restrictions make for an expensive, lengthy process to print things in mass. Adding more to the cost is the fact that it's not cheap to constantly heat material to the temperatures required to melt and build up a part for hours on end.

HOW LONG UNTIL WE HAVE REPLICATORS?

In theory 3D printers are similar to *Star Trek* replicators. You are taking one material and changing how it is constructed, but there are currently limitations on how you can go from one form to another. 3D printers don't rearrange molecular structure like replicators do. Currently, 3D printers take some form of solid material and "melt" it into another shape. This not only changes the original format of the material but also its durability and strength.

In addition, you still have to store all the material to print things. So while a printer could be relatively small, the amount of material required to feed a whole ship and create various supplies via 3D printing wouldn't save much space from actually storing and carrying the fully formed items themselves. Plus, most 3D printers currently only function with one material at a time, so if you were printing food it would be pretty bland and boring. Looking back at the consistent and repeatable issue, if you want food to taste the same every single time, getting that balance could be tricky. On the flip side, with a ship full of different tastes buds you may want to customize what you are printing, in which case getting the right balance could also be tricky with all the 3D printer settings.

At this point, some of you are probably thinking, hey, they've 3D printed a car, why can't we just print a whole spaceship or other stuff already? It can't honestly be that hard. But it is in fact very difficult. The cars that have been 3D printed are mostly just the frame, with additional parts added. This is perfectly fine because the cars do run, but they run much slower than your average vehicle and are typically much smaller than a standard car.

So what is 3D printing actually good for today? 3D printing is currently useful for one-off parts, trinkets, smaller parts, and parts that aren't required to support huge loads. If you have something that will experience limited use or is solving a function other than weight bearing, 3D printing might be the right route. It's also great for complex shapes and/or reducing part count. Many times, other machining techniques make complex shapes difficult or expensive to manufacture, which can drive up part count and assembly time. But if you can 3D print something, you can do difficult shapes in one run instead of building multiple parts and then assembling them.

We're still a ways off from a lot of far future science fiction applications, but with the current interest in 3D printing and the amount of research going into it, we may get there one day. Not exactly to the replicators seen in *Star Trek*, but we may be printing products on demand from our own homes or somewhere across the universe.

ABOUT THE EXPERTS

The forty experts who contributed to this book represent a wide array of scientific, technological, and medical expertise. They include scientists, engineers, physicians, laboratory managers, and nurses who've collectively endured more than one hundred years of graduate study in their chosen fields. Many are aspiring or established science fiction and fantasy (SF/F) authors. Although they have different backgrounds and interests, they all have one thing in common: a love of SF. Their articles reference many popular books and movies that illustrate how (or how *not*) to put the science in fiction, with the goal of helping authors create realistic, compelling stories.

DAN ALLEN, FIELD OF EXPERTISE: PHYSICS

Dan Allen is a physicist and system architect for a smartphone sensor manufacturer. He has designed lasers for the government that see through envelopes and (eek!) clothing, lit a three-story electron accelerator on fire, and created nanoparticles in a radioactive hot lab.

KATHLEEN S. ALLEN, R.N., M.S.W., D.N.P., FIELD OF EXPERTISE: PSYCHIATRY

Kathleen S. Allen is a psychiatric registered nurse who specializes in depression. She has experience working as a psychiatric nurse practitioner, social worker, and educator.

TOM BENEDICT, FIELD OF EXPERTISE: ASTRONOMY

Tom Benedict has a bachelor's degree in astronomy and has spent the last fifteen years working as an instrument specialist at the Canada-France-Hawaii Telescope at the summit of Mauna Kea, a dormant volcano on the island of Hawaii.

MEGAN CARTWRIGHT CHAUDHURI, PH.D., FIELD OF EXPERTISE: TOXICOLOGY

Megan Cartwright Chaudhuri has a Ph.D. in toxicology and works as a freelance medical writer and editor. Her science nonfiction has appeared in *Slate* and Visionlearning.

REBECCA ENZOR, FIELD OF EXPERTISE: ENVIRONMENTAL SCIENCE
Rebecca Enzor is a fantasy author with a B.S. in biology and chemistry. She has spent the last eleven years working as a nuclear chemist at an environmental testing laboratory.

LEE A. EVERETT, D.V.M., M.S., FIELD OF EXPERTISE: BIOMEDICAL RESEARCH
Lee A. Everett is an SF/F writer who, in her other life, has advanced professional training within a niche intersection of biomedical research and medicine.

LYNN FORREST, PH.D., FIELD OF EXPERTISE: ATMOSPHERIC SCIENCE
Lynn Forrest is a lifelong weather geek and writing nerd. As an assistant professor, she teaches classes on and does research in atmospheric science.

ABBY GOLDSMITH, FIELD OF EXPERTISE: VIDEO GAME DEVELOPMENT
Abby Goldsmith is a video game industry veteran, with credits on more than twenty games for Nintendo DS and Wii, Sony PlayStation 2, and mobile platforms. She earned a B.F.A. in Film and Animation from the California Institute of the Arts.

JIM GOTAAS, PH.D., FIELD OF EXPERTISE: PHYSICS
Jim Gotaas passed through the gates of a Ph.D. in physics to a career in research and teaching physics, with occasional stops along the way to enjoy astrophysics and space travel.

MARIA GRACE, PH.D., FIELD OF EXPERTISE: EDUCATIONAL PSYCHOLOGY
Maria Grace has her Ph.D. in educational psychology and is a sixteen-year veteran of the university classroom, where she taught courses in human growth and development, learning, test development, and counseling.

MIKE HAYS, FIELD OF EXPERTISE: MICROBIOLOGY
Mike Hays lives in the heart of Kansas and has worked as a microbiologist for more than twenty-five years. He also coaches high school sports and writes middle-grade fiction. In his microbial research, he uses the tools of molecular biology to study the interactions between pathogens and their hosts.

RACHEL HEAPS-PAGE, FIELD OF EXPERTISE: SPECIAL EDUCATION
Rachel Heaps-Page has a B.Ed. Honors degree and experience educating children with severe learning disabilities and/or behavior problems. She has taught children with behavioral, emotional, and social disabilities in both mainstream classrooms and one-to-one, in primary and secondary schools based in England.

PUTTING THE SCIENCE IN FICTION

WILLIAM HUGGINS, FIELD OF EXPERTISE: ENVIRONMENTAL SCIENCE

William Huggins is an environmentalist in the American southwest. He writes, works, and explores the desert with his wife, daughter, and three rescue dogs. His short fiction and critical essays have appeared in various media, including *Texas Books in Review,* Third Flatiron Anthologies, the *Journal for Critical Animal Studies,* and *Studies in American Indian Literatures.*

GARETH D. JONES, FIELD OF EXPERTISE: ENVIRONMENTAL SCIENCE

Gareth D. Jones has been managing hazardous waste for seventeen years, much of that time while working at pharmaceutical research and development establishments. He has a degree in environmental science and likes to entertain his family on days off by pointing out different wheelie bin sizes.

GWEN C. KATZ, FIELD OF EXPERTISE: CHEMISTRY

Gwen C. Katz has a B.A. in chemistry (it's complicated). She did conservation research in a museum, helping museums develop better ways to preserve art and prevent fading and damage, before quitting to become a full-time writer.

BENJAMIN C. KINNEY, PH.D., FIELD OF EXPERTISE: NEUROSCIENCE

Benjamin C. Kinney is an SF/F author with a Ph.D. in neuroscience. He leads the Neuroscience and Rehabilitation Laboratory at a major Midwestern university, and somehow also finds time to serve as the assistant editor of the Hugo Award-nominated magazine-style podcast *Escape Pod.*

DAN KOBOLDT, M.S., FIELD OF EXPERTISE: GENETICS

Dan Koboldt is a principal investigator at the Institute for Genomic Medicine at Nationwide Children's Hospital and Research Assistant Professor of Pediatrics at The Ohio State University. In his fifteen years as a genetics researcher, he has co-authored more than seventy articles in *Nature, Science, The New England Journal of Medicine,* and other scientific journals.

JAMIE KRAKOVER, FIELD OF EXPERTISE: AEROSPACE ENGINEERING

Jamie Krakover has bachelor's and master's degrees in aerospace engineering. She has worked on spacecraft, rotorcraft, and numerous commercial and military aircraft.

PHILIP A. KRAMER, PH.D., FIELD OF EXPERTISE: BIOMEDICAL SCIENCE

Philip A. Kramer has a Ph.D. in the biomedical sciences and studies metabolism in the muscle and blood of cooperative mice and not-so-cooperative humans. He has co-authored nearly twenty manuscripts in peer-reviewed journals.

K.E. LANNING, FIELD OF EXPERTISE: GEOPHYSICS

K.E. Lanning is a scientist and writer with a B.S. in physics and a M.B.A. In her geophysics career, science met art, imagining landscapes beneath the surface of the Earth. She writes SF novels under the pen name of K.E. Lanning, exploring society, humanity and our future.

ANNE M. LIPTON, M.D., PH.D., FIELD OF EXPERTISE: NEUROLOGY

Anne M. Lipton is a behavioral neurologist who specializes in dementia. Her latest work on this subject is *The Common Sense Guide to Dementia for Clinicians and Caregivers* (Springer, 2013).

A.R. LUCAS, FIELD OF EXPERTISE: DECISION SCIENCE

A.R. Lucas is a decision scientist with degrees in cultural anthropology, psychology, and business. She's worked around the world in jobs ranging from archaeology to economics.

AMY MILLS, FIELD OF EXPERTISE: ENGINEERING

Amy Mills has a bachelor's degree in structural engineering and has passed the Seismic Principles Exam to become a licensed engineer in California. She also has over five years of civil engineering experience and twenty-eight years' worth of earthquake drills.

JUDY L. MOHR, PH.D., FIELD OF EXPERTISE: ASTRONOMY AND OPTICS

Judy L. Mohr is an engineer by background, but a writer at heart. Her Ph.D. specialized in astronomical instrumentation, where she used stellar light to measure the horizontal air movement above the 1-meter McLellan Telescope in Tekapo, New Zealand.

REBECCA MOWRY, FIELD OF EXPERTISE: BIOLOGY

Rebecca Mowry is a wildlife biologist who specializes in carnivore and big game research and management in the western United States. She's caught a few birds, bats, and hellbender salamanders along the way, and got a master's degree studying river otter poop.

TERRY NEWMAN, FIELD OF EXPERTISE: BIOLOGY

Terry Newman is a writer for film, television, stage, radio, and print. In a previous life he was a research biologist investigating changes in cell structure during activity, primarily using low-temperature techniques. Nobody called him Capt. Cold, no matter how hard he tried to make them.

PUTTING THE SCIENCE IN FICTION

BIANCA NOGRADY, FIELD OF EXPERTISE: SCIENCE JOURNALISM

Bianca Nogrady is a freelance science journalist who writes for national and international publications on everything from climate change to obesity to native foods to supernovas. She's the author of the nonfiction book *The End: The Human Experience of Death* (Penguin Random House Australia, 2013).

KARYNE NORTON, B.S.N., R.N., FIELD OF EXPERTISE: MEDICINE

Karyne Norton has worked as a labor and delivery nurse for thirteen years and been an avid reader for thirty years. She's also a photographer and writer of science fiction and fantasy.

BRIE PADDOCK, PH.D., FIELD OF EXPERTISE: BIOLOGY

Brie Paddock is a biology professor with a Ph.D. in biomedical science, focusing on molecular, cellular, and integrative neuroscience.

JONATHAN PEEPLES, M.D., FIELD OF EXPERTISE: PSYCHIATRY

Jonathan Peeples went to medical school at the University of Mississippi and completed his residency at Emory University School of Medicine. He is an emergency department psychiatrist in Atlanta, Georgia.

MATT PERKINS, FIELD OF EXPERTISE: COMPUTER SCIENCE

Matt Perkins writes code and fiction. He has over fifteen years of industry experience designing, building, and supporting web applications and enterprise software for clients large and small.

ERIC PRIMM, FIELD OF EXPERTISE: ENGINEERING

Eric Primm has spent the past decade making sure the wings don't fall off various aircraft as an engineer at Boeing. He writes fiction about space stations and nonfiction about martial arts.

PAUL REGIER, PH.D., FIELD OF EXPERTISE: NEUROSCIENCE

Paul Regier is a research associate at the University of Pennsylvania Perelman School of Medicine with a Ph.D. in neuroscience, investigating prior adversity and its relationship to addiction.

STEPHANIE SAUVINET, B.S.N., R.N., O.C.N., B.M.T.C.N., FIELD OF EXPERTISE: ONCOLOGY

Stephanie Sauvinet is an adult and young adult science fiction writer who has been practicing as an oncology and bone marrow/stem cell transplant nurse for more than ten years.

EFFIE SEIBERG, FIELD OF EXPERTISE: TECH INDUSTRY

Effie Seiberg is a science fiction and fantasy author and a marketing consultant who works with numerous tech and mobile startups in Silicon Valley. She's previously worked in 3D printing, on Google's mobile products and Android, and at IBM.

DANNA STAAF, PH.D., FIELD OF EXPERTISE: MARINE BIOLOGY

Danna Staaf is a science journalist and author of the nonfiction book *Squid Empire: The Rise and Fall of the Cephalopods* (ForeEdge, 2017). She has a Ph.D. in marine biology and loves to both consume and produce science fiction and fantasy.

GABRIEL VIDRINE, FIELD OF EXPERTISE: MICROBIOLOGY

Gabriel Vidrine is a microbiologist who has worked in research laboratories for over a decade and is now a laboratory manager.

ROBINNE WEISS, M.S., FIELD OF EXPERTISE: ENTOMOLOGY

Robinne Weiss has been known as The Bug Lady since she was seven years old. She eventually made it official with an M.S. in entomology from Penn State University. She now writes speculative fiction and teaches about bugs in beautiful New Zealand.

SYLVIA SPRUCK WRIGLEY, FIELD OF EXPERTISE: AVIATION

Sylvia Spruck Wrigley is a pilot and aviation journalist who has been obsessing about aviation safety for more than a decade. She writes about plane crashes and faeries, which have more in common than most people might imagine.

ACKNOWLEDGMENTS

First, I would like to thank all of the experts who contributed to this anthology. I'm also grateful to my literary agent Paul Stevens, who first suggested that we might put it together. Many thanks to Rachel Randall, Amy Jones, Cris Freese, Melissa Wuske, Alexis Estoye, and Jessica Zafarris, as well as the copy editing, promotion, and events teams at F+W Media. Finally, I'm grateful to the readers of the Science in Sci-fi blog series for their enthusiastic support.

INDEX